CAPITALISM, ALONE

CAPITALISM, ALONE

The Future of the System

That Rules the World

BRANKO MILANOVIC

THE BELKNAP PRESS OF
HARVARD UNIVERSITY PRESS
Cambridge, Massachusetts
London, England
2019

First printing

Library of Congress Cataloging-in-Publication Data is available from loc.gov
ISBN: 978-0-674-98759-3 (alk. paper)

CONTENTS

CAPITALISM, ALONE

CHAPTER 1

THE CONTOURS OF THE POST-COLD WAR WORLD

[The bourgeoisie] compels all nations, on pain of extinction, to adopt the bourgeois mode of production; it compels them to introduce what it calls civilization into their midst, i.e., to become bourgeois themselves. In one word, it creates a world after its own image.

—Marx and Engels, *The Communist Manifesto* (1848)

At the particular time when these discoveries [of the Americas and the East Indies] were made, the superiority of force happened to be so great on the side of the Europeans that they were enabled to commit with impunity every sort of injustice in those remote countries. Hereafter, perhaps, the natives of those countries may grow stronger, or those of Europe may grow weaker, and the inhabitants of all the different quarters of the world may arrive at that equality of courage and force which, by inspiring mutual fear, can alone overawe the injustice of independent nations into some sort of respect for the rights of one another. But nothing seems more likely to establish this equality of force than that mutual communication of knowledge and of all sorts of improvements which an extensive commerce from all countries to all countries naturally, or rather necessarily, carries along with it.

—Adam Smith, *Wealth of Nations* (1776)

1.1 Capitalism as the Only Socioeconomic System

I begin this chapter with two quotations. The first, from Karl Marx and Friedrich Engels, is some 170 years old; the second, from Adam Smith, almost 250 years old. These passages from two classic works of political economy capture, perhaps better than any contemporary writings, the essence of two epochal changes that the world is living through. One is the establishment of capitalism as not only the dominant, but the sole socioeconomic system in the world. The second is the rebalancing of economic power between Europe and North America on the one hand and Asia on the other, owing to the rise of Asia. For the first time since the Industrial Revolution, incomes on the three continents are edging closer to each other, returning to roughly the same relative levels they had before the Industrial Revolution (now, of course, at a much higher absolute level of income). In world-historical terms, the sole rule of capitalism and the economic renaissance of Asia are remarkable developments—which may be related.

The fact that the entire globe now operates according to the same economic principles—production organized for profit using legally free wage labor and mostly privately owned capital, with decentralized coordination—is without historical precedent. In the past, capitalism, whether in the Roman Empire, sixth-century Mesopotamia, medieval Italian city states, or the Low Countries in the modern era, always had to coexist—at times within the same political unit—with other ways of organizing production. These included hunting and gathering, slavery of various kinds, serfdom (with workers legally tied to the land and banned from offering their labor to others), and petty-commodity production carried out by independent craftspeople or small-scale farmers. Even as recently as one hundred years ago, when the first incarnation of globalized capitalism appeared, the world still included all of these modes of production. Following the Russian Revolution, capitalism shared the world with communism, which reigned in countries that contained about one-third of the human population. None but capitalism remain today, except in very marginal areas with no influence on global developments.

The global victory of capitalism has many implications that were anticipated by Marx and Engels in 1848. Capitalism facilitates—and when foreign profits are higher than domestic, even craves—the cross-border exchange of goods, the movement of capital, and in some cases the movement of labor. It is thus not an accident that globalization developed the most in the period between the Napoleonic Wars and World War I, when capitalism largely held sway. And it is no accident that today's globalization coincides with the even more absolute triumph of capitalism. Had communism triumphed over capitalism, there is little doubt that despite the internationalist creed professed by its founders, it would not have led to globalization. Communist societies were overwhelmingly autarkic and nationalistic, and there was minimal movement of goods, capital, and labor across borders. Even within the Soviet bloc, trade was carried out only to sell surplus goods or according to mercantilist principles of bilateral bargaining. This is entirely different from capitalism, which, as Marx and Engels noted, has an inherent tendency to expand.

The uncontested dominion of the capitalist mode of production has its counterpart in the similarly uncontested ideological view that money-making not only is respectable but is the most important objective in people's lives, an incentive understood by people from all parts of the world and all classes. It may be difficult to convince a person who differs from us in life experience, gender, race, or background of some of our beliefs, concerns, and motivations. But that same person will easily understand the language of money and profit; if we explain that our objective is to get the best possible deal, they will be able to readily figure out whether cooperation or competition is the best economic strategy to pursue. The fact that (to use Marxist terms) the infrastructure (the economic base) and superstructure (political and judicial institutions) are so well aligned in today's world not only helps global capitalism maintain its dominion but also makes people's objectives more compatible and their communication clearer and easier, since they all know what the other side is after. We live in a world where everybody follows the same rules and understands the same language of profit-making.

Such a sweeping statement does need some qualification. There are indeed some small communities scattered around the world that shun money-making, and there are some individuals who disdain it. But they do not influence the shape of things and the movement of history. The claim that individual beliefs and value systems are aligned with capitalism's objectives should not be taken to imply that all of our actions are entirely and always driven by profit. People sometimes perform actions that are genuinely altruistic or are driven by other objectives. But for most of us, if we assess these actions by time spent or money forgone, they play only a small role in our lives. Just as it is wrong to call billionaires "philanthropists" if they acquire an enormous fortune through unsavory practices and then give away a small fraction of their wealth, so it is wrong to zero in on a small subset of our altruistic actions and ignore the fact that perhaps 90 percent of our waking lives is spent in purposeful activities whose objective is improving our standard of living, chiefly through money-making.

This alignment of individual and systemic objectives is a major success achieved by capitalism—one I discuss more in Chapter 5. Unconditional supporters of capitalism explain this success as resulting from capitalism's "naturalness," that is, the alleged fact that it perfectly reflects our innate selves—our desire to trade, to gain, to strive for better economic conditions and a more pleasant life. But I do not think that, beyond some primary functions, it is accurate to speak of innate desires as if they existed independently of the societies we live in. Many of these desires are the product of socialization within the societies where we live—and in this case within capitalist societies, which are the only ones that exist.

It is an old idea, argued by writers as distinguished as Plato, Aristotle, and Montesquieu, that a political or economic system stands in harmonious relation with a society's prevailing values and behaviors. This is certainly true of present-day capitalism. Capitalism has been remarkably successful in imparting its objectives to people, prompting or persuading them to adopt its goals and thus achieving an extraordinary concordance between what capitalism requires for its expansion and people's ideas, desires, and values. Capitalism has been much more successful than its competitors in creating the conditions that, according to the political philosopher John Rawls, are necessary for the stability of any system: namely, that individuals in their daily actions manifest and thus reinforce the broader values upon which the social system is based.

Capitalism's mastery of the world has been achieved, however, with two different types of capitalism: the liberal meritocratic capitalism that has developed incrementally in the West over the past two hundred years (discussed in Chapter 2), and the state-led political, or authoritarian, capitalism that is exemplified by China but also exists in other parts of Asia (Singapore, Vietnam, Burma) and parts of Europe and Africa (Russia and the Caucasian countries, Central Asia, Ethiopia, Algeria, Rwanda) (discussed in Chapter 3). As has occurred so often in human history, the rise and apparent triumph of one system or religion is soon followed by some sort of schism between different variants of the same credo. After Christianity triumphed across the Mediterranean and the Near East, it experienced ferocious ideological disputes and divisions (the one between Orthodoxy and Arianism being the most notable), and eventually it produced the first big schism between the Western and Eastern churches. No different was the fate of Islam, which almost immediately after its dizzying conquest split into Sunni and Shia branches. And finally, communism, capitalism's twentieth-century rival, did not long remain a monolith, splitting into Soviet-led and Chinese versions. The worldwide victory of capitalism is, in that respect, no different: we are presented with two models of capitalism that differ not only in the political but also economic and, to a much lesser degree, social spheres. And it is, I think, rather unlikely that whatever happens in the competition between liberal and political capitalisms, one system will come to rule the entire globe.

1.2 The Rise of Asia and the Rebalancing of the World

The economic success of political capitalism is the force behind the second remarkable development mentioned above: the rise of Asia. It is true that the rise of Asia is not solely due to political capitalism; liberal capitalist countries like India and Indonesia are also growing very fast. But the historical transformation of Asia is without question being led by China. This change, unlike the rise of capitalism to global supremacy, has a historical precedent in that it returns the distribution of economic activity in Eurasia to roughly the position that existed before the Industrial Revolution. But it does it with a twist. While levels of economic development of western Europe and Asia (China) were roughly the same in, for example, the first and second centuries, or the fourteenth and fifteenth centuries, the two parts of the world barely interacted at the time and generally lacked knowledge about each other. Indeed, we know much more about their relative development levels now than contemporaries knew at the time. Today, in contrast, interactions are intense and continuous. Income levels in both regions are also many times greater. These two parts of the world, western Europe and its North American offshoots, and Asia, which are together home to 70 percent of world population and 80 percent of world output, are in constant contact through trade, investment, movement of people, transfer of technology, and exchange of ideas. The resulting competition between these regions is keener than it would be otherwise because the systems, while similar, are not identical. This is the case whether competition takes place by design, with one system trying to impose itself on the other and on the rest of the world, or simply by example, with one system being copied more readily by the rest of the world than the other.

This geographical rebalancing is putting an end to the military, political, and economic superiority of the West, which has been taken for granted during the past two centuries. Never in history had the superiority of one part of the world over another been as great as was the superiority of Europe over Africa and Asia in the nineteenth century. That superiority was most evident in colonial conquests, but it was also reflected in income gaps between the two parts of the world and thus in global income inequality among all citizens of the world, which we can estimate with relative precision from 1820 onward, as illustrated in Figure 1.1. In this graph, and throughout the book, inequality is measured using an index called the Gini coefficient, which ranges in value from 0 (no inequality) to 1 (maximum inequality). (The index is often expressed as a percentage, ranging from 0 to 100, where each percentage point is called a Gini point.)

Before the Industrial Revolution in the West, global inequality was moderate, and nearly as much of it was due to differences among individuals living in the same nations as among the mean incomes of individuals in

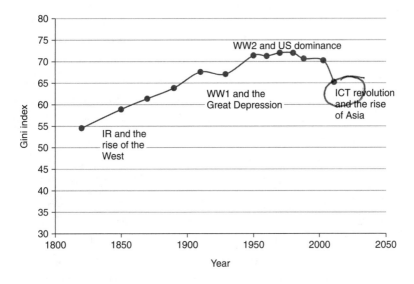

FIGURE 1.1. Estimated global income inequality, 1820–2013

IR = Industrial Revolution; ICT = information and communication technologies. *Data source:*
Data for 1820–1980 are based on Bourguignon and Morrisson (2002), with their GDPs per capita
replaced by new data from the Maddison Project (2018). Data for 1988–2001 are based on Lakner
and Milanovic (2016) and my own update. All incomes are in 2011 PPP dollars (purchasing power
parity) (the latest round of International Comparison Project at the time of writing in 2018). For
additional technical details, see Appendix C.

different nations. This changed dramatically with the rise of the West.
Global inequality increased almost continuously from 1820 to the eve of
World War I, rising from 55 Gini points (roughly the level of inequality
that currently exists in Latin American countries) to just under 70 (a level
of inequality higher than that in South Africa today). The rise of income
levels in Europe, North America, and later Japan (coupled with the stagnation of China and India) drove most of this increase, though rising income inequality within the nations of what was becoming the First World
also played a role. After 1918, there was a short drop in global inequality
caused by what—on the broad canvas on which we operate—appear as
the blips of World War I and the Great Depression, when Western incomes
failed to grow.

    After the end of World War II, global inequality stood at its highest level
ever, at about 75 Gini points, and it remained at that high plateau until

the last decade of the twentieth century. During this time the gap between the West and Asia—China and India in particular—did not grow any further, as Indian independence and Chinese revolution were setting the stage for the growth of these two giants. These two countries thus maintained their relative positions vis-à-vis the West from the late 1940s to the early 1980s. But those positions were highly skewed in favor of the rich countries: the GDP per capita of both India and China was less than one-tenth that of Western countries.

That income gap began to change, and dramatically so, after the 1980s. Reforms in China led to growth of approximately 8 percent per capita per annum over the next forty years, sharply narrowing the country's distance from the West. Today, China's GDP per capita is at approximately 30–35 percent of the Western level, the same point where it was around 1820, and shows a clear tendency to keep on rising (relative to the West); it will probably continue to do so until the time when incomes become very similar.

The economic revolution in China was followed by similar accelerations of growth in India, Vietnam, Thailand, Indonesia, and elsewhere in Asia. Although this growth has been accompanied by rising inequality within each of the countries (especially in China), the closing of the gap with the West has helped reduce global income inequality. This is what lies behind the recent drop in global Gini.

The convergence of Asian incomes with those in the West took place during another technological revolution, that of information and communication technologies (ICT)—a revolution in production that this time favored Asia (further discussed in Chapter 4). The ICT revolution contributed not only to the much faster growth of Asia but also to the deindustrialization of the West, which, in turn, is not dissimilar to the deindustrialization that happened in India during the Industrial Revolution. We thus have two periods of rapid technological change bookmarking the evolution of global inequality (see Figure 1.1). The effects of the ICT revolution are not over yet, but they are, in many respects, similar to those of the Industrial Revolution: a large reshuffle in worldwide income ranking as some groups advance and others decline, along with significant geographical concentration of such winners and losers.

It is useful to think of these two technological revolutions as mirror images of each other. One led to an increase of global inequality through the enrichment of the West; the other has led to income convergence among large swaths of the globe through the enrichment of Asia. We should expect that income levels will eventually be similar across the entire Eurasian continent and North America, thus helping reduce global inequality even further. (A big unknown, however, is the fate of Africa, which, so far, is not catching up with the rich world and whose population is rising the fastest.)

The economic rebalancing of the world is not only geographical; it is also political. China's economic success undermines the West's claim that there is a necessary link between capitalism and liberal democracy. Indeed, this claim is being undermined in the West itself by populist and plutocratic challenges to liberal democracy.

The rebalancing of the world brings the Asian experience to the forefront of thinking regarding economic development. Asia's economic success will make its model more attractive to others and may inform our views about economic development and growth, in a fashion not dissimilar to that in which the British experience and Adam Smith, who drew on that experience, influenced our thinking during the past two centuries.

For the past forty years, the five largest countries in Asia combined (excluding China) have had higher per capita growth rates than the Western economies in all but two years, and this trend is unlikely to change. In 1970, the West produced 56 percent of world output and Asia (including Japan) only 19 percent. Today, those proportions are 37 percent and 43 percent.[1] We can see this trend clearly by comparing the United States with China, and Germany with India (Figure 1.2). The remarkable rise of Asia during the era of globalization is reflected in popular support for globalization, which is the strongest in Asia, and notably in Vietnam (91 percent of people interviewed think globalization is a force for the good), and weakest in Europe, notably in France (where only 37 percent support globalization).[2]

Malaise in the West about globalization is in part caused by the gap between elites, who have done very well, and significant numbers of people who have seen little benefit from globalization, resent it, and, accurately

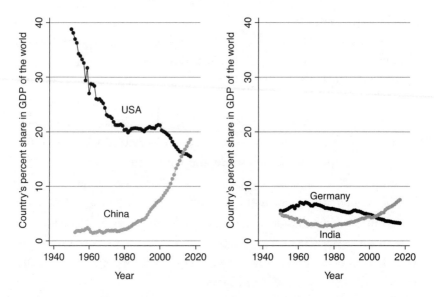

FIGURE 1.2. Percentage share of global GDP for the United States versus China (*left*) and Germany versus India (*right*), 1950–2016

Data source: Calculated from World Bank World Development Indicators 2017 version, with GDPs per capita expressed in international (PPP) dollars.

or not, regard global trade and migration as the cause of their ills (see Chapter 4). This situation eerily resembles the Third World societies of the 1970s, which also exhibited this dualistic character—with the bourgeoisie plugged into the global economic system and most of the hinterland left behind. The "disease" that was supposed to affect only developing countries (what was called "disarticulation" in neo-Marxist literature) seems to have now moved north and struck the rich world. At the same time, somewhat ironically, the dualistic character of many developing economies is being diminished by their full inclusion in the globalized system of supply chains.

The two types of capitalism, liberal meritocratic and political, now seem to be competing with each other. They are led, respectively, by the United States and China. But even independently of China's willingness to make available and to "export" an alternative political and, to some extent, economic version of capitalism,

The core of the book

political capitalism itself has certain features that make it attractive to the political elites in the rest of the world and not only in Asia: the system provides greater autonomy to political elites. It is also attractive to many ordinary people because of the high growth rates that it seems to promise. On the other hand, liberal capitalism has many well-known advantages, the most important being that democracy and the rule of law are values in themselves and both, arguably, can be credited with encouraging faster economic development through promoting innovation and allowing so-cial mobility, and thus providing approximately equal chances of success for all. It is the reneging on some crucial aspects of this implicit value system, namely a movement toward the creation of a self-perpetuating upper class and polarization between the elites and the rest, that repre-sents the most important threat to the longer-term viability of liberal capi-talism. This threat is a danger both to the system's own survival and to the general attractiveness of the model to the rest of the world.

In the next two chapters I discuss the main features of the two variants of modern capitalism, focusing on their inherent characteristics rather than on temporary aberrations. Keeping in mind the difference between sys-temic and incidental features is crucial if we wish to study the long-term evolution of liberal meritocratic and political capitalism, not just tempo-rary fluctuations. I focus in particular on the social and economic struc-tures that the two systems reproduce, especially as they affect matters of income inequality and class structure. The way the two systems deal with these matters will, I believe, determine their relative attractiveness and sta-bility. And consequently our desire to live under one or the other.

CHAPTER 2

LIBERAL MERITOCRATIC CAPITALISM

[Democracy] is a wonderfully pleasant way of carrying on in the short-run, isn't it?

—Plato, *The Republic*

The definition of liberal meritocratic capitalism is quite straightforward. I define capitalism in the fashion of Karl Marx and Max Weber, as the system

Definition of liberal meritocratic capitalism

where most production is carried out with privately owned means of production, capital hires legally free labor, and coordination is decentralized. In addition, to add Joseph Schumpeter's requirement, most investment decisions are made by private companies or individual entrepreneurs.[1]

The terms "meritocratic" and "liberal" come from the definitions of various forms of equality that John Rawls lays out in *A Theory of Justice* (1971). "Meritocratic equality" is a system of "natural liberty," in which careers are "open to talent"—that is, there are no legal obstacles preventing individuals from achieving a given position in society. It fully accepts inheritance of property. "Liberal equality" is more egalitarian because it corrects, in part, for inheritance of property by imposing high taxes on inheritance and includes free education as a way to reduce the intergenerational transmission of advantages. The term "liberal meritocratic capitalism" thus addresses how goods and services are produced and exchanged ("capitalism"), how they are distributed among individuals ("meritocratic"), and how much social mobility there is ("liberal").

In this chapter, I focus on how systemic forces within liberal meritocratic capitalism shape income distribution and lead to the formation of an upper-class elite. In Chapter 3, I examine similar issues with respect to political capitalism. In both chapters, the emphasis is on distribution of income, inequality in income and capital, and class formation, not on production.

2.1 Key Features of Liberal Meritocratic Capitalism

2.1a Historical Capitalisms

Liberal meritocratic capitalism can be best understood by contrasting its distinguishing features with those of nineteenth-century classical capitalism and with social-democratic capitalism, as it existed between approximately the end of the World War II and the early 1980s in Western Europe and North America. We are dealing here with "ideal-typical" features of the systems and ignoring details that varied among countries and across time. But in the following sections, where I focus on liberal meritocratic capitalism alone, I discuss these features in detail for a country that can be taken as prototypical, namely the United States.

Table 2.1 summarizes the differences between the three historical types of capitalism through which Western economies have passed. For simplicity, I take the United Kingdom before 1914 as representative of classical capitalism, Western Europe and the United States from the end of World War II through the early 1980s as representative of social-democratic capitalism, and the twenty-first-century United States as representative of liberal meritocratic capitalism.[2] Note that because the two key features that differentiate liberal from meritocratic capitalism, taxation of inheritance and broadly available public education, have weakened in the United States over the past thirty years, the country may have shifted toward a model of capitalism that is more "meritocratic" and less "liberal." However, since I am using the United States as an example of all rich capitalist countries, I

TABLE 2.1. Key features of classical, social-democratic, and liberal meritocratic capitalism

Form of capitalism	Classical capitalism	Social-democratic capitalism	Liberal meritocratic capitalism
Representative economy	UK before 1914	US, Europe after WWII	US in early 21st century
1. Rising share of capital income in net product	Yes	No	Yes
2. High concentration of capital ownership	Yes	Yes	Yes
3. Capital-abundant individuals are rich	Yes	Yes	Yes
4. Capital-income rich are also labor-income rich	No	No	Yes
5. Rich (or potentially rich) marry each other (homogamy)	Yes (to some extent)	No	Yes
6. High correlation of income between parents and children (transmission of advantages)	Yes	Yes, but in some cases weak	Yes

Note: "Rich" without an additional adjective indicates that a person is income-rich.

think it is still acceptable to speak of liberal meritocratic capitalism as a single model.

We start with the key characteristic of every capitalist system—the division of net income between the two factors of production: owners of capital (owners of property more generally) and workers. This division need not coincide with two distinct classes of individuals. It will do so only when one class of individuals receives income only from capital, and a different class receives income only from labor.[3] As we shall see, whether or not these classes overlap is what distinguishes different types of capitalism.

Division of the net product between owners and workers

Data on the division of total net income between capital and labor is murky for the period before 1914, since the first estimates for the United Kingdom, which were made by the economist Arthur Bowley, were not done until 1920. Based on this work, it has been argued that the income shares of capital and labor are more or less constant—a trend that came to be called Bowley's Law. Data produced by Thomas Piketty (2014, 200–201) for the United Kingdom and France have cast severe doubt on that conclusion, even for the past. For the United Kingdom in the period 1770–2010, Piketty found that the share of capital oscillated between 20 and 40 percent of national income. In France, between 1820 and 2010, it varied even more widely: from less than 15 percent in the 1940s to more than 45 percent in the 1860s. The percentages became more stable after World War II, however, reinforcing belief in Bowley's Law. Paul Samuelson, for example, in his influential *Economics,* included Bowley's Law among the six basic trends of economic development in advanced countries (although he did allow for some "edging upward of labor's share") (Samuelson 1976, 740). However, since the late twentieth century, the share of capital income in total income has been rising. While this tendency has been quite strong in the United States, it has also been documented in most developed countries, as well as developing countries, although the data for the latter must be taken with a strong dose of caution (Karabarbounis and Neiman 2013).

A rising share of capital income in total income implies that capital and capitalists are becoming more important than labor and workers—and thus acquiring more economic and political power. This trend occurred in both classical and liberal meritocratic capitalism, but not in the social-democratic variety (Table 2.1). A rising share of capital in total income also affects interpersonal income distribution because typically, (1) people who draw a large share of income from capital are rich, and (2) capital income is concentrated in relatively few hands. These two factors result almost automatically in greater income inequality between individuals.

To see why both (1) and (2) are indispensable for the automatic translation of higher capital share into greater interpersonal inequality, make the following mental experiment: assume that the share of capital in net income goes up, but that every individual receives the same proportion of income from capital and labor as every other individual.[4] A rising aggregate share of capital income will increase every individual income in the same proportion, and inequality will not change. (Measures of inequality are relative.) In other words, if we do not have a high positive correlation between being "capital-abundant" (that is, deriving a large percentage of one's income from capital) and being rich, a rising aggregate share of capital does not lead to higher interpersonal inequality. Note that in this example there are still rich and poor people, but there is no correlation between the percentage of income that a person draws from capital and that person's position in the overall income distribution.

Now, imagine a situation where poor people draw a higher proportion of their income from capital than rich people do. As before, let the overall share of capital in net income increase. But this time, the rising share of capital will reduce income inequality because it will increase proportionately more the incomes of the people at the low end of the income distribution.

But neither of these two mental exercises reflects what is happening in reality in capitalist societies: rather, there is a strong positive association between being capital-abundant and being rich. The richer a person is, the more likely they are to have a high share of their income coming from capital.[5] This has been the case in all types of capitalism (see Table 2.1, rows 2 and 3). This particular characteristic—that capital-abundant people are also rich—may be taken as an immutable characteristic of capitalism, at least in the forms that we have experienced it so far.[6]

The next feature to consider is the link between being well-off in terms of capital (that is, being capital-income-rich within the distribution of capital incomes) and being well-off in terms of earnings (that is, being labor-income-rich within the distribution of labor incomes). One might think that people who are capital-abundant rich are unlikely to be rich in terms of their labor income. But this is not the case at all. A simple example with two groups of people, the "poor" and the "rich," makes this clear. The poor have overall low income, and most of their income comes from labor; the rich are the opposite. Consider situation 1: The poor have 4 units of income from labor and 1 unit of income from capital; the rich have 4 units of income from labor and 16 units from capital. Here the capital abundant are indeed rich, but the amount of their labor income is the same as that of the poor. Now consider situation 2: Everything stays the same as in situation 1 except that the labor income of the rich increases to 8 units. They are

Capital-rich and labor-rich people

still capital abundant, since they receive a larger share of their total income from capital (16 out of 24 units = 2/3) than the poor do, but now they are also labor-rich (8 units versus only 4 for the poor).

Situation 2 is when the capital-abundant individuals are not only rich but also relatively well off in terms of labor income. Everything else being the same, situation 2 is more unequal than situation 1. This is indeed one of the important differences between, on the one hand, classical and social-democratic capitalisms, and on the other, liberal meritocratic capitalism (see Table 2.1, row 4). The perception and reality of classical capitalism was that capitalists (what I call here capital-abundant individuals) were all very rich but typically did not receive much income from labor; in the extreme case, they received no income from labor at all. It is no accident that Thorstein Veblen labeled them the "leisure class." Correspondingly, laborers received no income from capital at all. Their income came entirely from labor.[7] In this case there was a perfect division of society into capitalists and workers, with both sides receiving zero income from the other factor of production. (If we add landlords, who received 100 percent of their income from land, we have the tripartite classification of classes introduced by Adam Smith.) Inequality was high in such fragmented societies because capitalists tended to have lots of capital, and the return on capital was (often) high, but inequality was not compounded by these same individuals also having high labor incomes.

The situation is different in liberal meritocratic capitalism, as found in the United States today. People who are capital-rich now tend also to be labor-rich (or to put it in more contemporary terms, they tend to be individuals with high "human capital"). Whereas the people at the top of the income distribution under classical capitalism were financiers, rentiers, and owners of large industrial holdings (who are not hired by anyone and hence have no labor income), today a significant percentage of the people at the top are highly paid managers, web designers, physicians, investment bankers, and other elite professionals. These people are wage workers who need to work in order to draw their large salaries.[8] But these same people, whether through inheritance or because they have saved enough money through their working lives, also possess large financial assets and draw a significant amount of income from them.

The rising share of labor income in the top 1 percent (or even more select groups, like the top 0.1 percent) has been well documented by Thomas
Piketty, in *Capital in the Twenty-First Century* (2014), and other authors.[9]
We shall return to that topic later in the chapter. What is important to
realize here is that the presence of high labor income at the top of the income distribution, if associated with high capital income received by the
same individuals, deepens inequality. This is a peculiarity of liberal meritocratic capitalism, something that has never before been seen to this
extent.

Let's now move to the question of marriage patterns under different
forms of capitalism (Table 2.1, row 5). When economists study income or

*Marriage
patterns*

wealth inequality, we use the household as the unit of observation. For that unit, it matters a lot whether all members
are individually well off or not. Because many households
are formed through marriage, it is important to look at how people pair
up. As in the case of capital and labor income, liberal meritocratic capitalism again differs from the other two capitalisms.

To illustrate the difference, compare patterns of marriage pairing in the
United States in the 1950s and the twenty-first century. After World War
II, men tended to marry women from a similar status group, but the richer
the husband, the less likely the wife would work and have her own earnings. Today, richer and more educated men tend to marry richer and more
educated women. We can show what happens to inequality in these two
situations with a simple example. Consider two men, one who earns 50
units and another 100, and two women, one earning 10 units and the other
20. Now, suppose that there is some assortative mating (also called
homogamy), that is, a positive correlation between husbands' and wives'
earnings: thus the man with earnings of 100 marries the woman with earnings of 20, and the poorer man marries the poorer woman. But then assume
that the rich wife drops out of the labor force (as in the 1950s), while in the
other couple both continue to work. The ratio of the two family incomes
will be 100 to 60. Now let the assortative mating remain the same, but
both women (as today) stay in the labor force: the ratio of the two family
incomes becomes 120 to 60, that is, inequality increases.

The example shows that under conditions of assortative mating, inequality will go up if women's participation in the workforce increases. It will go up even more if mating was previously random or disassortative (with richer men marrying poorer women). Some have argued that assortative mating has become much more common in liberal meritocratic capitalism because social norms have changed such that more women are highly educated (in fact, their graduation rates now exceed those of men), and many more work. It is also possible (although it is entirely speculative) that people's preferences have changed, and that both men and women now prefer to be in a union with someone who is similar to them. Whatever the reasons for it, increasing homogamy is yet another factor that will push income inequality up. However, it will only push inequality up during the period of transition from nonassortative mating (or assortative mating with nonparticipation of wives in the labor force) to assortative mating. Once assortative mating and labor force participation rates have reached their limits, the inequality-enhancing effect disappears. Inequality stabilizes, albeit at a high level.

The final characteristic of capitalism that we will examine is the transmission of acquired advantages, notably wealth and "human capital," across generations, often measured by the correlation between parents' and children's incomes (Table 2.1, row 6). Although we lack data for earlier periods, it is reasonable to believe that such transmission must have been strong under all forms of capitalism. For later periods, when we do have

> *Intergenerational transmission of inequality*

better data, we know that it is significantly weaker in more equal contemporary societies, where access to education is easy, the cost of education is borne by taxpayers, and inheritance taxes are high. Nordic societies have particularly low intergenerational correlation of incomes, and it is likely that during the golden age of social-democratic capitalism such correlation was low, especially in Western Europe.[10] In contrast, the United States today has both high intergenerational transmission of inequality and high income inequality. Studies comparing multiple countries find a relatively strong relationship between the two, so this is not surprising (Corak 2013, 11; Brunori, Ferreira, and Peragine 2013, 27). We would expect the highly unequal United States to also have high transmission of intergenerational inequality.

What do we find overall, then, when we compare inequalities in the different versions of capitalism? In all six aspects examined here, liberal meritocratic capitalism displays features that enhance inequality. It differs from classical capitalism most distinctively in the feature that capital-rich individuals are also labor-rich, and probably also in greater assortative mating. It differs significantly from social-democratic capitalism in several respects: it exhibits a rising aggregate share of capital in net income, it has labor-rich capitalists, it almost certainly has a greater prevalence of assortative mating, and it most likely has greater intergenerational transmission of inequality.

| Complex nature of liberal meritocratic capitalism |

Three points need to be made, however, before we move on to a more detailed review of each of these six characteristics. The fact that liberal meritocratic capitalism scores "yes" on all six does not immediately imply that it must be more unequal than the other forms of capitalism. And in fact, it is certainly not more unequal than classical capitalism (Milanovic 2016, chap. 2). I have not included here the forces of redistribution, through direct taxes and transfers, which liberal capitalism has "inherited" from social-democratic capitalism and which classical capitalism lacked. These forces do reduce inequality below the level determined by market income alone.

Second, a "yes" score on an individual characteristic does not tell us how strongly that characteristic advances inequality. For example, while both classical and liberal capitalism have a high concentration of capital income, the level of concentration was much greater under the classical form. Around 1914, 70 percent of British wealth was in the hands of the top 1 percent of wealth-holders; that number today is around 20 percent (Alvaredo, Atkinson, and Morelli 2018). Wealth is still highly concentrated, but much less so than it was previously.

Third, some of the distinctive inequality-enhancing features of liberal meritocratic capitalism may be morally acceptable, and even, in some cases, desirable. Yes, inequality is greater where there is a greater share of labor-rich capitalists, but isn't it a good thing for people to be able to become rich by working? Isn't it better if people earn high incomes from both labor and ownership, rather than solely from the latter? And, yes, homogamy increases inequality, but isn't it something desirable, since it reflects much greater participation of women in the labor force, social norms that value paid work, and a preference for partners who are similar to ourselves? It is this deep ambivalence between the inequality-enhancing effects of some features of modern capitalism and the fact that most people may see them as socially desirable (leaving aside their effect on inequality) that we should keep in mind as we further examine the characteristics of liberal meritocratic capitalism and discuss remedies for high inequality in such societies.

2.1b Systemic and Nonsystemic Causes of Increase in Inequality in Liberal Meritocratic Capitalism

So far, in discussing the forces that drive inequality in liberal meritocratic capitalism, we have focused on systemic, or fundamental, factors. These do indeed appear to be the dominant factors that drive income distribution. But nonsystemic, or incidental, factors also play a role. For example, some of the increase in income inequality in the United States and other countries is a result of the increasing skill premium paid to more educated labor, which is not a systemic feature of liberal capitalism. This rising premium is due to a shortage in the supply of highly skilled labor and to technological change that has made skilled labor more productive and thus in greater demand (Goldin and Katz 2010). But nothing fundamental to liberal capitalism prevents an adequate increase in the supply of highly skilled labor. There are no legal obstacles preventing people from going on to advanced studies; moreover, in most Western European countries, higher education is either free or relatively cheap. The lack of response of labor to technological change does not result from systemic factors intrinsic to liberal capitalism.

To better understand the difference between systemic and nonsystemic factors, take the first characteristic of capitalism discussed in the previous section, the rising share of capital income. This phenomenon is a systemic feature of liberal meritocratic capitalism because it results from the weakened bargaining power of labor. This weakened power is in turn the outcome of (a) a change in the organization of labor in postindustrial capitalism, in which large physical accumulations of workers in one place have been replaced by a decentralized labor force of workers who often do not physically interact with each other and cannot be easily organized, and (b) globalization in general, and more specifically, the increased global supply of labor, including the outsourcing of production. Such features derive from deep changes in the nature of work in more advanced capitalism and globalization, and neither is likely to be overturned in the medium run.

Assortative mating is also a systemic factor to the extent that it derives from the equalization of access to education for women and men, which itself stems from a systemic feature of meritocratic (and even more so of liberal) capitalism: commitment to the equal treatment of all individuals regardless of gender, race, sexual orientation, and the like. There is an additional, more subtle, reason why it may be regarded as systemic. In a society where discrimination is, at least formally, excluded, a preference to partner with a person who is similar to oneself may be more freely expressed than in a system where marriages are arranged. In other words, the preference for one or another type of spouse itself is not ahistorical, but changes with the type of society in which one lives.[11]

The common failure of economists to distinguish between systemic and incidental factors is illustrated by the lack of understanding of some of Thomas Piketty's key formulations, especially the expression $r > g$ (meaning that the rate of return on capital is greater than the economy's growth rate). Debraj Ray (2014), for example, has pointed out that this relationship depends on capitalists' saving propensity: if capitalists just spent the entire return they earned from their capital, then $r > g$ would not have any effect on subsequent capital incomes because both the stock of capital and the income derived from it would stay the same. Thus, Ray argues that neither an increase in the capital-output ratio nor an increase in the share of income received by capitalists is inevitable. This argument is correct, but irrelevant. It is correct in the sense that if capitalists indeed consumed their entire profit, there would be no increase in capital and no rising inequality. But then there would be no capitalism either! In fact, one of the principal features of capitalism—perhaps the most important one—is that it is a system of growth, where capitalists do not behave like feudal lords and consume the surplus, but rather invest it. The function of the capitalist or capitalist-cum-entrepreneur has always been seen, from Smith and Marx to Schumpeter and John Maynard Keynes, to involve accumulating savings and reinvesting profits. If capitalists were to cease behaving in such a manner, the regularity uncovered by Piketty would not hold, but then the system we are discussing would not be capitalist but something else.

Keeping in mind these differences between systemic and incidental features is absolutely crucial if we wish to study the evolution of liberal meritocratic and (in Chapter 3) political capitalism. When we look at systemic features, we abstract from incidental variations and national idiosyncrasies; we focus on the elements that define a system and how they might affect the system's evolution.

2.2 Systemic Inequalities

2.2a Increasing Aggregate Share of Capital in National Income

About a decade ago, it became noticeable that the share of income from capital in net national income was rising. The common wisdom in economics was that the shares of capital and labor were supposed to be stable, at, say, approximately 70 percent of national income going to labor and 30 percent going to capital (as enshrined in Bowley's Law, discussed in Section 2.1a). There were, moreover, theoretical arguments about why this should be so, implied in the so-called unitary elasticity of substitution between capital and labor, which says that as the relative price of labor increases by x percentage points with respect to capital (that is, labor becomes relatively more expensive), the relative use of labor as opposed to capital will go down by x percent. Decreased use of a more expensive factor of production would exactly offset its increase in price, such that the aggregate income share of that factor of production (and by definition of the other, since there are only two) would remain unchanged.

The view that the shares of labor and capital are constant was so prevalent that economists paid very little attention to how income was distributed between capital and labor and even to what was happening to the concentration of capital income. They focused entirely on labor income and the rising wage premium of more educated versus less educated workers. That alone was supposed to explain the entire increase in inequality. An influential book by Claudia Goldin and Lawrence Katz, *The Race between Education and Technology* (2010), made this argument. It went back to Jan Tinbergen's idea that technological change raises the productivity of highly skilled labor, and that in the absence of sufficient increase in the supply of such labor, inequality of labor incomes will tend to rise.

But capital was ignored. That was a mistake, because the share of capital in national income has been rising, as has been shown by Elsby, Hobijn, and Şahin (2013) for the United States, and Karabarbounis and Neiman (2013) for both rich and developing countries.[12] They find that labor share in the United States, which was approximately 67 percent in the late 1970s, had declined by some 4–5 percentage points around 2010. The capital share must then have risen by 4–5 percentage points, which, given that the initial capital share was about one-third of national income, is quite a lot.[13] In a study that included advanced, emerging, and developing economies, Dao et al. (2017) found that most of the decline in the labor share in advanced economies was due to the decreasing income share of middle-skill workers, mostly through reduction in their wages.

The reasons behind the increase in capital share are being debated, and it is unlikely that this debate will be fully settled any time soon. It may even be impossible to answer the question definitively because each of the factors adduced as an explanation may show the expected effect if that factor only is changed and all others are kept constant. But it is possible that many of the factors are interdependent and that they all changed at the same time, so that taking them one by one, although it makes econometric sense, may not provide a satisfactory analytic explanation.

Karabarbounis and Neiman (2013) argue that the increase in capital share is not the result of changed composition of output (say, an increase in sectors where capital share is high) because they find rising capital share within different sectors, and even within different regions of the United States. They argue that the rising share of capital was driven by a decline in the cost of capital goods (think of relatively cheap computers); this increased the use of capital (by replacing low-skilled labor with technology) and drove up its share in net product. But that does not explain the full increase, they argue: part of it is due to increasing monopoly power and markups, a finding that others have confirmed.[14]

According to Robert Solow, the rising share of capital comes from a change in the relative bargaining power of labor and capital. When organized labor was relatively powerful, as exemplified in the 1949 Treaty of Detroit between the auto workers' unions and employers, labor was able to push the distribution of income in its favor.[15] But when the power of organized labor declined—with the shift toward services as well as toward a global capitalist system that more than doubled the number of wage workers worldwide—the power of labor waned, and the functional distribution of income moved in favor of capital.[16]

In an interesting take on the evidence, Barkai (2016) has argued that both capital and labor shares have shrunk while a third factor of production, entrepreneurship (which is normally lumped together with capital) has increased in importance. According to this view, the share of capital—defined as income received by owners of capital only—has gone down while corporate profits (the earnings of entrepreneurs) have skyrocketed.[17] The cause, according to Barkai, is the rising monopolization of the economy, especially in sectors that have grown the fastest, such as information and communication.[18]

In *The Vanishing American Corporation* (2016), Gerald Davis emphasizes changes in company structure and size in the United States. According to Davis, companies with the highest revenues also used to employ the most people. They observed tacit agreements with workers, paying them somewhat above the market-determined wage. They might have been doing this for selfish reasons, to promote loyalty to the company, better working relations, fewer strikes, or fewer work-to-rule conflicts. But, Davis argues, when these companies outsourced many of the services that had been supplied in-house, their relationship to the labor force changed: contractors were not part of the company workforce, and there was no longer any need to reward loyalty or to ensure that the working atmosphere was pleasant and congenial. They could pay contractors the minimum market-determined rate. Hence the labor share shrank.

There may be other explanations for the shrinking labor share (and thus rising capital share), but the interesting fact for our purposes is that the rising aggregate share of capital income will, because of how concentrated it is and where in the income distribution the recipients of higher capital incomes are, have a direct effect on interpersonal income inequality.

2.2b High Concentration of Capital Ownership

Wealth has always been more concentrated (that is, more unequally distributed) than income. This is practically a truism: wealth distribution is the product of accumulation over time and transmission within households and across generations; it also tends to grow exponentially not only if invested wisely, but even if invested in risk-free assets. We know empirically that the only serious shocks to the high concentration of wealth in history have come from wars, revolutions, and, in some cases, unanticipated hyperinflation.[19]

In his monumental book *A Century of Wealth in America*, Edward Wolff, who has studied wealth inequality in the United States for several decades, showed that in 2013, the top 1 percent of wealth-holders owned one-half of all stocks and mutual funds, 55 percent of financial securities, 65 percent of financial trusts, and 63 percent of business equity. Perhaps even more revealing is that the top 10 percent of wealth-holders owned more than 90 percent of all financial assets (Wolff 2017, 103–105). Simplifying somewhat, we can say that almost all financial wealth in the United States is held by the wealthiest 10 percent. Moreover, these shares have been mildly increasing over the past thirty years, and are much higher than the share of disposable income received by the top US income decile, which is around 30 percent.[20]

Because wealth is more unequally distributed than overall income, it follows that revenues from that wealth will also be more unequally distributed than overall income (and especially so compared with other income sources, like earnings or self-employment income).[21] Income from capital will be received by people who are also ranked high in income distribution. These are the reasons why an increasing share of income from capital will tend to raise inequality.

Looking at levels of inequality in income from capital and labor in the United States, the United Kingdom, Germany, and Norway over the past thirty years (Figure 2.1), we see two interesting things: income from capital is much more unequally distributed than income from labor, and inequalities in both capital and labor income have increased over time.[22] The increase in capital income inequality is rather mild (amounting to only a few Gini points) because the level of inequality was already exceedingly high: it is around 0.9 in the United States and the United Kingdom, between 0.85 and 0.9 in Germany, and between 0.8 and 0.9 in Norway.[23] It is thus in all cases close to a theoretical maximum inequality of 1 (when the entire capital income would be earned by one individual or one household). What is also remarkable is that such high concentrations of capital income exist in all Western countries, and that the United States and the United Kingdom, which are often found to be the outliers in terms of high inequality of after-tax income, are not very much so in this case. In short, it is a systemic feature of liberal meritocratic capitalism that *capital income is extremely concentrated and is received mostly by the rich.*[24]

Note too that inequality in labor income (before taxes) in these countries has increased during this period, from a Gini coefficient of under 0.5 to about 0.6.

Looking at a snapshot of capital and labor income inequalities in rich countries from around 2013, we see that with the exception of Taiwan, all the countries shown have extremely concentrated income from capital, with Gini coefficients above 0.86 (Figure 2.2). Labor income Ginis are much lower, generally between 0.5 and 0.6, and even lower for Taiwan. I will return to the case of Taiwan later in the chapter.

To see how important the combination of rising capital income and heavy concentration of capital ownership is to total income inequality, one has to look at it dynamically. As countries grow richer, they acquire more wealth from savings and successful invest-

> *The curse of wealth*

ments (just like individuals do). Moreover, the increase in their capital overtakes the increase in their income, and they gradually become more "capital-intensive" or "capital-rich." This relationship—the ratio between capital and income—was a central feature of Piketty's *Capital in the Twenty-First Century.* Countries with higher income (GDP per capita) not only have more wealth per person, but their wealth-income ratio (denoted by β) is higher (Table 2.2). Thus in terms of GDP per

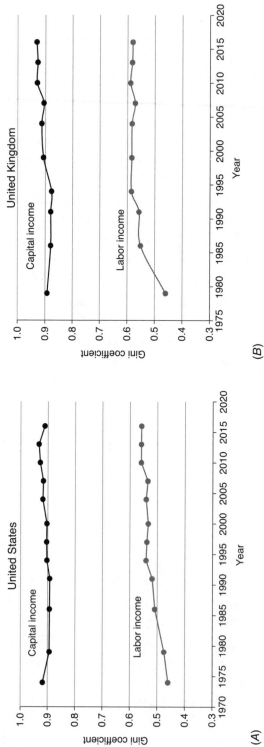

(A)

(B)

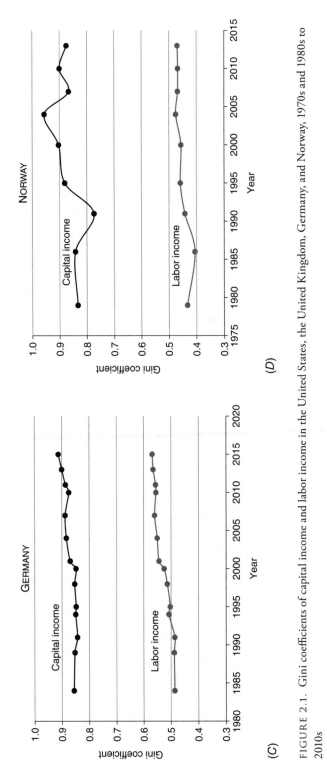

(C)

(D)

FIGURE 2.1. Gini coefficients of capital income and labor income in the United States, the United Kingdom, Germany, and Norway, 1970s and 1980s to 2010s

Both capital and labor incomes are pretax. Since capital incomes among the top of the income distribution tend to be underestimated (see Yonzan et al. 2018), true capital income Gini may be even higher. For the definitions of capital and labor income, see Appendix C. *Data source:* The calculations are based on Luxembourg Income Study data (https://www.lisdatacenter.org), which provide individual-level information from household surveys and harmonize the definitions of the variables so that capital and labor incomes are defined consistently over time and between countries.

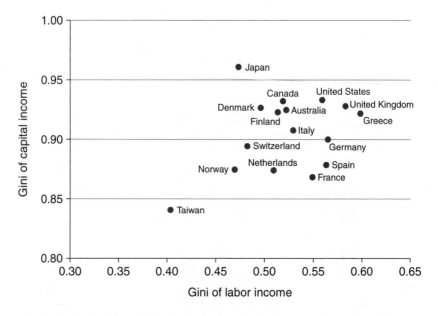

FIGURE 2.2. Capital and labor income inequalities in rich countries, around 2013

Data source: Luxembourg Income Study database (https://www.lisdatacenter.org).

capita, Switzerland is 53 times better off than India, but it has almost 100 times more wealth per adult than India.

As capitalist countries become richer, the share of capital income in total net income is bound to increase (unless the rate of return on wealth goes down commensurately), and as long as wealth is heavily concentrated, inequality will also increase. Moreover, the transmission of higher wealth into greater interpersonal inequality is generally stronger in more capital-rich countries because the correlation between having lots of capital and being ranked high in the income distribution is stronger (Milanovic 2017). If the correlation between having more capital and being rich were close to zero (i.e., if everybody had wealth proportional to their income), the increase in capital share would not have an impact on interpersonal inequality. It would simply increase everybody's income in the same proportion. But when the rich hold most of capital, any increase in capital share raises their income more than proportionately and pushes inequality up.

TABLE 2.2. Household net wealth per adult and GDP per capita in selected countries, 2013 (in current US dollars, at market exchange rates)

	Wealth per adult	GDP per capita	Wealth-income ratio (β)
Switzerland	513,000	85,000	6.0
USA	301,000	53,000	5.7
Japan	217,000	40,000	5.4
China	22,000	7,000	3.2
Indonesia	12,000	3,600	3.3
India	4,700	1,500	3.1

Data source: Wealth data from Credit Suisse Research Institute (2013) and Jim Davies (pers. comm.). GDP data from World Bank, World Development Indicators.

The fact that development leads to countries becoming wealthy by a greater degree than the increase in their income may be seen, from the point of view of distribution, as a curse of wealth. Why? Because richer countries will "naturally" tend to be more unequal. For that reason, efforts to curb high inequality ought to be correspondingly greater. If no additional measures are taken on the policy side to offset the forces pushing inequality up as countries become richer, their inequality will tend to rise.

But the increase in inequality will be even stronger if the returns to wealth are not uniform across the board but are higher for people who own more wealth. This is the topic to which we turn next.

2.2c Higher Rate of Return on the Assets of the Rich

The rich not only own more wealth, but they own more wealth in proportion to their income, and, in addition, they own different types of wealth than the rest of the population. In 2013, some 20 percent of households in the United States had zero or negative net wealth, while the middle 60 percent of households had almost two-thirds of their wealth tied up in housing and 16 percent in pension funds (Wolff 2017, chap. 1).[25] Middle-class wealth is not diversified (since most of it is in housing) and is highly leveraged (that is, debt is a substantial component of gross wealth). This has been the case for the entire post–World War II period, as Kuhn, Schularick, and Steins (2017) have shown, using historical data from US wealth surveys. The amount of leverage increased with the financialization of the economy: by 2010, middle-class leverage attained a "stunning" 80 percent (out of each $5 of gross wealth, $4 were debt and only $1 represented net assets), compared with 20 percent in 1950 (Kuhn, Schularick, and Steins 2017, 34). Being so undiversified and so highly leveraged, the wealth of the middle class is dependent on housing price fluctuations and is very volatile. With leverage of 80 percent, the price of housing only has to go down by 20 percent for the entire net wealth to be wiped out. This indeed happened during the 2008 financial crisis.

But when we look at the top 20 percent and above, the composition of wealth changes: equity and financial instruments become the dominant asset class, representing almost three-quarters of their wealth for the top 1 percent. Housing wealth is correspondingly small, accounting for less than one-tenth of the wealth of the top 1 percent.

This difference in the composition of wealth has a crucial effect on the average rate of return on wealth obtained by different income groups. If the rates of return are fairly constant within asset classes (that is, the rate of return on housing is approximately the same whether one owns a huge mansion or a small studio apartment), then the overall rate of return will depend on the difference in rate of return between different asset classes—for example, whether the return on housing differs from the return on financial assets. Although few studies have been done on the relationship between returns for a given asset and the amount of that asset one owns, Wolff (2017, 119) concluded that rates of return varied little within asset classes. In other words (to go back to our example), whether one owns a mansion or a studio apartment, the rate of return will be approximately the same; and that is also true whether one owns $1,000 or $1 million of bonds.

So the issue then boils down to the difference in returns between asset classes. Over the thirty-year period from 1983 to 2013, richer households did better because financial assets outperformed housing (Wolff 2017, 116–121). The average real (after inflation) annual return on financial assets was 6.3 percent, while the average real return on housing was a meager 0.6 percent (Wolff 2017, 138, appendix table 3.1). The return on gross assets for the top 1 percent was on average 2.9 percent per year versus only

1.3 percent for the middle three quintiles. Capitalized over thirty years, this difference yields an advantage for the rich of around 60 percent.

If the rich systematically outperform the middle class and the poor in the returns they obtain on their assets, we are dealing with an important long-term contributor to greater inequality. Remedying this (if one wished to do so) would require progressive taxation of greater fortunes. One needs to keep in mind, however, that the kinds of assets held by the rich do not always prove more valuable. During a housing bubble, as in the United States between 2001 and 2007, housing often outperforms financial assets. Although it did not do so during the first three years of the Great Recession (when housing returns were more negative than financial returns), it often does: when stock markets plummet and housing prices do not change much, the rich realize an overall rate of return that is lower than that of the middle class. The opposite, as we have seen, has happened over the past thirty years.

It theoretically could be that the asset classes held by the rich are more risky and more volatile, so that their higher return might be ascribed partially to a premium for risk. However, thirty years is a long enough period to even out the consequences of risk, and over the longer term, rich wealthholders did do better than the middle class.

Asset classes held by the rich are also more valuable because they tend to be taxed less than asset classes held by the middle class. Thus capital gains and, in the United States, carried interest (income received by investment fund managers) are, in most cases, taxed at lower rates than interest from savings accounts.[26]

The rich also enjoy the advantages of size: entry costs (the minimum amount required for investment) to high-yield assets are high and discourage small investors; rich investors can also avail themselves of much better advice about where to invest and, per unit of dollar invested, pay lower fees. Feldstein and Yitzhaki (1982) found that rich investors consistently outperformed small investors in returns on their assets.[27]

Overall, the higher returns that the rich earn on their assets derive from three sources: (1) the rich hold proportionally more assets whose long-term return is higher (the asset composition effect), (2) the rich pay less tax per dollar earned from wealth (the tax advantage), and (3) entry fees and management costs per dollar of assets are lower (the effect of lower barriers to entry).

2.2d Association of High Capital and High Labor Income in the Same Individuals

A unique and markedly different feature of liberal meritocratic capitalism compared with its classical form is the presence of people with high labor income among the richest income decile or percentile, and even more interestingly the rising share of the population that has both high labor and high capital income. Creating a neologism based on Greek roots, I call the association of high capital and high labor income within the same household (or individual) *homoploutia* (*homo* for "same," and *ploutia* for "wealth").

The share of people who have both high labor (or capital) income and also high capital (or labor) income has been increasing in the past few decades (Figure 2.3). In 1980, only 15 percent of people in the top decile by capital income were also in the top decile of labor income, and vice versa. This percentage has doubled over the past thirty-seven years. In a hard version of classical capitalism, we would expect that almost no top capitalists would have high labor income. They would be rich anyway, with their capital income alone, and would have neither the desire nor the time to double up as hired laborers. Similarly, no wage-earner in classical capitalism would be able to have sufficiently high capital income to be placed among the top decile of capitalists. But conditions have now changed.

The end point of homoploutia (if such a point can be imagined) would occur when the top capitalists and the top workers were the same people (the value on the vertical axis of Figure 2.3 would be 100 percent). The correspondence between high-capital and high-labor earners adds to inequality but, more importantly, it makes it much more difficult to institute economic policies aimed at reducing inequality. The reason for this is political. In classical capitalism, most rich people did not need to exert much daily effort to achieve (or maintain) their status, whereas in liberal meritocratic capitalism, many of them are workers, even when an important part of their income comes from ownership of capital. We may observe that they are rich, but we do not know what percentage of their total

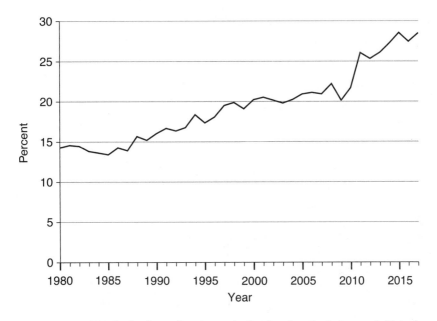

FIGURE 2.3. Top decile of capitalists in top decile of workers (and vice versa), United States, 1980–2017

Individuals are ranked by their household per capita labor or capital income; thus the richest "capitalist" decile includes people living in the 10 percent of households with the highest capital incomes (and the same for labor). Therefore, the shares of richest capitalists among richest workers and of richest workers among richest capitalists are the same. *Data source:* Calculated from US Current Population Surveys, https://www.census.gov/programs-surveys/cps.html.

income is derived from capital as opposed to labor. Politically, therefore, it is more difficult to apply to them the very high tax rates that were used in the past, since their high incomes are viewed as being more deserved (that is, as resulting from their labor).

The growth of homoploutia may be the product of either capital-rich people acquiring high levels of education and earning high wages, or of high-wage earners saving portions of their salaries and becoming rich capitalists. It is impossible to judge the importance of one versus the other without additional data. What is known, however, is that the concentration of wealth has remained extremely high in the United States, and direct stock ownership has not changed much. In 1983, 13.7 percent of the population owned at least some stocks directly; that percentage was unchanged thirty years later (Wolff 2017, 122). If we include mutual funds and pension accounts, stock ownership did increase from less than a third of the US population to just under one half, but the amounts owned are mostly minimal. This suggests that homoploutia is a product of extremely high wages "joining" (in the same individuals) an already highly concentrated ownership of capital.

2.2e Greater Homogamy (Assortative Mating)

It may be useful to open this topic with an anecdote. Some ten years ago, I found myself in an after-dinner conversation, lubricated by wine, with an American who had been educated at an Ivy League college and was then teaching in Europe. As our conversation drifted toward matters of life, marriage, and children, I was initially surprised by his statement that whomever he had married, the outcome in terms of where they lived, what type of house they owned, what kind of holidays and entertainment they would enjoy, and even what colleges their children would attend would be practically the same. His reasoning was as follows: "When I went to [Ivy League institution], I knew that I would marry a woman I met there. Women also knew the same thing. We all knew that our pool of desirable marriage candidates would never be as vast again. And then whomever I married would be a specimen of the same genre: they were all well educated, smart women who came from the same social class, read the same novels and newspapers, dressed the same, had the same preferences about restaurants, hiking, places to live, cars to drive, and people to see, as well about how to take care of the kids and what schools they should attend. It really made almost no difference socially whom among them I married." And then he added, "I was not aware of that at the time, but I can surely see it now."

The story struck me then and stayed in my mind for a long time. It contradicted the cherished myths that we are all deeply different, unique individuals, and that personal decisions such as marriage, which have to do with love and preferences, matter a lot and have a big effect on the rest of our lives. What my friend was saying was precisely the opposite: he could have fallen in love with A, or B, or C, or D, and ultimately would have ended up in virtually the same house, in the same affluent neighborhood—whether in Washington, DC, Chicago, or Los Angeles—with a similar set of friends and interests, and with children going to similar schools and playing the same games. And his story made a lot of sense. Of course, this scenario assumed that people who attended the same college would couple up. Had he dropped out of college, or not found anyone suitable to marry there, the outcome might have been different (say, a house in a less affluent neighborhood). His story dramatically illustrates the power of socialization: almost everyone at the top schools comes from more or less equally affluent families, and almost everyone adopts more or less the same values and tastes. And such mutually indistinguishable people marry each other.

Recent research has documented a clear increase in the prevalence of homogamy, or assortative mating (people of the same or similar education status and income level marrying each other). A study based on a literature review combined with decennial data from the American Community Survey showed that the association between partners' level of education was close to zero in 1970; in every other decade through 2010, the coefficient was positive, and it kept on rising (Greenwood, Guner, and Vandenbroucke 2017). A different database (Yonzan 2018) provides another perspective on this trend; it looks at marriage statistics for American women and men who married when they were "young," that is, between the ages of twenty and thirty-five. In 1970, only 13 percent of young American men who were in the top decile of male earners married young women who were in the top decile of female earners. By 2017, that figure had risen to almost 29 percent (Figure 2.4A). At the same time, the top decile of young male earners have been much less likely to marry young women who are in the bottom decile of female earners. The rate has declined steadily from 13.4 percent to under 11 percent. In other words, high-earning young American men who in the 1970s were just as likely to marry high-earning as low-earning young women now display an almost three-to-one preference in favor of high-earning women. An even more dramatic change happened for women: the percentage of young high-earning women marrying young high-earning men increased from just under 13 percent to 26.4 percent, while the percentage of rich young women marrying poor

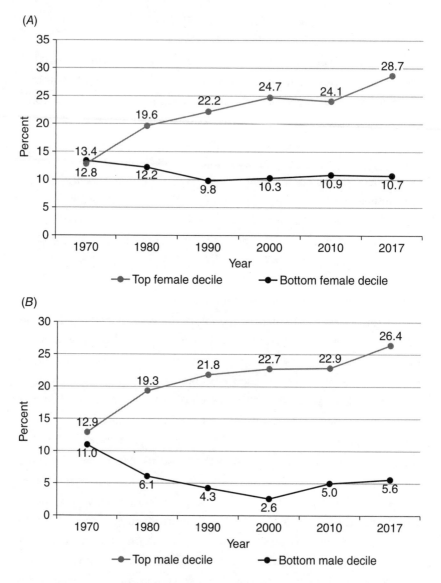

(A)

(B)

Top female decile ● Bottom female decile

Top male decile ● Bottom male decile

FIGURE 2.4A. Percentage of men aged 20 to 35 in the top male decile of labor earnings who married women aged 20 to 35 in the top and bottom female deciles by labor earnings, 1970–2017

FIGURE 2.4B. Percentage of women aged 20 to 35 in the top female decile by labor earnings who married men aged 20 to 35 in the top and bottom male deciles by labor earnings, 1970–2017

The sample for each survey is composed of men and women who at that time were (i) between 20 and 35 years old, (ii) married, and (iii) employed (with positive earnings). The underlying number of matches (top decile of men to top decile of women, and the reverse) is the same in Figures 2.4A and 2.4B, but the percentages are slightly different because the sizes of the men's and women's deciles differ. *Data source:* Yonzan (2018), as calculated from US Current Population Surveys, https://www.census.gov/programs-surveys/cps.html.

young men halved (Figure 2.4B).[28] From having no preference between rich and poor men in the 1970s, women currently prefer rich men by a ratio of almost five to one.[29]

In a very ambitious paper, Chiappori, Salanié, and Weiss (2017) tried to explain both the rise of assortative mating and the increasing level of education among women (which contrasts with a lack of increase in educational attainment for men). They argued that highly educated women have better marriage prospects, and thus, there is a "marriage education premium" which is perhaps as important as the usual skill premium that education provides. While the skill premium is, in principle, gender neutral, the marriage education premium is, the authors argue, much higher for women. Underlying this must be greater "pure preference" for homogamy among men because if that did not exist, the rising education level of women might be as much of a deterrence in the marriage market as an attraction.

Marriage education premium

There is a further link between, on the one hand, assortative mating, and, on the other hand, increasing returns to investment in children, which only more educated couples are able to provide. They can, for example, expose their children to a learning-conducive atmosphere at home and introduce them to cultural experiences that less-educated parents may have little interest in (concerts, libraries, ballet), as well as to elite sports. The importance of linking these seemingly unrelated developments—women's education, greater work participation by women, assortative marriage patterns, and the increasing importance of early childhood learning—is that it illuminates one of the key mechanisms of within-generation creation of inequality and its intergenerational transmission.

If educated, highly skilled, and affluent people tend to marry each other, that by itself will tend to increase inequality. About one-third of the inequality increase in the United States between 1967 and 2007 can be explained by assortative mating (Decancq, Peichl, and Van Kerm 2013).[30] For countries in the OECD (Organization for Economic Cooperation and Development), assortative mating accounted for an average of 11 percent of increased inequality between the early 1980s and early 2000s (OECD 2011).[31]

But if, in addition, the returns to children's early education and learning are sharply rising, and if these early advantages can be provided only by very educated parents, who, as the data show, spend much more time with their children than less educated parents, then the road to a strong intergenerational transmission of advantages and inequality is wide open. This is true even if—and it is important to underline this—there is high taxation of inheritance, because inheritance of financial resources is merely one of the advantages that the children of educated and rich parents enjoy. And in many cases, it may not even be the most important part. Although, as I shall argue in Section 2.4, taxation of inheritance is a particularly good policy for leveling the playing field and increasing equality of opportunity, it is an illusion to believe that such taxation will by itself be sufficient to equalize the life chances of children born to rich and poor parents.

2.2f Greater Transmission of Income and Wealth across Generations

High income and wealth inequality in the United States used to be justified by the claim that everyone had the opportunity to climb up the ladder of success, regardless of family background. This idea became known as the American Dream. The emphasis was on equality of opportunity rather than equality of outcome.[32] It was a dynamic, future-oriented concept. Schumpeter used a nice metaphor to explain it when he discussed income inequality: we can see the distribution of incomes in any one year as being like the distribution of occupants who are staying on different floors of a hotel, where the higher the floor, the more luxurious the room. If the occupants move around between the floors, and if their children likewise do not stay on the floor where they were born, then a snapshot of which families are living on which floors will not tell us much about which floor those families will be inhabiting in the future, or their long-term position. Similarly, inequality of income or wealth measured at one point in time may give us a misleading or exaggerated idea of true levels of inequality and can fail to account for intergenerational mobility.[33]

The American Dream has remained powerful both in the popular imagination and among economists. But it has begun to be seriously questioned during the past ten years or so, when relevant data have become available for the first time. Looking at twenty-two countries around the world, Miles Corak (2013) showed that there was a positive correlation between high inequality in any one year and a strong correlation between parents' and children's incomes (i.e., low income mobility). This result makes sense, because high inequality today implies that the children of the rich will have, compared to the children of the poor, much greater opportunities. Not only can they count on greater inheritance, but they will also benefit from better education, better social capital obtained through their parents, and many other intangible advantages of wealth. None of those things are available to the children of the poor. But while the American Dream thus was somewhat deflated by the realization that income mobility is greater in more egalitarian countries than in the United States, these results did not imply that intergenerational mobility had actually gotten any worse over time.

Yet recent research shows that intergenerational mobility has in fact been declining. Using a sample of parent-son and parent-daughter pairs, and comparing a cohort born between 1949 and 1953 to one born between 1961 and 1964, Jonathan Davis and Bhashkar Mazumder (2017) found significantly lower intergenerational mobility for the latter cohort. They used two common indicators of relative intergenerational mobility: rank to rank (the correlation between the relative income positions of parents and children) and intergenerational income elasticity (the correlation between parents' and children's incomes).[34] Both indicators showed an increase in correlation between parents' and children's incomes over time (rank to rank increased from 0.22 to 0.37 for daughters and from 0.17 to 0.36 for sons, and intergenerational income elasticity increased from 0.28 to 0.52 for daughters and from 0.13 to 0.43 for sons). For both indicators, the turning point occurred during the 1980s—the same period when US income inequality began to rise. In fact, three changes happened simultaneously: increase in inequality, increase in the returns to education, and increase in the correlation between parents' and children's incomes. Thus, we see that not only across countries, but also across time, higher income inequality and lower intergenerational mobility tend go together.

Decline of relative mobility

So far, we have only looked at relative mobility. We should also consider absolute intergenerational mobility, that is, the change in real income between generations. Here too, we see a decline: absolute mobility in the United States declined significantly between 1940 and the 2000s, as a result of a slowdown in economic growth combined with increased inequality (Chetty et al. 2017b).[35] We should keep in mind that absolute mobility is very different from relative mobility, since it depends largely on what happens to the growth rate. For example, absolute mobility can be positive for everyone if the income of every child exceeds the income of their parents, even if the parents' and children's positions in the income distribution are exactly the same. In this example, complete intergenerational absolute mobility would coincide with a complete lack of intergenerational relative mobility. Throughout this book I rely more on relative than absolute mobility because it better reflects systemic features of an economy.

2.3 New Social Policies

In this section I discuss new social policies with respect to capital and labor, and the pressure on the welfare state under conditions of globalization.[36]

2.3a Why Twentieth-Century Tools Cannot Be Used to Address Twenty-First-Century Income Inequality

The remarkable period of reduced income and wealth inequalities in rich countries that lasted roughly from the end of World War II to the early 1980s relied on four pillars: strong trade unions, mass education, high taxes, and large government transfers. Since income inequality began increasing about forty years ago, attempts to stem its further rise have relied on undertaking, or at least advocating, the expansion of some or all of these four pillars. But this approach will not do the job in the twenty-first century. Why not?

Consider trade unions first. The decline in trade union membership, which has occurred in all rich countries and has been especially strong in the private sector, is not only the product of inimical government policies. The underlying organization of labor has also changed. The shift from manufacturing to services and from enforced presence on factory floors or offices to remote work has resulted in a multiplication of relatively small work units, often not located physically in the same place. Organizing a dispersed workforce is much more difficult than organizing employees who work in a single huge plant, continuously interact with each other, and share the same social environment and same interests regarding pay and working conditions. In addition, the declining role of unions reflects the diminished power of labor vis-à-vis capital, which is due to the massive expansion of the pool of labor working under capitalist systems since the end of the Cold War and China's reintegration into the world economy. Although the latter event was a one-off shock, its effects will persist for at least several decades and may be reinforced by future high population growth rates in Africa, thus keeping the relative abundance of labor undiminished.

Turning to the second pillar, mass education, we can see that it was a tool for the reduction of inequality in the West in the period when the average number of years of schooling went up from between four and eight in the 1950s to thirteen or more today. This led to a reduction in the skill premium, that is, the wage gap between those with and without a college education. The belief that the supply of high-skilled labor would remain plentiful led Jan Tinbergen, the Dutch economist who was the recipient of the first Nobel Memorial Prize in Economic Sciences, to forecast, in the mid-1970s, that by the turn of the century the skill premium would be reduced almost to zero, and that the race between technology that demands ever more skilled workers and its supply would have been won by the latter.[37]

But further mass expansion of education is impossible when a country has reached fourteen or fifteen years of education on average, simply because the maximum level of education is bounded from above. Not only is it bounded by the number of years of schooling, but it is bounded even in terms of cognitive gains. When a country enters a transition period from elitist to mass education, as most Western countries did in the second half of the twentieth century, gains in knowledge, acquired through both longer and better education, were massive. But when most people have gone to school about as much as they wish and have learned about as much as they care or are able to, societies reach an educational ceiling that cannot be overcome: technology ultimately wins the race with education. Thus, we cannot rely on small increases in the average education level to provide the equalizing effect on wages that mass education once did.

High taxation of current income and high social transfers constituted the third and fourth pillars in reducing income inequality in the twentieth century. But it is politically difficult to increase them further. There are two main reasons. With globalization and the greater mobility of capital and labor, higher taxes might lead to both capital and highly skilled labor leaving the country in search of jurisdictions with lower tax levels, and thus to a loss of tax revenue for the original country.[38] The second reason lies in a skeptical view of the role of government and of tax-and-transfer policies, which is now much more prevalent among the middle class in many rich countries than it was half a century ago. This is not to say that people are unaware that without higher taxes the systems of social security, free education, and modern infrastructure would collapse. But people are skeptical about the gains to be achieved from additional increases in taxes imposed on current income, and such increases are unlikely to be voted in.

To illustrate what can be done using the old tools of tax-and-transfer redistribution and what problems remain, consider the examples of the United States and Germany for the past half century, shown in Figure 2.5.

Limits to what taxes and transfers can do

Look first at the lines for market income inequality, which measures inequality in income before taxes and transfers. In both countries (as in practically all rich countries), market income inequality increased dramatically, driven by the factors discussed earlier. The increase was even sharper in Germany than in the United States. The middle line in both graphs shows gross income inequality, that is, the inequality level that exists after taking transfers (such as public pensions and welfare benefits) into account, and the bottom line shows disposable income inequality—after the effects of direct taxes have been included as well. If policymakers or legislators want to curb inequality at the level of disposable income, they must either increase taxes and transfers or make them more progressive.

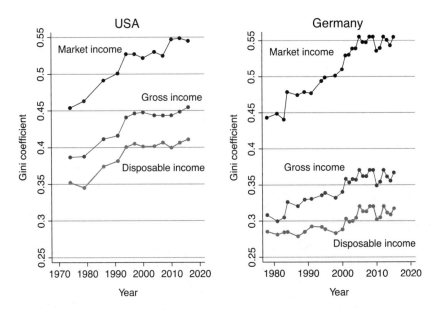

FIGURE 2.5. Inequalities of market, gross, and disposable income in the United States (1974–2016) and Germany (1978–2015)

Market income includes wages and other employment-related pay, income from property, and self-employment income. Gross income is equal to market income plus cash social transfers like public pensions, unemployment benefits, and welfare payments (such as SNAP, formerly known as food stamps, in the United States). Disposable income is equal to gross income minus direct taxes. Government-provided benefits in kind (health and education) are not included. All calculations are done on a per capita basis (that is, Ginis are calculated across household per capita incomes). *Data source:* Calculated from Luxembourg Income Study data (https://www.lisdatacenter.org).

Germany has almost succeeded in offsetting rising market income inequality; inequality in disposable income (the bottom line) shows only a modest increase since the early 1980s. This was achieved through large social transfers (notice the widening gap between the top and middle lines) and to a lesser extent through higher or more progressive taxation (the gap between the middle and the bottom lines has been about the same since 1990). Income redistribution in the United States, in contrast, has become only slightly more progressive, such that disposable income inequality has risen by a similar amount as market income inequality (shown by the parallel movements of the top and bottom lines). This comparison shows that policy can make a difference, but it also illustrates its limitations.

Higher transfers and direct taxes can neutralize higher underlying inequality. But if that underlying inequality has a tendency to keep on rising, this policy has to work against ever stronger headwinds. At some point, the old tools of redistribution are likely to be overwhelmed.

If inequality is bound to continue increasing, and if the old tools used to combat it will no longer work as well, what tools should be used now?

Here we not only need to think outside the box to find some new tools, but we must set ourselves an entirely new objective: *We should aim for an egalitarian capitalism based on approximately equal endowments of both capital and skills across the population.*

> *Libertarian utopia of a small state can be reached only through protocommunist policies*

This form of capitalism would generate egalitarian outcomes even without large redistributions of income. If the rich had only twice as many units of capital and twice as many units of skill as the poor, and if returns per unit of capital and skill were approximately equal, then overall inequality could not be more than two to one. Looking again at Figure 2.5, equalizing endowments would directly affect the underlying market inequality: doing so would slow down and even reverse the increase in the top line, to such an extent that the amount of redistribution (the gap between the top and the two bottom lines) could even go down without affecting the overall inequality of disposable income. The closest real-world example is that of Taiwan, where distribution of both labor and capital incomes is markedly more egalitarian than in any other rich country (see Figure 2.2) and where, as a result, the level of disposable income inequality is similar to that of Canada, an outcome achieved with minimal redistribution. To continue the example to the extreme, consider an imaginary world with absolutely equal endowments of capital and labor: market income inequality would be zero, and no redistribution would be needed; disposable income inequality would be zero as well.[39]

But how can the distribution of capital and skill endowments be made less unequal? As far as capital is concerned, it could be done by deconcentrating ownership of assets. As for labor, it could be accomplished by equalizing the returns to the approximately same skill levels. In the case of capital, inequality would be reduced by equalizing the stock of endowments; in the case of labor, it would be reduced mostly by equalizing the returns to the stocks (of education).[40]

Let us start with capital. As we saw in Section 2.2b, in all advanced countries, the concentration of income from property has remained at an incredibly high level since the 1970s. This is a key reason why the continued increase in the relative power of capital over labor and the increase in the capital share in net output were, and will continue to be, directly translated into higher interpersonal inequality.

Deconcentration of capital ownership

National policies may not be able to affect how total net income is shared between capital and labor (since this trend is often driven by technological change and globalization), but they can surely affect the distribution of capital ownership among individuals within national borders. With less concentrated capital ownership, an increase in the share of capital in net income need not lead to higher inequality among individuals. The rise in interpersonal inequality could be curbed or thwarted altogether.

Methods for reducing capital concentration are not new or unknown—they have just never been used seriously and consistently. We can divide them into three groups. First, one could institute favorable tax policies to make equity ownership more attractive to small and medium shareholders and less attractive to big shareholders (a policy exactly the opposite of what exists today in the United States). Currently, the middle class holds relatively few financial assets, which are, over the long term, better performing assets than housing. If we wish to help equalize returns received by the middle class and the rich, it follows that the middle class should be encouraged to hold more stocks and bonds. A common objection to this proposal is that small investors are risk-averse, since even a small negative return can wipe out most of their financial wealth. This is true, but there are ways to both improve the return they may obtain and ensure lower volatility. Many tax advantages that are currently available only to rich investors could be expanded to cover small investors, or even better, new tax advantages for small investors could be introduced. Lower volatility and greater security of investments could be ensured through a government-guaranteed insurance scheme that would set a floor (of, say, zero real return) for some classes of sufficiently small investments. Small investors could avail themselves of that guarantee on an annual basis when they submitted their tax returns.[41]

A second group of methods involves increasing worker ownership through employee stock ownership plans (ESOPs) or other company-level incentives that would encourage employee-shareholding. Here the legal regulations already exist in the United States and many other countries. This idea is not new, either. In 1919, Irving Fisher presented the idea in his presidential speech to the American Economic Association (Fisher 1919, 13); in the 1980s, Margaret Thatcher similarly spoke of "people's capitalism." However, after a relatively successful period in the 1980s, ESOPs have fallen into oblivion. When employee shares are used, it is more in the context of providing incentives to the top management rather than instituting some form of workers' capitalism. The objection to this idea is that workers would prefer to diversify rather than having both their wages and property income depend on the performance of one company; they would be better off "investing" their labor in one company and their capital in other companies or in government bonds or housing. That argument, in theory, is correct. Everything else being the same, it makes more sense to invest your assets in companies other than the one where you are employed. However, most people own hardly any financial assets at all, so they have all their eggs in the same basket, anyway—that of the company where they work. If there were more opportunities for the middle class to invest in financial capital, then ESOPs might be an inferior strategy. But as long as opportunities to profitably invest in small amounts are few, ESOPs make sense as a step toward less concentrated asset ownership.[42]

Third, an inheritance or wealth tax could be used as a means to even out access to capital if the tax proceeds were applied to giving every young adult a capital grant. (This has been proposed by Atkinson [2015] and Meade [1964].) A tax on inheritance has, in principle, many advantages. It has less effect on decisions regarding work or investment than taxes that are assessed on income, and it represents a tax on (nonearned) wealth received by future generations. Moreover, the perpetuation of an upper class is made possible through its ability to transfer, often tax-free, many assets across generations. Thus, a tax on inheritance also has an important role to play in reducing inequality of opportunity.

It is important to situate the inheritance tax within an intellectual and ideological framework. John Rawls, in his taxonomy of various equalities, introduces taxation of inheritance as the first (and lowest) complement to equality before the law (1971, 57). In Rawls's lowest state of equality, there are no legal constraints to people achieving the same position in life. This level of equality satisfies Rawls's first principle of justice, namely, that everyone has the same political liberty regardless of economic or social class. This is Rawls's system of natural liberty, or "meritocratic capitalism." After the mid- to late nineteenth century in Europe, Russia, and the Americas, and after Indian independence and the Chinese revolution in the mid-twentieth century, the entire world began to operate under a system of natural liberty. Since then countries have moved, to varying degrees, toward satisfying Rawls's second principle of justice, namely, equality of opportunity. Achieving equality of opportunity requires applying correctives to make up for the advantages enjoyed by people born into the "right" families or with the "right" genetic abilities. The correction can never be complete because it would involve correcting for differences in talent and for the intangible advantages enjoyed by children who are born into richer or more educated families. But significant corrections are possible, and the first corrective policy that Rawls introduces is taxation of inheritance. That, combined with free schooling, brings us into the system of Rawls's liberal equality (what I call "liberal capitalism" in this book). Therefore, inheritance tax, which is desirable in itself (according to Rawls and others who care about equality of opportunity), can also be used to reduce the concentration of wealth if the proceeds are distributed to all citizens. It is thus a tax that is desirable on two grounds: current equality and future opportunity.[43]

It is unfortunate that inheritance taxes have diminished in most advanced economies. Even in countries that have such a tax and where the marginal tax rate is high (e.g., Japan and South Korea, with marginal tax rates of 50 percent, and the United Kingdom, France, and the United States, with marginal rates of 40–45 percent), revenues from the tax have been severely reduced because of very high exemptions (that is, the level below which inheritances are not taxed). In the United States the exemption was $675,000 in 2001, but it was raised to $5.49 million in

2017 ($22 million for a married couple). Caroline Freund (2016, 174) points out that "in 2001, estate tax revenues could have covered the cost of the [US] food stamps program 14 times over. In 2011 the revenue could have covered just two-thirds of the program." A weakened inheritance tax, reduced through both increased exemptions and reduced marginal tax rates, cannot do much to accomplish its intended role of leveling the playing field. To return to Rawls's classification of equality, it seems that many countries may be backtracking even on liberal equality and moving back to a system of natural liberty alone, one that provides for equality before the law but not equality of opportunity.

Having discussed how to equalize capital endowments, we now turn to labor. In a rich and well-educated society, the issue is not just to make education more accessible, but to equalize the returns to education between equally educated people. Wage inequality is no longer due only to differences in individuals' years of schooling (a difference that will likely be further reduced). Today, wage inequality (for the same number of years of education, experience, and other relevant variables) is also driven by the perceived or actual differences in the qualities of different schools. The way to reduce this inequality is to equalize teaching standards among schools. In the United States, and increasingly in Europe, doing so would require improving the quality of public schools. This can be achieved only by large investments in public education and by the withdrawal of numerous advantages (including tax-free status) enjoyed by private universities and secondary schools, many of which command huge financial endowments.[44] Without leveling the playing field between private and public schools, a mere increase in the number of years of schooling, or the admission of some students from lower-middle-class families into elite colleges, will not reduce inequality in labor income or equalize opportunity.

Equal access to the same quality of education

2.3b The Welfare State in the Era of Globalization

It has become a truism to say that the welfare state is under stress from the effects of globalization and migration. It will help to understand the nature of this stress if we go back to the origins of the welfare state.

As Avner Offer and Daniel Söderberg have recently reminded us in their book *The Nobel Factor* (2016), social democracy and the welfare state emerged from the realization that all individuals go through periods when they are earning nothing but still have to consume. This applies to the young (hence children's benefits), the sick (health care and sick pay), those injured at work (worker's accident insurance), new parents (parental leave), people who lose jobs (unemployment benefits), and the elderly (pensions). The welfare state was created to provide these benefits, delivered in the form of insurance, for unavoidable or very common conditions. It was built on an assumed commonality of behavior, or, differently put, cultural and often ethnic homogeneity. It is no accident that the prototypical welfare state, born in the homogeneous world of 1930s Sweden, had many elements of national socialism (not used here in a pejorative sense).

In addition to depending on common behavior and experiences, the welfare state, in order to be sustainable, requires mass participation. Social insurance cannot be applied to only small parts of the workforce because it then naturally leads to adverse selection, a point well illustrated by the endless wrangles over health care coverage in the United States. If it is possible to opt out, anyone who thinks they may not require the insurance (for example, the rich, those unlikely to be unemployed, or healthy people) will do so, since they do not want to subsidize the "others." A system that relies only on the "others" is unsustainable because of the huge premiums it would require. Thus, the welfare state can work only when it covers all, or almost all, of the labor force or all citizens.

Globalization erodes these requirements. Trade globalization has led, in most Western countries, to a decline in the share of the middle class and its relative income. This has produced income polarization: there are more people at the two ends of the income distribution and fewer around the median.[45] With income polarization, the rich come to realize that they are better off creating their own private systems because sharing a mass system with those who are substantially poorer and face different risks (such as a higher probability of unemployment or of certain diseases) would lead to sizeable income transfers from the rich. Private systems also provide better quality for the rich (per unit of expense) because they allow savings for the types of risks that the rich do not face. If very few among the rich smoke or are obese, they do not have an incentive to pay for the health care of smokers or obese people. This leads to a system of social separatism, reflected in the growing importance of private health plans, private education, and private pensions.[46] Once these private systems are created, the rich are increasingly unwilling to pay high taxes because they benefit little from them. This in turn leads to erosion of the tax base. The bottom line is that a very unequal, or polarized, society cannot easily maintain an extensive welfare state.

Economic migration, another aspect of globalization, to which most rich societies have been exposed in the past fifty years—and some of them, especially in Europe, for the first time ever—also undercuts support for the welfare state. This happens through the inclusion in the social system

Migration and the welfare state

of people with social norms, behavior, or lifecycle experiences that are, or are perceived to be, different. Natives and migrants may display different behavior and have different preferences; a similar gap may also exist among different native-born groups. In the United States, a perceived lack of "affinity" between the white majority and African Americans has rendered the US welfare state smaller than its European counterparts (Kristov, Lindert, and McClelland 1992). The same process is now taking place in Europe, where large pockets of immigrants have not been assimilated and where the native population believes that the migrants are getting an unfair share of the benefits. The fact that natives feel a lack of affinity need not be construed as discrimination. Sometimes discrimination could indeed be a factor, but often this belief can also be grounded in evidence that one is unlikely to experience lifecycle events of the same nature or frequency as other people, and as a result one becomes unwilling to contribute to insurance against such events. In the United States, the fact that African Americans are more likely to be unemployed or incarcerated probably led whites to support less generous unemployment benefits and an often dysfunctional penitentiary system. Similarly, the fact that migrants are likely to have more children than natives might lead to the curtailment of children's benefits in Europe. In any case, the difference in expected lifetime experiences undermines the homogeneity necessary for a sustainable welfare state.

In addition, in the era of globalization, more highly developed welfare states may experience the perverse effect of attracting less skilled or less ambitious migrants. Other things being equal, a migrant's decision about where to emigrate will depend on the expected income in one country versus another. In principle, that would favor moving to richer countries. But we also have to consider the migrants' views about where in the income distribution of the recipient country they might expect to end up. If a migrant expected to be in the lower part of the income distribution, perhaps because of a lack of skills or ambition, then a more egalitarian country with a larger welfare state would be more attractive. A migrant who expected to reach the higher end of a recipient country's income distribution would make the opposite calculation. Hence the adverse selection among migrants who choose more developed welfare states.

Figure 2.6 shows empirically, based on calculations done for 118 countries in 2008 (Milanovic 2015), how much income equality will be worth to migrants depending on where in the recipient country's income distribution they expect to be. The results in the figure should be interpreted as follows. If migrants are pessimistic or low-skilled and expect to be among the poorest five percent (poorest ventile) in the recipient country, their income will be the same if they select a country that is 8 percent poorer in terms of GDP per capita but with 1 Gini point lower inequality as it would be if they went to a richer but more unequal country. This is shown at point A. For the second ventile in Figure 2.6, greater equality will be worth slightly less— around 5 percent of income—and so forth. Migrants who would expect to end up in the sixteenth ventile or above in the recipient country, however, prefer more unequal countries, since at that point they benefit from inequality. For such optimistic or high-skilled migrants inequality is a benefit, and they may be willing to accept to migrate to a *poorer* country provided that it is *more* unequal. Such migrants might prefer to migrate to, say, Colombia rather than Sweden, even if Colombia is poorer. Since they expect to haul themselves high up in the recipient country's distribution, they will attach greater importance to a country's inequality than to its mean income. The reverse, as we saw, holds for pessimistic or low-skilled migrants who expect to be placed low in the recipient country's distribution: they will

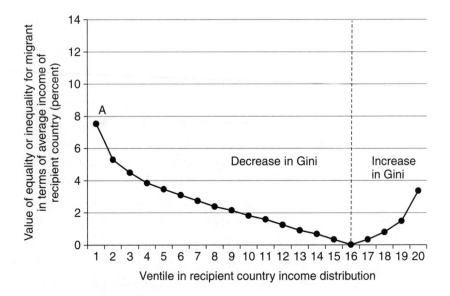

FIGURE 2.6. Trade-off between income equality and average income of the recipient country as faced by migrants

The graph shows how much a country with a more equal income distribution (lower Gini) (if a migrant expects to be in the lower parts of the recipient country's income distribution), or more unequal country (higher Gini) (if a migrant expects to be in the higher parts of the recipient country's income distribution) is worth to a migrant, in percentage of the recipient country's average income. In other words, for migrants who expect to end up in the first through sixteenth ventile of the recipient country's income distribution, it may be better to move to a poorer country that has less income inequality (say, Sweden), than to a richer country (say, the United States) that is more unequal. The opposite holds for migrants who expect to end up in the top four ventiles of the recipient country's income distribution. *Data source:* Recalculated from Milanovic (2015).

tend to choose more equal countries. For that reason, there may be adverse selection of pessimistic migrants moving to countries with more developed social safety nets. If more pessimistic migrants are indeed also effectively less ambitious or less skilled, rich countries with extensive social welfare systems will tend to attract the "wrong" kinds of migrants.[47] The existence of such an adverse selection dynamic is documented by Akcigit, Baslandze, and Stantcheva (2015), who show that inventors (who may be supposed to be highly skilled or highly ambitious) tend to migrate from high-tax to low-tax jurisdictions, that is, to places with a less-developed welfare state. Borjas (1987) found the same result for the United States with respect to the countries of migrants' origin: migrants coming from more economically equal countries than the United States tended to be more skilled.

The countries that would face the worst problems would be those with both well-developed welfare systems and low income mobility. Migrants going to such countries could not expect their children to climb up the income ladder. In a destructive feedback loop, such countries would attract the least skilled or the least ambitious migrants, and once they created an underclass, the upward mobility of their children would be limited. Such a system works like a self-fulfilling prophecy: it attracts ever more unskilled migrants who fail to assimilate. The native population will tend to see these migrants as lacking in skills and ambition (which, as I just argued, may be true) and hence as "different." At the same time, the failure to be accepted as an equal member of the community will be seen by the migrants as confirmation of natives' anti-migrant prejudices, or, even worse, as religious or ethnic discrimination.

Thus, large welfare states face two types of adverse selection, which are mutually reinforcing. On the domestic side, polarization between the poor and the rich encourages the private provision of social services and leads the rich to opt out of government-provided services. This leaves in the system only those whose premiums may be unaffordably high, and many of them may leave the system altogether. On the international side, adverse selection works by bringing in low-skilled migrants—a process that leads to the opting out of the native-born.

There is no easy solution to the vicious circle faced by developed welfare states during a time of globalization. Two major initiatives, however, would make a significant difference:

1. The pursuit of policies that would lead toward equalization of endowments, so that taxation of current income could be reduced and the size of the welfare state brought down (as discussed in Section 2.3a).
2. A fundamental change in the nature of migration, so that it is much more akin to the temporary movement of labor that does not come with automatic access to citizenship and the entire gamut of welfare benefits (discussed further in Chapter 4).

2.4 Self-Perpetuating Upper Class?

The formation of a durable upper class is impossible unless that class exerts political control. Only politics, used for that purpose, can guarantee that the upper class stays on top.

In principle, this should be impossible in a democracy; the right to vote belongs to everybody, and the majority of people have an interest in ensuring that those who are powerful and rich do not retain their status permanently. A great deal of evidence, however, demonstrates convincingly that the rich in the United States exert a disproportionate influence on politics. The political scientists Martin Gilens (2012, 2015), Benjamin Page (with Gilens, 2014), and Christopher Achen and Larry Bartels (2017) have, for the first time in history, provided empirical confirmation that the rich have more political clout and that the political system has moved from being a democracy to being an oligarchy—a system where, to use Aristotle's definition, "the possession of political power is due to the possession of economic power or wealth."[48] For example, Gilens (2015) has found that members of the US Congress are much more likely to discuss and vote on issues that are of interest to the rich than those that are important only for the middle class and the poor.[49] Gilens concludes that middle-class issues have a chance to be considered only when they coincide with what the rich care about.

These findings are remarkable not only for their empirical strength and political implications but also because they apply to one of the most established democracies in the world, where, moreover, the middle class has traditionally been regarded as playing a key role in both politics and economics. If the middle class in even the most pro–middle-class society in the world (at least in terms of ideological discourse) has political power only when it holds opinions shared by the rich, then the middle classes and the poor in the rest of the world are likely to be politically even less relevant.

But how do the rich control the political process in a democracy? This is not easy to explain, not only because the rich are not legally a separate group with special rights, but also because politicians in modern democracies are not automatically selected from the privileged layers of the population. One might argue that in the past under conditions only approximating full franchise, the political class came mostly from the rich, which would imply a certain commonality of views, shared interests, and mutual understanding between politicians and the rest of the rich. But this is not the case in today's democracies: politicians come from various social classes and backgrounds, and many of them share sociologically very little, if anything, with the rich. Bill Clinton and Barack Obama in the United States, and Margaret Thatcher and John Major in the United Kingdom, all came from modest backgrounds but quite effectively supported the interests of the top 1 percent.

Where does the influence of the rich then come from? The answer is quite clear: through the funding of political parties and electoral campaigns. The United States is the prime example, thanks to the ability of corporate entities to finance politicians and the virtual absence of limits on private contributions. This leads to an extremely high concentration of political contributions from the people at the very top of the income or wealth distributions: in 2016, the top 1 percent of the top 1 percent (this is not a typo) contributed 40 percent of total campaign donations.[50] In fact, the distribution of political contributions is even more concentrated than the distribution of wealth.[51] If we consider political contribution as an expenditure, it would be without doubt one of the expenditures most restricted to the rich, along the same lines as expenditures on yachts and sports cars.

> *Politics controlled by the top 1 percent*

This finding is not new except in the amounts of money needed to influence elections and its pervasiveness. In his 1861 essay "On Representative Government," John Stuart Mill wrote: "There has never yet been, among political men, any real and serious attempt to prevent bribery, because there has been no real desire that elections should not be costly. Their costliness is an advantage to those who can afford the expense, by excluding a multitude of competitors" (Mill 1975, 316). The problem is not limited to the United States; it also exists in Germany and France, where in principle campaign spending is more controlled (Schäfer 2017; Bekkouche and Cagé 2018). It is probably even more serious in many young democracies, where the rules of political funding are even less clear and often unenforced. Most of the recent political scandals in Europe (involving

Helmuth Kohl, Nicolas Sarkozy, and Silvio Berlusconi, for example) have been related not to personal corruption, but to politically motivated corruption in which the politicians were accused, and in some cased convicted, of illegally accepting money and using it for political campaigns. The problem has reached gargantuan proportions in India, where massive under-the-table donations are common, and candidates take some money for themselves and some for their party (Crabtree 2018). In eastern and southern Europe, there is a glaring disproportion between the amounts needed to conduct campaigns (to pay for pollsters and activists and to run ads in newspapers, electronic media, and TV) and what is reported as having been received from legal sources. The issue is generally passed over in silence and ignored: winners are not asked how they won the elections, and losers know that the same questions could be asked regarding their own finances.

The next issue is to ask whether the rich get value for their contributions. Do politicians do what the rich want? Earlier in this section, I mentioned empirical evidence showing that politicians do pay more attention to issues that matter to the rich. But economics also provides methodological insight on this point. It is perhaps odd that this question should be asked at all, given how obvious the answer is: it is equivalent to asking whether the rich really like the big houses that they buy. The fact is that nobody spends money without expecting to receive something in return, whether it be utility from owning a large house or favorable tax policy from politicians. To argue that rich people donate money to political campaigns without expecting any favors in return is not only totally antithetical to the normal behavior of the rich (most of whom have become rich by squeezing maximum surplus from employees, suppliers, and customers); it goes against common sense and our understanding of human nature. Only politicians can say such illogical things in public, as for instance Hillary Clinton, who pretended to be surprised that people would think that Goldman Sachs might expect something in return for giving substantial amounts to her campaign.[52] We can believe Hillary Clinton's statement only if we are ready to believe that rich donors, as a class, temporarily lose their minds at regular biennial or quadrennial intervals. In other words, the rich (like everybody else) expect a return on their money, be it in bond financing or campaign contributions; it is simply a part of normal behavior.[53]

What the rich purchase with their political contributions are economic policies that benefit them: lower taxes on high incomes, greater tax deductions, higher capital gains through tax cuts to the corporate sector, fewer regulations, and so on. These policies in turn increase the likelihood that the rich will stay on top. This is the ultimate link in the chain that runs from higher share of capital in net income to the creation of a permanent, or at least durable, upper class in liberal meritocratic capitalism. Without that last link in the chain, the upper class would still enjoy very strong tailwinds helping them maintain their position, but with the closing of the political link in the chain their position becomes all but unassailable. The circle is closed. Thus political control is an indispensable component for the existence of a durable upper class, the point with which this section began.

Tying up the knot on power and wealth

But we would be remiss to see the new capitalist upper class as a replica of the old. Its members differ in several ways that I have already discussed: they are better educated, they work harder and get a greater share of their income from labor, and they tend to intermarry. They also pay much greater attention to their children's education. The modern "new capitalist" upper class is keen to make sure that their assets, together with manifold nontangible advantages, like connections and the best education that money can buy, are transferred to their children. The role of expensive private education, in this context, can be seen in an entirely new light. The cost of private higher education, which has increased several times faster than the general cost of living or the real income of households in the United States, makes it very difficult for middle-class families to afford to educate their children.[54] In the top thirty-eight US colleges and universities, more students come from families in the top 1 percent than from the entire bottom 60 percent of the income distribution.[55] Assuming that the number of children per family is approximately equal in rich and poor families, that means that the chance of attending the best schools for children born in very rich families is some sixty times greater than that of children born not just in poor families, but

The elite prefer expensive education because it reinforces their power

also in middle-class families.[56] "Legacy admissions" (students who are accepted because one of their relatives went to the same school) account for between one-tenth and one-quarter of the students in the top one hundred US colleges and universities (Levy and Tyre 2018).

In addition, since in the American system of higher education being admitted to a university is tantamount to graduating from it, the principal effort of parents and children is directed toward college admissions—and this is precisely where the rich enjoy enormous advantages.[57] This is also where private secondary and, further down the chain, private primary and even kindergarten education matter, since they are conduits to elite colleges and universities. It is thus misleading simply to compare the cost of top private colleges with, say, that of state universities. One should look at the private-public cost differential throughout a child's education, a period of some fourteen to sixteen years before college. Once such an investment pays off by ensuring admittance, the fact that admitted students almost always graduate means that progeny of the rich who in a more competitive environment would never have graduated do not have much to worry about.[58] For George W. Bush, to take one example, getting into Yale was all that mattered, and his family made sure that happened. Once there, he just had to put in a perfunctory effort and avoid making a huge scandal or dropping out.[59]

The high cost of education, combined with the actual or perceived educational quality of certain high-status schools, fulfills two functions: it makes it impossible for others to compete with top wealth-holders, who monopolize the top end of education, and it sends a strong signal that those who have studied at such schools are not only from rich families but must be intellectually superior.[60]

Note that both of these factors (high cost and high educational level) are necessary. If costs were less, the competition faced by rich parents' children would be much tougher. And if the quality of such schools were seen to be inferior, they could be branded as outfits that merely provide professional legitimation for the children of the rich but are not especially esteemed in the real world. But because these schools are expensive (thus reducing competition) and good (signaling intellectual superiority) at the same time, the rich are able to avoid both of these problems. The advantages show up not only in the rising education premium for those with college or graduate degrees but in the increasing differences between graduates who have had the same number of years of education. Ten years after starting college, the top decile of earners from all colleges had a median salary of $68,000, while graduates from the ten top colleges had a median salary of $220,000 (Stewart 2018, 22).

This is also why we can expect that if nothing dramatic is done to improve the relative quality of public education and to equalize the chance of access to top schools, the current situation in the United States will become even more extreme and will spread to more countries. Although still at an early stage, the same process is beginning to occur in European countries that have historically had strong systems of public education.

As the rich realize the advantages of expensive private education, their willingness to pay high tuition enables those schools to attract the best professors and gradually guts the public system of its best teachers and of children from wealthy families. Further, as the rich continue to separate themselves, their willingness to pay taxes for public education diminishes. The eventual result is a bifurcated education system that replicates the distribution of wealth: a small group of top schools attended mostly by the rich, and a large group of mediocre schools open to everyone else.

Members of the top class are thus able to transfer their advantages to the next generation. The children, in addition to receiving money while their parents are alive, inheriting wealth, and benefiting from their parents' social capital, also enjoy a huge start-up advantage of excellent education that begins with private pre-K schools and ends with advanced degrees. In his 2015 commencement address at Yale Law School, Daniel Markovits estimated the additional education investment received by the children of the rich (as compared with those from the middle class) to be equivalent to an inheritance of between $5 and $10 million. He concluded that "children from poor or even middle class households cannot possibly compete . . . with people who have imbibed this massive, sustained, planned, and practiced investment, from birth, or even in the womb." Unbiased employers will, if they consult only their own interest, have all the reason in the world to give better jobs to this privileged group. As in many other cases, the simultaneous existence of two equilibria, one for the rich, at the high level, and another for the middle class, at the low level, generates forces that reinforce this double equilibrium and make its reversal more difficult.

Let's conclude with inherited wealth. To see the importance of financial inheritance alone, consider a calculation that has been done for France but is probably even stronger for countries with higher inequality of wealth, like the United States. In *Capital in the Twenty-First Century*, Piketty (2014, 377–429) asks the following two-part question: How much of total wealth is inherited annually, and what percentage of the population in a given year

> Inherited wealth

acquires inherited wealth greater in value than the capitalized lifetime earnings of an average worker in the lower half of the wage distribution (called here for simplicity a "median worker"). The question is important because the higher the percentage of the population receiving such an amount, the greater—everything else being the same—the share of the rentiers would be. But even if the issue is not the share of the rentiers—people aspire to be more than just coupon-clippers—the higher the number the greater the advantage of the rich. The formula for inherited wealth as a share of GDP is $\mu m \beta$, where m = annual mortality rate, μ = wealth of the deceased compared with wealth of the living, and β = country's wealth-output ratio. Now (as we have seen before) as countries grow richer their β goes up; also as people live longer, the wealth of decedents tends to be much higher than the average wealth per adult (because people accumulate more wealth as they age). Both of these variables will therefore tend over time to increase the flow of inheritance as a share of national income. In France, the current inheritance-to-GDP ratio is around 15 percent of national income (Piketty 2014, fig. 11.1). And what percentage of the French population receives inheritances equal to or greater than the capitalized lifetime earnings of the median worker? Between 12 and 15 percent. This group of people could live at the standard of living of a median worker for their entire life without working even for a day. In more wealth-unequal countries the percentage is likely to be greater, mostly because of a higher value of μ. And even when we adjust for the fact that in very wealth-unequal countries, where the distribution of inheritances is strongly skewed toward the wealthy, the percentage of very high inheritances (that is, those whose value exceeds the capitalized lifetime earnings of a median worker) may be smaller, it is still true that an important portion of the population will enjoy a tremendous advantage compared with those who inherit nothing or very little.[61]

One of the characteristics of the upper class under liberal meritocratic capitalism is its relative openness to outsiders. Since the upper class is not legally different from the rest of the population (the way an aristocracy is), and since its key and, in reality, only distinguishing feature is money, it does not close itself off to those individuals who, through skill or luck, have managed to become rich despite all the obstacles. Unlike in the past, the modern upper class is open to them and does not hold them in any lower esteem; it might even hold them in higher esteem because of the more difficult path they have had to traverse to reach the top. This openness to new arrivals from below reinforces the top class in two ways: it co-opts the best members of the lower classes, and it sends the message that the path of upward mobility is not entirely closed off, which in turn makes the rule of the top class seem more legitimate and thus more stable.

> How open is the upper class to outsiders?

The openness to new arrivals may be greater when technological progress is fast and large fortunes are made quickly, as has been the case in the past several decades. Even a cursory look at the new billionaires suffices to show that, while many came from well-off families, very few came from the top 1 percent or enjoyed disproportionate social advantages. This is confirmed by the data on US billionaires: the share of inherited wealth in total wealth of US billionaires has consistently gone down from about 50 percent in 1976, to 35 percent in 2001, to just over 30 percent in 2014 (Freund and Oliver 2016, 30).[62] Most billionaires and probably many millionaires enjoy income levels and relative positions that are much higher than those of their parents. They have experienced both absolute and relative intergenerational upward mobility.

This finding might suggest a positive relationship, over a limited period of time, between fast economic growth and a fast increase in income inequality on the one hand, and high intergenerational mobility on the other. But such a relationship seems to conflict with the data discussed earlier showing an association between a high level of inequality and a *low* level of mobility. The way to reconcile the two may lie in distinguishing temporary from more enduring changes in both variables (inequality and mobility). Consider the following situation, illustrated in Figure 2.7. Assume that mobility and inequality are negatively correlated, as long-term data from the United States and other countries confirm. This relationship is represented by the line A–A. Now suppose that a country like the United States starts at point Z, but then inequality goes up, driven by fast technological progress and new large fortunes. Both inequality and mobility may increase, resulting in a move to point Z_1. This point, however, lies on a new (higher) line connecting inequality and mobility, and the longer-term relationship between the two is still negative (higher inequality leads to lower mobility). This scenario shows why temporary movements in inequality and mobility should be distinguished from their longer-term relationship, and what appears to be a good development (increased intergenerational mobility) may over the longer term simply maintain the underlying "bad" relationship between inequality and mobility.

In practical terms, this means that once technological progress slows down, and it becomes increasingly difficult to generate new fortunes, the durability of the upper class will be reinforced. We would then have a less open upper class, higher inequality, and lower social mobility, represented

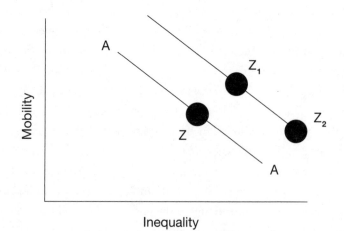

FIGURE 2.7. The long- and short-term relationship between inequality and intergenerational mobility

by point Z_2. This of course would be a recipe for the creation of a (semi-) permanent upper class.

It is perhaps not sufficiently appreciated how similar were the views of Marx and the Italian economist Vilfredo Pareto on the role of the ruling class (in Marx's terminology) or the elite (in Pareto's). Both believed that every society contains, or has contained, a distinct upper class, and that such an upper class uses ideology to present its own interests as general interests and thus to maintain its hegemony over those it rules.

> How to think about today's elite in liberal meritocratic capitalism

Their view differed, however, about the importance of ownership of the means of production as the principal basis for class distinction, and about the importance of the way in which production is organized. Marx saw these factors as determining the characteristics of societies and those of the ruling classes, while Pareto's view was more open-ended: even within a single social formation, the elite may be formed according to different criteria and may maintain its dominion in different ways. Pareto identified two types of ruling classes: "lions," a militarized class that maintains its position through violent means, and "foxes," a more sophisticated ruling class that avoids the use of violence and prefers to rule through economic power and ideological domination.[63]

Pareto's classification leads us to ask the following question: Given the nature of liberal meritocratic capitalism, what would be the principal characteristics of its ruling elite? Or to put it differently, what type of elite or ruling class (I use the two terms interchangeably here) is associated with, and prospers, in liberal meritocratic capitalism?

There is no doubt that, to use Pareto's terminology, the ruling class in liberal capitalism is composed of foxes. It does not use militaristic means to retain power, and it has other characteristic features that I have discussed in this chapter. It may be useful to summarize them here:

1. The ruling class controls most of the financial capital of the country. We have seen that in the United States, the top 10 percent of wealth-holders control more than 90 percent of financial assets.

2. The ruling class is highly educated. Many members of the ruling class work, and their labor income tends to be high (because of their high level

of education). Members of the ruling class therefore combine high income from labor and capital—what I have called *homoploutia*.

3. The elite invest heavily in their progeny and in political control. Investment in their children's education enables the children to maintain high labor income and the high status that is traditionally associated with knowledge and education. Investment in political influence enables the elite to write the rules of inheritance, so that financial capital is easily transferred to the next generation. The two together (acquired education and transmitted capital) enable the reproduction of the ruling class.

4. The objective of the investment in political control is done not only to improve the contemporaneous economic power of the ruling class, but to ensure its domination over time.

5. The ability of women to access the same level of education as men and to enjoy the same rules regarding inheritance makes women increasingly indistinguishable from men, when measured by income or power. Thus, the ruling class in liberal meritocratic capitalism is probably the least gendered of all historical ruling classes.

6. Increasing economic and educational similarity between men and women leads to family formation of similarly educated and rich couples (homogamy), which also contributes to intergenerational maintenance of these advantages.

7. Because the upper class is not defined according to hereditary or occupational criteria but is based on wealth and education, it is an "open" upper class. It co-opts the best members of the lower classes who are able to become wealthy and highly educated.

8. Members of the ruling class are hard-working and have an amoral outlook on life (see Chapter 5). Everything that enables this class to maintain and reinforce its position and is within the bounds of the law is, ipso facto, desirable. Its ethics are defined by the existing legal framework, and its use of money to control the political process extends to the use of money to change laws. This flexible interpretation of the rules enables it to stay within the confines of the law even if its practices increasingly diverge from general ethical standards.

CHAPTER 3

POLITICAL CAPITALISM

An oligarchy can expect to ensure its safety only by enforcing good order.

—Aristotle, *Politics*

This chapter takes a historical, or rather genealogical, approach to the study of political capitalism. Political capitalism, I argue, is in many cases a product of communist revolutions conducted in societies that were colonized or de facto colonized, such as China. I begin by discussing the place of communism in global history and the effects of communist revolutions in colonized societies. I then proceed to define political capitalism more abstractly and to illustrate and discuss its main features and contradictions as well as its global role, using the example of China. Because of its economic and political power, China plays the paradigmatic role in the chapter, analogous to that of the United States in Chapter 2. (For more on the implications of my particular reinterpretation of communism, which differs from the conventional view, see Appendix A.)

3.1 The Place of Communism in History

3.1a Inability of Marxist and Liberal Views of the World to Explain the Place of Communism in History

There is a difficulty in trying to place communism, its rise and fall, in the history of the world, that is, history with a big H.[1] That difficulty is great for Marxist thought because it regards communism as the pinnacle of human evolution, toward which history is striving. But the difficulty is no less for the liberal view of human history, or for what used to be called the Whig view of history. In fact, every *histoire raisonée* from Plato to Hegel to Fukuyama presents the rise and decline of socioeconomic or political systems as obeying some discoverable laws of social change. These laws were divided into two types, "Athens" and "Jerusalem," by the Russian philosopher Nikolai Berdyaev: Athens stands for cyclical laws (as in Plato's "Athenian" idea that regime types come and go in a cyclical pattern), and Jerusalem for teleological laws (with societies going from "lower," or less-developed states, to "higher," or more-developed states—toward "Jerusalem").[2]

Both liberal and Marxist conceptions of history are Jerusalem-like. This is the case whether we deal with regularities of History on a very broad canvas—as, for example, asking what comes after capitalism—or on a smaller scale—as, for example, when we look for empirical evidence that there is income convergence among countries (as economic theory predicts) or that economic development tends to be associated with societies that are more democratic. In all such reasoning, we expect to find some unidirectional regularities of development, that is, evolution toward something "better." Social evolution is viewed not as random or as cyclical, but rather as following a linear progression toward richer and freer societies.[3]

This is where we encounter the difficulty of understanding communism. If we believed that socioeconomic systems rose and fell randomly, there would be nothing to explain. If we believed that there were cyclical movements between, say, liberty and tyranny, or, to take Plato's four-way cycle, timarchy, oligarchy, democracy, and tyranny, there might also be less of a problem, although no one has yet attempted to situate communism within such a cyclical order of development. But the situation is more difficult when we take a teleological view.

I need to make a terminological clarification at the outset. The term "communism" is used in several different senses. Outside of Marxism it is generally used for political parties, and by extension the societies they rule, that are characterized by single-party governments, state ownership of assets, central planning, and political repression. But in Marxist terminology, communism is the highest stage of development of humankind; the societies that in the previous sentence were described as communist would, in the Marxist view, be considered "socialist," that is, societies that are in transition from capitalism to communism. Most of the time I adhere to the former (non-Marxist) definition since it seems simpler, but when I discuss the performance of an economy ruled by a communist party, I use the more common appellation of "socialist economy." The reason is that the term "communist economy" is more appropriate either for limited time periods, such as under War Communism in the early years of Soviet power, when markets were totally suppressed, or for a hypothetical economy based on noncommodification of labor, generalized abundance of goods, and the principle of "from everyone according to his abilities, to everyone according to his needs." Since the latter economy has never existed, and the former was a very specific experiment driven by the civil war and lasting only three years, it would be misleading to use the term "communist" for the normally functioning post–World War II economies of Eastern Europe, the Soviet Union, or China. "Socialist economy" is not only more accurate, but it also agrees with the (not unreasonable) Soviet description of such societies in the late Brezhnev era as societies of "really existing socialism" (often abbreviated as "real socialism").[4]

Terminological clarification: "communism" and "socialism"

The issue of the placement of historical communism within Marxist thought is especially difficult. This is not only because Marxism originally (and still to this day) regards communism as the highest developmental stage of human society. The problem for Marxism is how to explain why socialism, an ostensible prelude to the highest stage of human evolution, after having won in several countries and

The role of communism within Marxist and liberal historical narratives

then spread and established itself even further, suddenly disappeared by transforming itself officially into capitalism (as in the Soviet Union and Eastern Europe) or evolving de facto toward capitalism (as in China and Vietnam). Such an evolution is simply inconceivable from within Marxism.

The problem is not so much that "real socialism" did not have all the characteristics that it was theoretically supposed to have (although that too is a problem, since its classless character was put in doubt by Marxist sociologists); the key and seemingly unsolvable problem that Marxist historiography needs to explain is how a superior socioeconomic formation like socialism could regress back to an inferior one. It is, within Marxism, the equivalent of trying to explain how a society might go through capitalist and industrial revolutions, create the bourgeoisie and the working class, and then suddenly regress to a feudal order with labor, formerly free, now being chained once again to the land and an aristocracy exacting forced labor and paying no taxes. It would seem absurd to Marxists, as well as to pretty much everyone else, that such a development could happen. But the "fall" of communism back to capitalism is equally absurd, and cannot be explained within the traditional Marxist framework.

It can be explained better, albeit not fully, within the liberal framework. In the liberal view, which Francis Fukuyama captured quite well in the 1990s with *The End of History and the Last Man*, liberal democracy and laissez-faire capitalism represent the terminus of socioeconomic formations invented by humankind. What Marxists see as an incomprehensible reversal to a much lower (inferior) system, liberals see as a perfectly understandable movement from an inferior, dead-end system (communism) back onto the straight path leading to the end point of human evolution: liberal capitalism.

It is worth stopping here for a moment to note how similarly communism and fascism are treated from the liberal point of view. Fascism was—obviously for a shorter period—also a very powerful alternative socioeconomic system. For liberalism, both communism and fascism represent detours in two wrong directions—one too much to the left, another too much to the right. The fall of fascism, whether as the result of a lost war (Germany, Italy, Japan) or internal evolution (Spain, Portugal), is thus seen as almost symmetrical to the fall of communism: the two detours have been overcome, straightened out as it were, and while the countries that went through those detours may have endured tremendous material and human losses, they were eventually able to return to the normal path and progress to a higher socioeconomic system, namely liberal capitalism. Thus, the liberal explanation for the place of communism within twentieth-century history is relatively coherent and has the advantage of treating symmetrically all departures from a straight line leading humanity toward the best system.

It is only "relatively" coherent, however, because it has no clear explanation for failure to follow the straight line. Fascism and communism appear as mistakes, which are ultimately correctible, but there is no understanding or explanation at all for why such mistakes were committed in the first place. Why did fascism and communism become powerful if humanity—and certainly the advanced liberal capitalist countries—was on the right path in 1914? We encounter here a fundamental problem that the liberal capitalist view of history faces: explaining the outbreak of the most destructive war in history (up to that point) within a system that, from a liberal point of view, was fully consonant with the highest, most developed and peaceful way of organizing human society.[5] How to explain that a liberal international order where all the key players were capitalist and globalist, and, moreover, were actual, partial, or aspiring democracies (as was certainly the case for the Western Allies but also for Germany, Austria-Hungary, and Russia, which were all moving in that direction) could end up in a state of general carnage?

The existence of World War I creates an insurmountable obstacle to the Whiggish interpretation of history: it just should not have happened. The fact that it happened at the heyday of liberal dominance, both nationally and in international relations, opens up the possibility that the liberal order might lead to a similar outcome in the future. And it is clearly impossible to claim that a system that might regularly end up in worldwide wars somehow represents the pinnacle of human existence, as defined by the quest for prosperity and freedom. This is the key stumbling block of the liberal explanation of twentieth-century history, and the weak explanations (or complete lack of an explanation) for the rise of fascism and communism follow directly from it. Since the liberal view of history cannot explain the outbreak of the war, it likewise treats the existence of fascism and communism (both, indeed, outcomes of the war) cavalierly, as "mistakes." Saying that something is a mistake is not a satisfactory historical explanation. Liberal theory thus tends to ignore the entire short twentieth century and to go directly from 1914 to the fall of the Berlin Wall in 1989, almost as if nothing had happened in between—1989 brings the world back to the path it was on in 1914, before it slipped in error. This is why liberal explanations for the outbreak of the war are nonexistent, and the explanations proffered are based on politics (Fritz Fischer, Niall Ferguson), the remaining influence of aristocratic societies (Joseph Schumpeter), or, least convincing of all, the idiosyncrasies of individual actors, mistakes, and accidents (A. J. P. Taylor).

Marxism is much better able to explain the war and the rise of fascism. Its adherents hold that the war was the outcome of "the highest stage of capitalism," that is, the stage at which capitalism had created cartels and national monopolies that fought each other for control of the rest of the world. Fascism, in turn, was the weakened bourgeoisie's response to the threat of social revolution. Thus the straight civilizational line of development from capitalism to socialism and ultimately to communism is maintained, although the bourgeoisie might from time to time organize virulent movements like fascism that briefly stop the wheels of history. Marxist views regarding both the war and the rise of fascism are consistent with historical evidence. What is not consistent with historical evidence, and remains a big stumbling block, possibly even an insuperable obstacle, for the Marxist explanation of twentieth-century history is how communism failed to spread to the more advanced countries, and why communist countries turned capitalist again. As I already mentioned, these events not only cannot be explained but cannot even be fathomed within the Marxist view of History.

We thus reach the conclusion that two of the most important events in the global history of the twentieth century, World War I and the fall of communism, cannot both be consistently explained within the liberal or Marxist paradigms. The liberal paradigm has problems with 1914, the Marxist paradigm with 1989.

The difficulty of dealing with communism theoretically and conceptually is widespread. In two influential books (*Economic Origins of Dictatorship and Democracy* and especially *Why Nations Fail*), Daron Acemoglu and James Robinson provided a comprehensive theory that aimed to explain why democracies develop and fail and to demonstrate the close relationship between political and economic inequalities. Their view was very influential, especially in the period before the 2008 global financial crisis, because it unified two strands then dominant in liberal thought: the

> *Difficulty of dealing with communism is widespread*

Washington Consensus (which promoted privatization internally and globalization externally) and the Fukuyama-style celebration of liberal democracy.

One of Acemoglu and Robinson's central concepts is that of "extractive" institutions: political and economic institutions that are controlled by an elite in order to extract economic resources and concentrate political power, with political and economic power occurring together and reinforcing each other. But this concept cannot handle the case of communism, where political power and economic power are at best very weakly related. Within the Acemoglu-Robinson framework, we would expect that the high concentration of political power found in communist countries must also result in a high concentration of economic power. But that was patently not the case under communism; nor were economic advantages, once acquired, transmitted in any meaningful way across generations. Thus communism, a system under which up to a third of the world population lived for the better part of the twentieth century, is almost entirely absent from their scheme and cannot be explained by it. Neither does it explain China's and Vietnam's economic successes. These societies do not have what Acemoglu and Robinson call "inclusive" institutions—those that allow broad participation, operate under the rule of law, and, according to the authors, are essential for economic growth—yet their growth record is among the best in the world, and China's recent record is the best in all of human history. Acemoglu and Robinson thus have to dismiss these countries' success by arguing in *Why Nations Fail* that it cannot last forever, or to be more precise, that unless China democratizes, it must fail once it reaches the technological level at which countries with extractive institutions are allegedly unable to innovate (Acemoglu and Robinson 2012, 441–442). This "China must ultimately fail" theory of history is very weak except in the trivial sense that nothing can last forever.

3.1b How to Situate Communism within Twentieth-Century History

One remarkable feature of both liberal and Marxist theories so far is their sole concern with the West. The economies or societies of the so-called Third World hardly appear at all. They do make a cameo appearance in the Marxist concept of high imperialism, where they are the object over which the advanced capitalist economies fight. And they are sometimes present implicitly, as in Marx's comment in the preface to the first volume of *Capital* that "the country that is more developed industrially only shows, to the less developed, the image of its own future." The non-Western world is thus seen by Marxists as a capitalist, and ultimately socialist, society *in potentia*. Otherwise, there is nothing special about it. According to the standard Marxist view, these societies are behind the advanced societies, but they follow the same route—a route from primitive communism, to slavery, to feudalism, to capitalism that I call here the Western path of development, or WPD. When subscribers to this view discuss the future evolution of advanced economies, they are ipso facto also discussing the future evolution of developing economies. Imagine a train with different cars. To determine the future trajectory of the train, there is no point focusing on individual cars, some of which are ahead of the others; it suffices to know where the locomotive is heading to know where the whole train will end up.

There are only two places in Marxism where the WPD chain is "broken": in the so-called Asiatic mode of production, and in the cautious statement Marx made in his 1881 letter to the Russian revolutionary Vera Zasulich, in which he stated that socialism in Russia could develop directly from the peasant commune, bypassing the stage of capitalist development.[6] The latter has been very influential because it raised the possibility that less-advanced societies could move to socialism as it were directly. ("Legal" Marxists in Russia thought this absurd, but it led them into a no less absurd practical position of having to work for the development of capitalism in Russia so that its full blossoming might, at some near point, create a working class sufficiently large to overthrow it.) The introduction of the Asiatic mode of production (which was never very clearly defined) does allow for some non-linearity in the progression of social formations, but it does nothing to help Marxist schema explain the fall of socialism, the topic of interest here. It remains just as incomprehensible as before.[7]

The liberal view on the position of less-advanced countries is very similar to the standard Marxist view in its neglect of these countries' specificities. The two views are so alike in this respect that we can practically ascribe to liberals Marx's comment about more-advanced countries showing to the less advanced their future path. A number of British declarations expressed this linear, Whiggish view of history, contending that the Empire was a kind of school attended by colonized populations, where they were prepared for their future self-determination and the creation of capitalist economies. It is true that many such declarations can be thought of as thinly veiled justifications for the continuation of colonial rule—for example, that of the British secretary of state Edwin Montagu, who saw self-determination realized "over many years, . . . many generations," or of the United Kingdom's confirming sixty-six times between 1882 and 1922 that Egypt would "soon" be ready for self-government (Tooze 2014, 186; Wesseling 1996, 67). But it would be wrong, I think, to take them only as such. They also expressed a widely shared opinion that less "civilized" countries were on the road to achieving a more civilized or advanced state and that those that were already there should help them.[8] Colonialism involved just such a civilizing mission (*mission civilisatrice*). Thus in the liberal view of the world, as in the Marxist view, there was no specifically Third World issue or Third World path. In fact, there was no Third World in these global *histoires raisonées* at all.

It is precisely in the neglected history of the Third World that we shall find the place of communism within global history. I shall argue that *communism is a social system that enabled backward and colonized societies to abolish feudalism, regain economic and political independence, and build indigenous capitalism*. Or to put it another way, it was a system of transition from feudalism to capitalism used in less-developed and colonized societies. Communism is the functional equivalent of the rise of the bourgeoisie in the

World-historic role of communism

West. This interpretation provides the part of the Third World that was both colonized and went through communist revolutions with its own place in global history, which it lacks in both liberal and Marxist grand narratives.[9]

It is wrong, or fruitless, to think of communism within the standard Western-influenced conception of history because there, as we have seen, neither its rise (within liberalism) nor its fall (within Marxism) can be explained. It is wrong because the conditions that precipitated the evolution of Western societies from feudalism to capitalism were fundamentally different from those that prevailed in the Third World and led to its own transition from feudalism, or "petty-commodity production," to capitalism.

From the sixteenth century onward, most of the Third World, because of its lower level of economic and military development, was conquered by the West. The most difficult conquest was in Asia, where populations could not be eliminated or enslaved as they were in the Americas and Africa and where the level of economic and cultural development was relatively high. From the perspective of the Western path of development, imperialism in Asia (and also in Africa) could be defended as a way of making these countries transit from feudalism to capitalism, and thus, according to Marxist teleology, opening the way to their transition to socialism. This idea was originally formulated by no less an authority than Marx himself, and more recently in an eloquent defense of imperialism from a Marxist perspective by Bill Warren in *Imperialism: Pioneer of Capitalism* (1980).[10] In other words, for the Third World to follow the WPD, developing nations had to be transformed from without into capitalist societies and, at the same time, accelerating this transformation, drawn into a globalized capitalist economy.[11] If the entire Third World were to be reduced to Hong Kong, this would be exactly the path that was followed.

But the world was not Hong Kong. The problem with that approach—which became clear after the end of World War II—was that the external introduction of capitalism could work only on a small scale. Capitalism was able to create and then integrate small entrepôt economies like Hong Kong and Singapore, and to develop cities on the coast of West and South Africa (such as Accra, Abidjan, Dakar, and Cape Town), but it utterly failed to transform most Third World economies. Neither did it lead to satisfactory growth performance: these economies actually continued to fall farther behind the advanced capitalist economies, thus falsifying the economic idea of convergence. Nor did internal relations of production develop in an unambiguously capitalistic direction: different modes of production continued to exist side by side.

Instead, the metropolis-driven development created structural duality in these economies, leading to the rise of neo-Marxist explanations for this dual structure. This period was the high point of Latin American structuralism and *dependencia* theory. Structuralists thought that underdevelopment could be overcome only by severing all ties with the advanced economies (called "the center" or "the core"), which, they argued, naturally imposed a dualistic structure on Third World economies by stimulating the output of export-oriented resource-based sectors and letting the rest of the economy languish. Instead of core-driven development, the Third World should focus on domestically generated growth. Since structuralists were not orthodox Marxists, they left it vague how the new domestic economy should be organized, although it was implicitly assumed that it would continue to be capitalistic (i.e., with privately owned capital and wage labor), even if the state were to play a more important role than it did in an analogous stage of development in the West. Structuralist policies, however, were never implemented. When structuralists like Fernando Cardoso in Brazil came to power they implemented entirely different, pro-capitalist and pro-globalization policies.

We should regard these structuralist, or periphery-core, theories simply as a reaction to the inability of global capitalism to transform Third World countries into full-fledged capitalist economies. If the optimistic Marxist view about the ability of imperialism and global capitalism to convert Third World economies into clones of Western capitalist economies had been correct, colonialism would have turned them into mirror images of Britain and France, and there would have been no need for structuralist explanations. Structuralists and dependency theorists thus merely tried to fill this gap, explaining why global capitalism was not more successful while at the same time shying away from suggesting a fully socialist economy (e.g., public ownership of the means of production) as a way to development, since the Soviet model was, by the time structuralists came to the scene, showing clear signs of senescence.

The structuralists came to the scene too late, and their approach, as well as the huge gap between what they advocated and what they actually implemented (when they had a chance to do so), reflects that lateness. In many countries, to effect a real transition from Third World feudalism to capitalism, communist revolutions were needed. *Communist revolutions in the colonized Third World played the same functional role that domestic bourgeoisies did in the West.* Bill Warren is right when he argues that the Comintern's "Eastern turn" (the shift of emphasis toward anti-imperialist struggle rather than revolution in developed countries), which occurred in the 1920s, "changed the role of Marxism from a movement for democratic working-class socialism [in rich countries], to a movement for the modernization of backward societies," but while he regards that shift as a mistake, it was, in reality, a big step forward that would eventually transform less-developed countries into autochthonous capitalist economies.[12] Section 3.2 explains why communism was uniquely able to effect this transformation—that is, the transformation that was supposed to be brought about either by imperialism, a task at which it failed, or by structuralists, a task that they never undertook.

3.2 Why Were Communist Revolutions Needed to Being Capitalism to (Some Parts) of the Third World?

3.2a *The Role of Communist Revolutions in the Third World*

To understand the key difference between the actual position of the Third World countries and their supposed position as theorized by the WPD, we need to realize that their position in the 1920s was characterized by (a) underdevelopment vis-à-vis the West, (b) feudal or feudal-like relations of production, and (c) foreign domination. Foreign domination was unpopular, but it brought to these societies (China being the prime example) awareness of their underdevelopment and weakness. Had they not been so easily conquered and controlled, they would not have realized how far behind they had fallen. Thus points (a) and (c) are specific to less-developed nations, and both were absent at an equivalent stage in the West.[13] This is the reason why Third World countries could not develop along the WPD path.

It then becomes clear that the task facing any social movement in the Third World was twofold: to transform the domestic economy by changing the dominant relations of production, that is, by getting rid of the stifling power of landlords and other magnates, and to overthrow foreign rule. These two revolutions—a social revolution whose ultimate objective was development, and a political revolution whose ultimate objective was self-determination—were rolled into one. And the only organized forces that could effect these two revolutions were communist parties and other parties that were both left-wing *and* nationalist. Leaving aside communist parties' other advantages—such as their level of organization and the quality of their leaders and adherents, many of whom were well-educated and willing to make sacrifices—only these parties and their affiliates were ideologically committed to combining social and national revolutions. In Mao Zedong's words: "Two big mountains lie like a dead weight on the Chinese people. One is imperialism, the other is feudalism. The Chinese Communist Party had long made up its mind to dig them up."[14] Thus, "Mao's socialism [was] both an ideology of modernization and a critique of Euro-American capitalist modernization" (Wang 2003, 149). Other pro-independence parties were by definition nationalist, but they stumbled and vacillated when it came to social transformation (e.g., the Congress Party in India, in both its Hindu and Muslim versions). They could deliver one part of the revolution but not the other. And for the daily life of peasants and workers, the social revolution was perhaps even more important than the national one.

China and Vietnam are the best examples of combined social and national revolutions. The obstacles that both parties overcame in order to come to power were daunting and even overwhelming, and no one in their right mind would have forecast in, say, 1925 or 1930, what ultimately did come to pass in those countries. Most important parts of China were divided into a number of foreign-controlled zones where Chinese law did not apply, while the rest of the country, nominally controlled by the Chinese, was ruled by multiple warlords in constantly changing coalitions and in more or less overt collaboration with foreign powers. Poverty was dreadful, disease and infanticide widespread. At the end of World War I, Woodrow Wilson's closest adviser, Edward ("Colonel") House, described China as a "menace to civilization": "[China] is in a deplorable condition. The prevalence of disease, lack of sanitation, . . . slavery, infanticide and other brutal and degenerate practices make it as a whole a menace to civilization." The solution, according to House, would be to place China under international "trusteeship."[15] As the Chinese Civil War and the Great Depression further impoverished China, a survey of villages undertaken by the China Cotton Mill Owners' Association for the purpose of estimating the demand for textiles "found disastrous conditions: women in Szechuan were not wearing skirts because the rural devastation had left farmers without the means to purchase cloth, and in many households family members shared one item of clothing" (Shiroyama 2008, 127). Vietnam at the same time was under the thumb of the French, who ran an efficient, extractive, and oppressive administration.[16] The ideas of national liberation, territorial unification, and transformation of social relations were so remote and so weak that I do not think it is an exaggeration to say that not one bet in a million could rationally have been placed on their becoming a reality. And yet they did, precisely for the reasons advanced above.

There are two aspects, social and national, to the victory of communist parties in the Third World countries. I shall illustrate them with the most important example, that of China. The Chinese Communist Party (CCP)

Social and national revolutions

advocated and implemented, first in the areas that it controlled in the 1920s–1930s, and then after its victory in 1949 throughout China, a comprehensive land reform, the abolition of quasi-feudal relations in rural areas, and a weakening of clan-based social relations, which were replaced by a more modern nuclear family structure and gender equality. It also promoted widespread literacy and education with "affirmative action" in education and employment in favor of children from peasant and workers' families. This was no less than a complete overturning of historical hierarchical relationships.[17] It all went together with the rejection of Confucianism, which, through its emphasis on filial piety, unquestioning respect of authority, and meekness, permitted such iniquitous structures to endure for centuries. The nationalist Kuomintang not surprisingly never engaged, nor would it have engaged, in such wholesale change. Moreover, during the periods when the Kuomintang and the CCP "cooperated," in the late 1920s and during the Japanese occupation, the CCP agreed, to please the Kuomintang and maintain a joint front, to shelve some of its most important reforms, especially the most controversial of all: agrarian reform.

The second, national, aspect is also well illustrated by the CCP and the Maoist leadership that came to power in 1935. Although Mao and the CCP paid lip service to Stalin's and the Comintern's instructions, and while ideologically and in their plans for the future organization of the state they were Stalinists, they prosecuted a national revolution that had very little to do with Moscow or even with internationalism. The emphasis on the role of the peasantry as opposed to the urban working class as the key force to bring about the socialist revolution was not only unorthodox in a Marxist sense, but was against the long-standing policy of the Comintern, which saw workers in Shanghai as the nucleus of a future Soviet state. Mao ignored that view and, in 1935, replaced the Moscow-approved leadership of Wang Ming with himself and his own nationalist cadres. It is worth quoting here the judgment on Mao by Wang Fan-hsi, one of the early leaders of the CCP (who was later expelled for his Trotskyist leanings, along with many others, and had no reason to be sentimental about Mao and the CCP): "Mao has never been a Stalinist in terms of [belonging to a Stalinist] faction [within the CCP]. The Stalinists would have never recruited anyone as opinionated as Mao. . . . He built his ideological foundation on the Chinese classics; . . . acquired knowledge of modern European thought, in particular Marxism-Leninism . . . by building a rough superstructure of foreign style on a solid Chinese foundation . . . nor will [he] ever cast aside that self-conceited pride peculiar to old-style Chinese scholars."[18] In fact, the CCP looked at foreign Communist "advisers" and those Chinese who followed them without demurring as "red compradors."[19]

What this reveals is the open nationalism of the Chinese revolution, not only in the way it came to power and whose class interests it represented (disregarding Marxist theory), but in its ideological independence from what was supposed to be the center of worldwide communism. Of course, the CCP was not nationalist solely in its relations with other communists. It was also nationalist in its attitudes and actions toward Japanese occupiers and against the Western powers that had divided China. Thus, nationalism is reflected both in the rejection of the classical Marxist WPD and the Comintern's policies, and also in the struggle against Japanese and Western imperialisms.

Prosecuting a social and a national revolution at the same time enabled left-wing and communist parties to make a tabula rasa of all ideologies and customs that were seen as retarding economic development and creating artificial divisions among people (such as the caste structure, which the much less radical Indian revolution never succeeded in erasing) and to do away with foreign rule. These two simultaneous revolutions were a precondition for successful domestic development and, over the longer run, for the creation of an indigenous capitalist class that would, as such a class did in Western Europe and North America, pull the economy forward. Here, however, the transformation from feudalism to capitalism took place under the control of an extremely powerful state, a different process from what happened in Europe and North America, where the role of the state was much less important and where countries were free of foreign interference.[20] But this is a fundamental difference; and this difference in the role of the state explains why capitalism in China, Vietnam, and many other places, either in the past (South Korea) or currently (Ethiopia, Rwanda), has so often had an authoritarian edge to it.

3.2b Where Was Communism Successful?

The argument that communism was the system that enabled the transition from feudalism to indigenous capitalism in countries that were colonized or dominated by the West is also supported by the fact that communism was more successful in less-developed countries. When we measure the success of communism either by a crude growth rate or, preferably, by comparing the performance of communist countries against capitalist countries at the same level of development, we find a negative correlation between the income level of a country at the time when it became communist and its subsequent absolute growth rate, or its growth rate relative to its capitalist counterparts. In simple terms, this means that communism was least successful in developed industrial economies like East Germany and Czechoslovakia and most successful in poor agricultural societies like China and Vietnam.

The relative failure of communism in more developed countries was clear from the mid-1970s onward as the gap between central European communist countries and similar capitalist countries (like Austria) began to widen. This has led to a significant literature, some of it published after the fall of communism, that examined communism's historical economic performance and the reasons for its decline. The two most common explanations point to the system's inability to innovate and its inability to substitute capital for labor. Both could be seen as an inability to create and manage technological change. The first explanation (Broadberry and Klein 2011) puts the emphasis on the fact that communist countries were unable to successfully move beyond the relatively simple level of network industries with large economies of scale (dams and electricity generation, integrated steel plants, railroads, etc.) and thus entirely missed the technological revolution that followed. In the words of Broadberry and Klein, "Central planning was able to achieve a satisfactory productivity performance during the era of mass production, but could not adapt to the requirements of flexible production technology during the 1980s" (2011, 37). Communist-ruled countries would probably have missed the ICT revolution, too, had communism not collapsed first. The second explanation (Easterly and Fischer, 1995; Sapir 1980) puts more emphasis on the lack of substitutability between capital and labor, which meant that final output was produced with quasi-fixed proportions of the two factors. In this situation, the level of output is determined (limited) by the less abundant factor: if population ceases to grow, a shortage of workers cannot be compensated by more capital. According to the authors, this is what happened in the Soviet Union and Eastern Europe.

Both explanations imply that the more sophisticated the economy, the less efficient the socialist economic system was. Recent evidence confirms this. In a detailed study covering the entire postwar period during which socialism existed in Eastern Europe, Vonyó (2017) reports three important results, shown in Figure 3.1. First, countries that were more developed in 1950 had lower average growth rates in the subsequent thirty-nine years. This result implies income convergence, and it is true for both socialist and capitalist European countries. This is why the two lines in Figure 3.1 are both downward sloping. Second, socialist countries, at any (initial) income level, performed worse than capitalist countries. This is why the line for socialist countries lies below the line for capitalist countries. Third, the gap in performance between the two types of countries increases as initial income level increases (that is, the more developed the country, the greater the gap). This is why the distance between the two

> **Contra *Marx*, *socialism was least successful in developed countries***

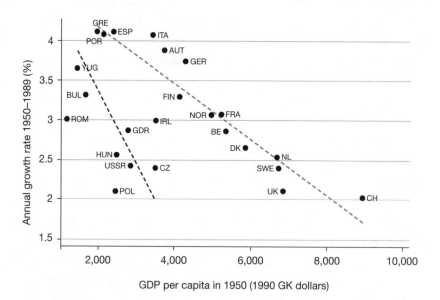

FIGURE 3.1. Performance of socialist versus capitalist economies in Europe, 1950–1989

Country abbreviations: *Socialist countries*: BUL Bulgaria, CZ Czechoslovakia, GDR German Democratic Republic, HUN Hungary, POL Poland, ROM Romania, USSR Soviet Union, YUG Yugoslavia; *Capitalist countries*: AUT Austria, BE Belgium, CH Switzerland, DK Denmark, ESP Spain, FIN Finland, FRA France, GER West Germany, GRE Greece, IRL Ireland, ITA Italy, NL Netherlands, NOR Norway, POR Portugal, SWE Sweden, UK United Kingdom. GK dollars are Geary-Khamis PPP (purchasing power parity) 1990 dollars. *Data source:* Vonyó (2017, 255). Reproduced with permission.

lines is greater for countries that were richer in 1950 than for those that were poorer.

A comparison between capitalist and socialist (that is, communist-run) countries is extremely important not only because it shows the inferior performance of socialist countries, but because it enables us to decompose the inferior performance of the richer socialist countries into two parts: (1) the part due to economic convergence (that is, the non-system-specific part which exists whether we compare the performance of the United Kingdom to that of Spain, or of Czechoslovakia to Bulgaria), and (2) the part that is system-specific and is reflected in the much worse performance of the richer socialist countries than the richer capitalist countries. It is part 2 that is of key importance for my argument that socialism was economically much less successful in rich than in poor countries. This in turn undermines the linear Marxist, or WPD, approach, which holds exactly the opposite: that socialism's failures stem from having been applied not in rich Western countries but in peripheral countries like Russia. Actually, the very opposite is true: had socialism been applied in Western Europe, it would have been even less successful than in Eastern Europe. It is the very failure of socialism in rich countries that falsifies simple-minded Marxist teleology.

Carlin, Shaffer, and Seabright (2012) came to the same conclusion, that the performance of socialist economies differed according to income level. They showed that relatively poor countries benefited more from some advantages of central planning (such as improved infrastructure and better education) than they suffered from the absence of market incentives. Expressed in terms of the long-run growth rate, poor socialist countries therefore benefited, compared with their capitalist equivalents. However, the opposite holds for richer countries, where the absence of markets reduced the long-term growth rate below that of their capitalist counterparts.

Both theory and empirical evidence therefore suggest that less-developed countries (that is, precisely those in which communism enabled the transition from feudalism to indigenous capitalism) would most likely benefit from changes brought about by communism. By looking at their performance over an even longer period that includes the past three decades, during which some of the communist countries transformed into political capitalist countries, we see that that advantage has widened. Figure 3.2 shows the annual rate of GDP per capita growth from 1990 through 2016 for China, Vietnam, and the United States (which may be seen as the representative of liberal meritocratic capitalism). China's growth rate is on average about 8 percent, Vietnam's around 6 percent, and the United States' only 2 percent. Not only is the gap between the growth rates high, but it is constant across all years: over a twenty-six-year period, there was only one year when Vietnam and the United States displayed the same growth rate (in 1997, the year of the Asian financial crisis), and in no year was Chinese growth equal to or lower than American growth. As we shall see below, this remarkable performance of political capitalist countries is something that puts them, at least if prosperity is a key criterion, in competition with liberal capitalism as to the best way to organize society. Whether this gap in performance will remain in the future is not obvious: as China,

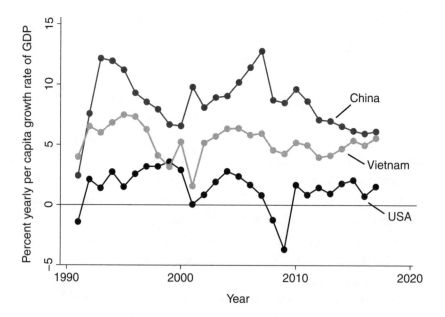

FIGURE 3.2. Growth rates of GDP per capita in China, Vietnam, and the United States, 1990–2016

Growth rates are in real terms, based on 2011 PPP (purchasing power parity) dollars. *Data source:* World Bank World Development Indicators, 2017 version.

Vietnam, and others approach the production possibility frontier and their growth depends more on innovation, it might slow down (see also Appendix C). But we do not know if it would slow down all the way to the level of today's rich countries, or if the slowdown would—despite the truly remarkable journey of these countries, which have gone in the span of a couple of generations from very poor to very rich—make them less of a model for others to follow.

3.2c Is China Capitalist?

But is China really capitalist? This is a question that is often asked—sometimes rhetorically and sometimes genuinely. We can dispose of it quickly if we use the standard Marx-Weber definition of capitalism introduced in Chapter 2. To qualify as capitalist, a society should be such that most of its production is conducted using privately owned means of production (capital, land), most workers are wage-laborers (not legally tied to land or working as self-employed using their own capital), and most decisions regarding production and pricing are taken in a decentralized fashion (that is, without anyone imposing them on enterprises). China scores as positively capitalistic on all three counts.

Before 1978, the share of industrial output produced by state-owned enterprises (SOEs) in China was close to 100 percent, since most of the industrial enterprises were state owned. They worked within a central plan, which, although more flexible and covering many fewer commodities than in the Soviet Union, nevertheless included all the key industrial products (coal and other mined materials, steel, petroleum, utilities, etc.), some of which are still predominantly supplied by the SOEs. By 1998, the state's share in industrial output had already halved to just above 50 percent, as shown in Figure 3.3. Since then it has consistently, year after year, declined, and it is currently just slightly above 20 percent.

The situation in agriculture is even clearer. Before the reforms, most of the production was carried out by village communes. Since 1978 and the introduction of the "responsibility system," which allowed private leasing of land, almost the entire output has been produced privately—although of course farmers are not wage-workers but are mostly self-employed, in

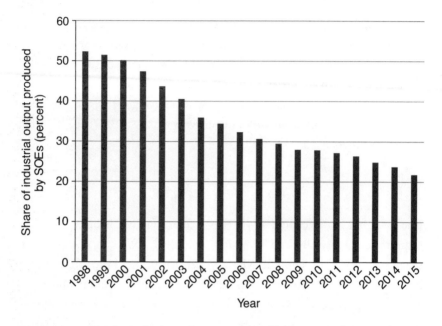

FIGURE 3.3. The share of industrial output produced by state-owned enterprises in China, 1998–2015

Data source: Chinese official data kindly provided by Chunlin Zhang, World Bank Beijing office.

what Marxist terminology calls "petty-commodity production." This was historically the typical way Chinese agriculture was organized, so the present ownership structure in rural areas is somewhat of a return to the past (with one significant difference—the absence of landlords). But as the rural exodus to cities continues, more capitalistic relations are likely to be established in agriculture as well. We may also mention the township and village enterprises (collectively owned enterprises), which, although less important now than in the past, grew rapidly using surplus rural labor to produce nonagricultural commodities. They use wage labor, but their ownership structure, which combines in varying proportions state ownership (albeit at the communal level), some cooperative ownership, and purely private ownership, is extremely complicated and varies between different parts of the country.

Private firms are not merely numerous; many are large. According to official data, the share of private companies in the top 1 percent of firms ranked by total value added has increased from around 40 percent in 1998 to 65 percent in 2007 (Bai, Hsieh, and Song 2014, fig. 4).

Ownership patterns in China are complex because they often involve central state, provincial state, communal, private, and foreign ownership in various proportions, but the role of the state in total GDP, calculated from the production side, is unlikely to exceed 20 percent,[21] while the workforce employed in the SOEs and collectively owned enterprises is 9 percent of the total rural and urban employment (China Labor Statistical Yearbook 2017). These percentages are similar to those in the early 1980s in France (Milanovic 1989, table 1.4). As we shall see in Section 3.3, one of the characteristics of political capitalism is indeed that the state plays a significant role, easily exceeding its role as proxied by its formal ownership of capital, but my point here is simply to dispose of some doubts about the capitalistic nature of the Chinese economy—doubts that are made not on empirical grounds (since the data clearly invalidate them) but on the specious grounds that the ruling party is called "communist," as if that alone were sufficient to determine the nature of an economic system.

The distribution of fixed investment by sector of ownership also shows a very clear trend toward a greater share of private investment (Figure 3.4).

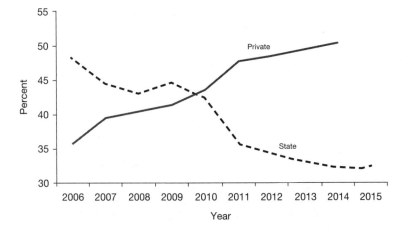

FIGURE 3.4. Fixed investment by sector of ownership in China, 2006–2015

Data source: World Bank (2017, figure 1.6).

Private investment already accounts for more than half of fixed investment, while the state share is around 30 percent (the remainder is composed of the collective sector and foreign private investment).[22]

The change is also starkly reflected in the share of SOE workers in total urban employment (Figure 3.5). Before the reforms, almost 80 percent of urban workers were employed in SOEs. Now, after a decline that has continued year after a year, their share is less than 16 percent. In rural areas, de facto land privatization under the responsibility system has transformed almost all rural labor into private sector farmers.

Finally, the contrast between socialist and capitalist modes of production is seen most dramatically in decentralized production and pricing decisions. At the beginning of the reforms, the state set prices for 93 percent of agricultural products, 100 percent of industrial products, and 97 percent of retail commodities. In the mid-1990s, the proportions were inverted: prices were market-determined for 93 percent of retail commodities, 79 percent

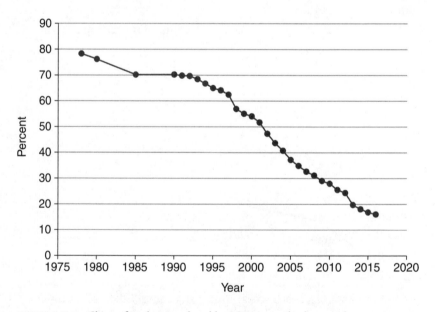

FIGURE 3.5. Share of workers employed by SOEs in total urban employment in China, 1978–2016

Data source: National Bureau of Statistics, Statistical Yearbooks, various years. Data kindly provided by Haiyan Ding.

of agricultural products, and 81 percent of production materials (Pei 2006, 125). Today even a higher percentage of prices are market determined.

3.3 Key Features of Political Capitalism

3.3a Three Systemic Characteristics and Two Systemic Contradictions

Max Weber's definition of politically motivated capitalism in *The Protestant Ethic and the Spirit of Capitalism* was "the use of political power to achieve economic gains." In Weber's words, "The capitalism of promoters, large-scale speculators, concession hunters and much modern financial capitalism even in peace-time, but, above all, the capitalism especially concerned with exploiting wars, bears this stamp [acquisition of wealth by force, political connection, or speculation] even in modern Western countries, and some . . . parts of large-scale international trade are closely related to it" (1992, 21). Weber developed this idea further in *Economy and Society*: "Political capitalism has existed . . . wherever there has been tax farming, the profitable provision of the state's political needs, war, piracy, large-scale usury, and colonization" (1978, 480).

The states that practice political capitalism today, especially China, Vietnam, Malaysia, and Singapore, have modified this model by putting a highly efficient and technocratically savvy bureaucracy in charge of the system. This is the *first* important characteristic of the system—that bureaucracy (which is clearly the primary beneficiary of the system) has as its main duty to realize high economic growth and implement policies that allow this goal to be achieved. Growth is needed for the legitimization of its rule. The bureaucracy needs to be technocratic and the selection of its members merit-based if it is to be successful, especially since the rule of law is absent. The absence of a binding rule of law is the *second* important characteristic of the system.

Deng Xiaoping, China's preeminent leader from the late 1970s to the mid-1990s, could be considered the founding father of modern political capitalism, an approach—more than an ideology—that combines private-sector dynamism, efficient rule of bureaucracy, and a one-party political system.

Deng as the founding father of modern political capitalism

Zhao Ziyang, who was prime minister of China and, for a brief period, secretary general of the Communist Party (but was deposed in 1989 after the Tiananmen events), described in his memoirs Deng's political views thus: "[He] was particularly opposed to a multiparty system, tripartite separation of power and the parliamentary system of western nations—and firmly rejected them. Almost every time he mentioned political reform, he was sure to note that the western political system absolutely could not be adopted" (2009, 251). For Deng, economic reform was based on "learning from the facts" and allowing the private sector wide latitude, but never so wide and powerful as to be able to dictate its preferences to the state and the Communist Party. Political reform, Zhao writes, meant improvement in the efficiency of the system; it amounted to no more than an "administrative reform."

In the economic arena, Deng's view was not very different from that of the conservative "elder" Chen Yun (father of China's first five-year plan), who used the metaphor of a bird in a cage to explain the proper role of the private sector: if the private sector is controlled too tightly, it will, like an imprisoned bird, suffocate; if it is left entirely free, it will fly away.[23] So the best approach is to place the bird in a spacious cage. Although the metaphor was associated with the conservative interpretation of Chinese reforms, it could be said that Deng's view differed only in terms of the size of the cage within which he wanted to enclose the private sector. It was not, however, the size of the private sector that Deng wanted to limit but its political role—that is, its ability to impose its preferences on state policy. In Ming Xia's apt summary, Deng was "the Chief Architect [who] designed a smooth transition from state socialism to capitalism" but who was also "not hesitant to destroy any ideas he deemed dangerous. . . . He stopped the tendency of 'bourgeois liberalization' [in 1986] and brutally clamped down on the student demonstrations [in 1989]" (2000, 186). It is this double legacy that defined not only Deng's China but more broadly the model of political capitalism.

Deng's approach is similar to what Giovanni Arrighi, in *Adam Smith in Beijing* (2007), calls Smithian "natural" market development, where capitalists' interests are never allowed to reign supreme, and the state retains significant autonomy to follow national-interest policies and, if needed, to rein in the private sector. This dual ability of the state to be guided by national interests (a very mercantilist feature) and to control the private sector is the key feature of modern political capitalism, or what we may call its *third* important characteristic. This requires, in order for the state to be able to act decisively, its independence from legal constraints—in a word, arbitrary decision-making by people, and not decision-making by laws (our second characteristic).

Like all countries, those with political capitalism do have laws, and those laws are in most cases applied. However, the rule of law cannot be generalized (i.e., made to apply to all regardless of their political connections and affiliations) because that would destroy the set-up of the system and affect its main beneficiaries. The elite benefits from the arbitrariness since it can, *le cas échéant,* simply not apply the law, either to itself or to its supporters, when the law is inconvenient. Alternatively, it can apply it with full force (and even add a bit more) when an "undesirable" political actor, or business competitor, needs to be punished. Thus, for example, the rules do not apply when Xi Jinping needs to extend his presidency beyond the usual two terms, or when Vladimir Putin needs to circumvent the spirit of the law by running for the top office four times. But the full strength of the law can be used to bludgeon companies owned by politically inconvenient actors. It is not necessarily the case that such actors are innocent (as in the example of the exiled Russian billionaire Mikhail Khodorkovsky, who probably was not), but that the law is used selectively against them. The Chinese tycoon Xiao Jianhua, a man with complex connections to the Chinese leadership, faced a similar fate to Khodorkovsky's when he was suddenly abducted from the most luxurious Hong Kong hotel. This arbitrary use of power is what Flora Sapio (2010, quoted in Creemers 2018) calls a "zone of lawlessness," where the normal operation of the law is suspended. Such zones of lawlessness are not an aberration but are an integral part of the system.

This brings us to the *first contradiction* that exists in modern political capitalism: that between the need for a technocratic and highly skilled elite and the fact that the elite must operate under the conditions of selective application of the rule of law.[24] The two are in contradiction: a technocratic elite is educated to follow the rules and to operate within the confines of a rational system. But arbitrariness in the application of the rules directly undermines these principles.

The *second contradiction* is that between (i) inequality-increasing corruption, which is endemic in such systems because the discretionary power granted to bureaucracy is also used by its various members to obtain financial gain, the greater the higher their position, and (ii) the need, for reasons of legitimacy, to keep inequality in check. This is where Weber's

Endemic corruption

more detailed definition of political capitalism becomes fully applicable. Decisions on such matters as taxation, the enforcement of regulations, borrowing and lending, and who will profit from public works are often discretionary. They may be based in part on objective criteria, and in part on the identity of potential beneficiaries and what might be the financial gain by the elite. The elite should not be seen simply as bureaucracy, because the lines between where bureaucracy ends and business begins are blurred: individuals may move between these two roles, or the different roles may be maintained by different individuals within the same "organization" that has its "representatives" dispersed, some in business, others in politics. Using a pejorative term, one could say that such organizations are not too dissimilar from mafias. They create politico-entrepreneurial clans and represent the skeleton of political capitalism upon which everything else hangs. The accumulation of such clans creates what may be called the politico-capitalist class.[25]

Corruption is endemic to political capitalism. Any system that requires discretionary decision-making must have endemic corruption. The problem with corruption, from the point of view of the elite, is that, taken too far, it tends to undermine the integrity of bureaucracy and the ability to conduct economic policies that produce high growth. The key part of the social compact that maintains political capitalism is then exploded. The population may tolerate its lack of voice (or in some cases, may not care whether it has a voice or not) as long as the elite delivers tangible improvements in living standards, provides tolerable administration of justice, and does not allow glaring inequalities. But if corruption goes overboard, that compact no longer holds: high growth cannot be maintained in a high-corruption environment; nor is administration of justice tolerable any longer; nor can ostentatious consumption be held in check. All become much worse.

The system is always in precarious equilibrium. If corruption gets out of hand, the system may collapse. But if the rule of law is fully implemented, then the system changes radically and moves from the control of one party or one elite to a system of elite competition. To keep the system functioning, the elite therefore has to find a middle path between the two courses, neither of which it can implement fully. At certain times it may lean toward one, and at other times it may lean toward the other. One course is to reinforce the rule of law, even if it cannot be fully implemented, because discretion is, as we have seen, essential to the elite's power. This is the strategy that Hu Jintao, president of China from 2003 to 2013, tried to adopt. Some analysts saw Hu's strategy, wrongly, as a first move toward the ultimate objective of liberal capitalism. Although that was not the objective, it is nevertheless true that a more law-observant political capitalism begins to look much more like liberal capitalism. The alternative strategy is the one used by Xi Jinping, where the emphasis is on fighting corruption. That strategy does not address the principle of discretion in decision-making, but cracks down on its most egregious misuses. This is why commentators generally see this strategy as more conservative; it leaves the basic features of political capitalism unchanged, does not reduce the power of bureaucracy, and keeps the ideological gap between political and liberal capitalism as wide as before. But it stabilizes political capitalism.

Since corruption is endemic to political capitalism, it is impossible to eradicate it. To do so, the system would either have to change in the direction of liberal capitalism or would have to become autarkic. Autarkic systems, for the reasons explained in Chapter 4, do not have difficulties keeping corruption in check (but they do have other problems).

It may be useful at this point to summarize the systemic characteristics and the key contradictions of political capitalism, the way I see them.

> *System summarized*

The three systemic characteristics are:

(1) Efficient bureaucracy (administration)
(2) Absence of the rule of law
(3) Autonomy of the state

The contradictions are:

First, the clash between systemic characteristics (1) and (2), namely the contradiction between the need for impersonal management of affairs required for a good bureaucracy and discretionary application of the law.

Second, the contradiction between endemic corruption generated by the absence of the rule of law and the basis on which the system's legitimacy rests.

We see that, in some sense, the contradictions are derived from the main characteristics of the system.

3.3b Which Countries Have Systems of Political Capitalism?

China and Vietnam are the paradigmatic examples of political capitalism. But they are not alone. At least nine other countries have systems that fit the requirements of political capitalism, as shown in Table 3.1. To be included in this list, the country's political system must be either single party or de facto single party, with other parties permitted to exist but not to win elections, and / or with one party having stayed in power for several decades.[26] The political system must also have been "born" after a successful struggle for national independence, whether the previous conditions were formally colonial or just very close to being so. Finally, note that all countries listed, save possibly Singapore, became independent after a violent struggle.[27] Some, in addition, went through a period of civil war. The list also indicates the countries in which the transition to indigenous capitalism was carried out by a communist or an explicitly left-wing party (that is, the countries that fit into my discussion of the role of communism in effecting the transition to capitalism).[28] Seven of the eleven countries satisfy that last requirement. The table also shows the growth rates of these countries over the past thirty years and their current ranking by level of corruption.

With the exception of Angola and Algeria, all of the countries have had a per capita growth rate over the past quarter century above the world average. In 2016, the eleven countries listed here contained more than 1.7 billion people (24.5 percent of the world population) and produced 21 percent of the world output (calculated at 2011 PPPs [purchasing power

TABLE 3.1. Countries that have systems of political capitalism

Country	Political system	Number of years in power (up to 2018)	Average GDP per capita growth rate between 1990/1991 and 2016	Corruption ranking in 2016[4]
China[1]	Single party rule since 1949	69	8.5	79
Vietnam[1]	Single party rule since 1945, extended in 1975 to South Vietnam	73	5.3	113
Malaysia	One party in power since 1957 (ended in May 2018)	61	3.7	55
Laos[1]	Single party rule since 1975	43	4.8	123
Singapore	One party in power since 1959	59	3.4	7
Algeria[1]	Single party rule since 1962	56	1.8[2]	108
Tanzania[1]	One party in power since 1962	56	3.5	116
Angola[1]	Single party rule since 1975	43	1.1	164
Botswana	One party in power since 1965	53	2.8	35
Ethiopia[1]	Single party rule since 1991	27	4.1	108
Rwanda	Single party rule since 1994	24	2.6[3]	50
World			2.0	88

1. Ruling party is communist or quasi-communist.
2. Calculated after the end of the civil war in 2002.
3. Calculated after the end of the civil war in 1993.
4. Countries are ranked from the least corrupt (number 1) to the most corrupt (number 176).
Note: "Single party rule" means that other parties do not exist or are irrelevant; "one party in power" means that the multiparty system exists but one party always wins elections. *Data source:* GDP data from World Bank World Development Indicators 2017. Corruption ranking from Transparency International, https://www.transparency.org/. This corruption index measures "perceived levels of public sector corruption according to experts and businesspeople."

parity]). In 1990, their share of world population was 26 percent, while their share of world output was only 5.5 percent. In other words, their share of world output almost quadrupled in less than thirty years, a fact that may not be unrelated to the attractiveness that they, and China especially, have for the rest of the world.[29]

In the area of corruption, six of the eleven countries score significantly worse than the median country (the median rank is 88, since 176 countries were ranked in 2016). China's score is slightly better than the world median. Botswana and Singapore are the real exceptions here, since their perceived corruption, as measured by Transparency International, is very low.

China is by far the most important country among the eleven, a proto-type of the system of political capitalism, and it also touts its model as one that other countries should emulate. Certain features of the Chinese system, notably inequality, are thus worth looking at carefully in the same way that we looked closely at inequality in the United States, the emblematic country of liberal meritocratic capitalism, in Chapter 2. One difference, however, is that our knowledge of American inequality is vastly superior to our knowledge of Chinese inequality. Not only are the US data much more plentiful and available for a longer period, they are more reliable and high-light many aspects (including, very importantly, the transmission of in-equality across generations) that are almost nonexistent for China. My dis-cussion of Chinese characteristics will therefore, by necessity, be more limited.

3.4 A Review of Inequality in China

3.4a Rising Inequality Throughout

Knowledge about income and wealth inequality in China is much more limited than it is for the United States and other rich or middle-income economies. The multitude of income surveys that exist in China is matched only by their unreliability. The most trustworthy sources of information are the official household surveys of rural and urban areas that have been conducted by the National Bureau of Statistics (NBS) since 1954–1955. There was an interruption during the Cultural Revolution, and they were restarted in 1982. Until 2013 rural and urban surveys were technically dif-ferent (questionnaires differed as well), and it was not easy to put their results together to obtain a picture for all of China. In fact, official Chi-nese publications never combined rural and urban survey results or pub-lished the fractiles that purported to represent distribution for all of China until 2013, when the first all-China survey was conducted. One of the chief difficulties consisted (and still does consist to some extent) in the treatment of people who lived in cities without urban residence permits (hukou). Some surveys grouped these people as a peculiar "floating" population that stood between rural and urban residents; in other cases, this floating population was not included in the surveys: members of the group were not interviewed in urban areas because they were not official residents, and they could not be interviewed in rural areas because they were not physically present there. In some extreme cases, as in Shenzhen and Shanghai, the gap between the actual population and those with city permits exceeds several million.[30] The study of income distribution was made even more difficult because the Chinese authorities never released microdata (individual household characteristics and income) from the surveys but rather published only fragmentary data in the form of tabulations of income fractiles. At best, they provided, through the Chinese Academy of Social Sciences and Beijing Normal University, microdata subsamples from the original national surveys that did not cover all the provinces.

Since 2013, when urban and rural surveys were merged into a single all-China survey, in principle a big step forward, the published data have become even more sparse, and microdata have not been released. The government statistical offices currently publish only five quintiles of total population, and their urban and rural parts, ranked by household per capita income. So, ironically, an improvement in the methodology of the national flagship survey was followed by even more scant release of the data. Despite such problems, these are still the data that are most often used to study inequality in China, and, in their subsample version (China Household Income Project, or CHIP), they are included in the Luxembourg Income Study database, the premier source for harmonized worldwide surveys (that is, surveys where various variables are defined to be similar, or the same, across countries in order to allow meaningful international comparisons). More recently, several academic and private surveys with less than complete coverage of China have also become available, but only one (China Household Finance, CHFS) has acquired some acceptance. Not only are income inequality data for China unsatisfactory, but many of the other topics that can be studied for rich and middle-income countries (for example, the importance of capital income, homogamy, and intergenerational mobility), in the case of China, are studied using questionable sources or only very short time-series, or cannot be studied at all.[31]

Mentioning these severe problems with Chinese data will not only (hopefully) prod the authorities to become more open and forthcoming, but is also necessary to highlight the fact that we cannot speak with nearly the same level of confidence when we discuss inequality in China as when we discuss inequality in rich countries. It is with this caveat that we turn to the study of the main inequality trends in China.

Figure 3.6 shows the evolution of income inequality in China from the 1980s to 2016. Panel A shows urban and rural inequalities, calculated from the two surveys (urban and rural), while panel B shows one way of putting the two together to obtain an estimate of all-China inequality. Several things are worth noticing in panel A. First, rural inequality in China has typically been higher than urban inequality, which is very uncommon, especially in countries that are undergoing fast industrialization and urbanization. It can be explained by the very low initial level of inequality in cities, when most of the companies were state-owned and wage distribution was compressed, but also by the *hukou* system, which did not allow for urbanization to proceed too fast (leading to large pools of the poor and unemployed), and in addition, possibly by the failure of surveys to capture all actual city residents, precisely because of the unclear treatment of people without the *hukou*. Urban inequality would likely be greater if all residents were included.

Second, while rural inequality has, after an increase in the 1980s, stayed around the same level, urban inequality has substantially increased, with the result that the gap between rural and urban inequality levels was first reduced and then, by the early 2000s, apparently eliminated.

Third, there has recently been a noticeable slowdown, sometimes called a pause, in the increase of urban inequality. This is explained by what I termed elsewhere "Kuznets waves," that is, by the fact that China has reached a limit to the expansion of a cheap labor force and that consequently the wage gap between high- and low-skill wage workers has declined, curbing the increase or even driving income inequality down (Milanovic 2016, chap. 2).[32] These broad trends make sense despite a break in the rural series between 2007 and 2012, after which the rural data reappear with a substantially higher level of inequality than before (thus maintaining the unusual gap in inequality between rural and urban areas).

If we put rural and urban data together, given that urban incomes are much higher than rural incomes (even after adjusting for the differential

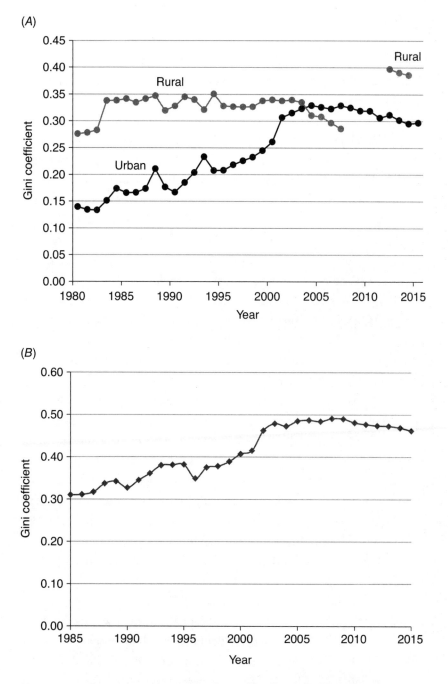

FIGURE 3.6. Income inequality in (A) urban and rural and (B) all China, 1980s–2015

Data source: Urban and rural Ginis calculated from income fractiles provided in various annual Statistical Yearbooks. All-China Gini for the period 1985–2001 is from Wu and Perloff (2005) and for the period 2003–2015 is the officially reported Gini (from Zhuang and Li 2016).

cost of living), we would expect that all-China inequality would be greater than either rural or urban inequality alone. This is indeed the case. Whereas rural and urban inequalities in the 2010s were between 30 and 40 Gini points, the all-China inequality was almost 50 Gini points, with a slight decreasing tendency starting around 2009 (Figure 3.6B).[33] This is a level of inequality that significantly exceeds US inequality, approaching inequality levels that we find in Latin America. It is also a level of inequality that is dramatically higher than in the 1980s, when China was, in terms of the share of the state sector in both employment and value added, still a socialist country. Thus, inequality has risen starkly in both rural and urban areas, and even more so (because of the increasing income gap between urban and rural areas) in China as a whole.

It is useful to place the Chinese increase in inequality in a comparative context. While US disposable income inequality increased by about 4 Gini points between the mid-1980s and 2013 (reaching a level of about 41 Gini points), Chinese inequality increased over approximately the same period by almost 20 Gini points (Figure 3.6B).

It is also useful to place the increase of Chinese inequality in the context of Kuznets waves, the upward and downward movements of inequality, as I have done in my book *Global Inequality*. The rise of inequality in China can then be seen as responding to the classical Kuznetsian mechanism of a transfer of the labor force from low-income agriculture to higher-income manufacturing (which by itself creates inequality) and from rural areas to cities. In China's case the upward swing was made stronger than usual by the fact that the structural transition also implied a systemic change, from rural-based socialism to urban capitalism. Thus both transitions pushed inequality up.

What were the main drivers of this rise? Wage inequality has obviously risen as the economy has moved toward capitalism, and the wages of more efficient or more-skilled workers have gone up much more than the wages of low-skilled workers (at least until recently; see Luo and Zhu 2008, 15–17; Zhuang and Li 2016, 7). In one of the very rare papers that uses microdata from the usually inaccessible large survey conducted by the National Bureau of Statistics, Ding, Fu, and He (2018) show that urban wage inequality increased between 1986 and 2009 within both state-owned and privately owned urban companies. Wage inequality in private companies in China has always been greater than in SOEs (a standard result that goes back to the studies of European inequality in the 1970s), and the gap between the two sectors shows a further increase from approximately 2004 until 2009, when the series ends.

Chinese inequality is also largely "structural." Urban areas have developed far faster than rural areas (so that when we combine the two the resulting inequality is very high), and, in a similar fashion, successful maritime provinces have outpaced the western provinces (and again when we put them together, overall inequality is high). In an interesting exercise comparing Chinese and American inequality, Xie and Zhou (2014) show that 22 percent of Chinese inequality is due to these two structural features (urban versus rural, and provincial gaps), whose importance in the United States is a mere 2 percent.

The explosion of growth in China has also been a prime driver of the explosion of inequality. It is thus the case that no matter how we slice the pie, that is, whether we look at inequality between regions, or between cities and villages, or between urban and rural workers, or between the private and the state sector, or between high- and low-skilled workers, or between men and women, inequality has increased for every such partition. It would be, I think, impossible to find any partition where inequality had not risen to a level higher than what it was before the reforms. The most interesting, and for our purposes the most important, recent development is the increase in the share of income from privately owned capital, which seems to be as concentrated in China as in the advanced market economies. Thus some of the features whereby rising share of capital pushes up interpersonal inequality hold for China just as they do for the United States.

Data on the overall share and concentration of capital income in China are much scarcer and less reliable than those for the advanced economies. However, evidence gathered from different sources points to a rising share of income from capital (which is consistent with the increasing capital-income ratio) and a very high degree of concentration of capital income in the hands of the rich. Private wealth has, according to Piketty, Yang, and Zucman (2017), increased from 100 percent of

Rising share of income from capital

national income in the 1980s to 450 percent of national income in 2015. The increase in private wealth is due to the large-scale privatization of housing (more than 90 percent of housing stock is now privately owned) and the growing importance of private equity. The latter is due to both privatization of state-owned enterprises and the growth of new private companies.

In a pioneering study, Chi (2012) showed the increasing importance of capital income in urban China, especially for rich individuals. Using individual-level data from the NBS urban survey that are not normally available, Chi found that the share of capital income (defined as the sum of investment income, rental income, and other property income) in total income is nearly zero for the bottom 95 percent of the urban population, then hovers around 5 percent for those between the 95th and 99th urban percentile, and reaches approximately one-third for the top 1 percent. In 2007, a year before the global financial crisis, the urban top 1 percent made 37 percent of its overall income from ownership of capital. That value is likely to be underestimated, since it does not include nonrealized capital gains; undistributed corporate profits, which are especially high in China; and "invisible" capital incomes, such as interest that is not withdrawn but is left on the accounts. For comparison, we may note that in the first decade of the 2000s, the top 1 percent in the United States received about 35 percent of its income from capital, including realized capital gains, a percentage comparable to the one reported for China (Lakner 2014, fig. 2).[34]

In this respect, as well as in the persistence of intergenerational correlation of incomes between fathers and sons (at least over the past two generations) and inequality of wealth, China shows features similar to those of the United States, except that the Chinese transition has been remarkably fast.[35]

The rise of capital income coincides, as we would expect, with the emergence of a new class structure in China. In a study of the Chinese middle class, Li (n.d.) divided the middle class into three groups: the capitalist class (entrepreneurs), the "new" middle class (managers and professionals, whether in the public or the private sector), and the "old" middle class (small owners).[36] Although the capitalist class is the smallest of these three middle classes, its numbers have risen the fastest: in the 1980s, the percentage of capitalists in the urban population was close to zero; in 2005, when the study ended, the percentage was 1.6. The small owners, whose main income also comes from capital, similarly rose from practical nonexistence in the early 1980s to about a tenth of the urban population in 2005. Capitalist-entrepreneurial classes have clearly increased in China, together with the new middle class of professionals (somewhat under 20 percent of the urban population), who also, thanks to their savings, are likely to draw some income from property.

The rise of a new capitalist elite is confirmed in a more recent study by Yang, Novokmet, and Milanovic (2019). Using household surveys, they documented the change in the professional composition of the Chinese top 5 percent. In 1988, workers, clerical staff, and government officials accounted for four-fifths of those in the top 5 percent. Twenty-five years later, their share had almost halved, and business owners (20 percent) and professionals (33 percent) had become dominant (Figure 3.7).

A remarkable feature of the new capitalist class is that it has emerged from the soil, so to speak, as almost four-fifths of its members report having had fathers who were either farmers or manual workers. This intergenerational mobility is not surprising in view of the nearly complete obliteration of the capitalist class after the revolution in 1949 and then again during the Cultural Revolution in the 1960s. But it does not tell us anything about the future, when—given the concentration of ownership from capital, the rising cost of education, and the importance of family connections—we can expect intergenerational transmission of wealth and power to be similar to what is observed in the West.

This new capitalist class in China, however, may be more of a "class by itself" than a "class for itself," compared with the analogous group in the West, because the role of the state and state bureaucracy is greater under the conditions of political than liberal capitalism. The capitalists' lack of political importance echoes aspects of the social structure in medieval China. According to Jacques Gernet (1962), wealthy merchants in Song China never succeeded in creating a self-conscious "class" with

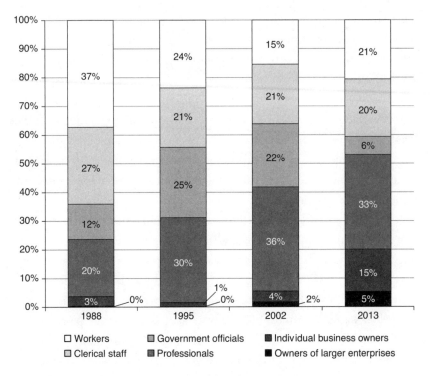

FIGURE 3.7. Professional composition of the Chinese top 5 percent, 1988–2013

Data source: Yang, Novokmet, and Milanovic (2019); calculations from Chinese Household Income Project (CHIP).

shared interests because the state was always there ready to check the power of merchants or any rival source of power. Although merchants continued to prosper as individuals (as capitalists largely do nowadays in China), they never formed a coherent class with its own political and economic agenda or with interests that were forcefully defended and propagated. This, according to Gernet, was very different from the situation at the same time (the thirteenth century) in Italian merchant republics and in the Low Countries. This pattern, in which capitalists enrich themselves without exercising political power, may be expected to continue in China, and, because of the power structure that by definition is created in societies of political capitalism, in other such countries as well.

3.4b Corruption and Inequality

Corruption is systemic and endemic to political capitalism and thus to China. This, as I have noted, is because the rule of law in systems of political capitalism must, by design, be interpreted flexibly. This situation not only helps the rulers control the system more effectively, but it also enables others (including the elite) to engage in embezzlement. There are two aggravating features that make Chinese corruption particularly serious. First, present-day corruption brings back memories (transmitted over generations) of the chaos of corruption and inflation that characterized the period of warlords and the rule of Chiang Kai-shek before the revolution. It cannot be a pleasurable or comforting thought for the Communist Party elite to realize that they have revived some of the conditions against which their communist predecessors had originally rebelled and to which they owed their popular support. Second, globalization has, as I shall argue in Chapter 4, facilitated worldwide corruption by having made it easier to hide stolen assets. That, in turn, has made the attractiveness of corruption in China (as elsewhere) greater. Corruption in China is also abetted by certain international conditions: first, there are a number of outfits that specialize in helping individuals hide their stolen gains, and second, because of lingering anticommunist feelings, US and Canadian authorities do not pursue Chinese citizens who flee the country with their booty with nearly as much alertness and rigor as they do similar criminals from other countries.[37]

The level of corruption in China is extraordinary by global standards; but even more politically salient is the fact that it is extremely high by the standards of Maoist China. A prominent Chinese sociologist, He Qinglian, could thus write, in a book that became a bestseller in China in the 1990s, that the Deng reforms had brought "inequality, generalized corruption and the erosion of the moral basis of society."[38]

To use a nice metaphor popularized by Vito Tanzi, former head of the Fiscal Affairs Department of the International Monetary Fund, corrupt practices are the "termites" gnawing at the foundations of the People's Republic. There are, in principle, two responses to this scourge. One, often advocated by Western and some Chinese commentators, is to strengthen the rule of law.[39] That, as I have argued above, is not a meaningful recommendation for a system of political capitalism because it would do away with the discretionary power of bureaucracy. Such discretionary power is used to control capitalists, punishing some and rewarding others. Strengthening the rule of law is directly antithetical to the system and is unlikely to be undertaken—at least by those who are sufficiently aware of what it would entail. Moreover, this advice ignores recent reality and is inspired by the example of countries that have made the transition to the rule of law over a much longer period and under very different circumstances. Attempts to introduce the rule of law in Russia and Central Asia have backfired in spectacular fashion, leading to even greater corruption than in the past, and, in Russia, to the rule of oligarchs who brought the country, after a decade of rapid economic and legal change (1990–1999), to the verge of either a breakup or an oligarch-fueled civil war. It is not a prospect that the Chinese or any other reasonable leadership would find appealing.

The other response, which is the one that China has chosen, is to ferret out corrupt officials using the tools of the system. Officially, it is called a campaign to "cage" the power within the system. This has included, among other things, the return to a Maoist-like campaign of "re-education," moral pressure, stiff penalties (up to execution by firing squad), and the decision not to stop the process (of requiring responsibility for corruption) at some arbitrarily high level—that is, to prosecute not only the "flies" but also the "tigers." Since the recent anticorruption campaign started, more than a million members of the Communist Party at different levels, about 1 percent of the total membership, have been punished.[40] Thus, in principle, no one is untouchable, although clearly some are more "touchable" than others.[41] However, for the first time ever a member of the Standing Committee of the Politburo was indicted, as well as 20 Central Committee members out of the 205 elected at the 2012 Party Congress, about 160 leaders at the vice-ministerial and provincial levels, and a number of top military leaders (Li 2016, 9).

Some of the cases of corruption brought to light are astonishing in the amounts that were embezzled and recovered. Xu Caihou, at the time of his arrest in 2014 the vice chairman of the Central Military Commission

and the highest official to be indicted to that date, had the entire base-
ment of his 20,000-square-foot house stocked with cash (renminbis, euros,
and dollars) that weighed more than a ton. The precious artifacts filled ten
military trucks. The largest seizure of cash since the founding of the
People's Republic concerned a deputy head of the coal department in the
National Energy Administration who was found with more than 200
million yuan in cash (about $26 million at the current exchange rate).
Sixteen money-counting machines were brought in; four burned out in
the process of counting the bills. Another official had stored 120 million
yuan and 37 kilograms of gold, and owned sixty-eight properties in
various Chinese cities (Xie 2016, 126, 149). The list goes on.

I do not think that one should conceive of the anticorruption campaign
as being intended to really eradicate corruption now and make it impossible in the future.[42] The systemic forces that are part of political capitalism
will always generate corruption. The real objective of the campaign is to
push these forces back for a while—to make the cost of engaging in embezzlement higher in order to reduce its incidence and merely keep corruption in check. Once the campaign weakens, as it is bound to do, corruption will again become more common. And then in ten or twenty years'
time, there may be yet another anticorruption drive with the same limited
objective. The goal of such campaigns is to keep the river of corruption
within its own riverbed and not to allow it to spread too much over the
rest of the society. Once corruption overflows, like a flood, it is very difficult to bring it back to a more sustainable level.

The blight of corruption in China is made more severe because corruption adds to the already high level of inequality. The injustice of high incomes is thus doubly resented. We saw this
dynamic in, for example, the forces that led to the Middle
Eastern revolutions (the so-called Arab Spring): while re-

*Distributional
effects of
corruption*

corded inequality had hardly changed during the previous decades, the
perception of its inequity—driven mostly by the inequity of corruption—had gone up (World Bank 2011). In his extremely detailed analyses
of corruption in China, Minxin Pei has emphasized the multiple corrosive
effects of corruption and provides a wealth of empirical detail (Pei 2006,

2016). While the distributional effects of corruption cannot be measured with much precision in China any more than they can be elsewhere, we can use pieces of information to form a picture of its effects. The data reported by Pei on the bureaucratic position of the corrupt officials, the length of time during which the corruption took place, and the number of official positions sold allow one to calculate the amount of money per position (office) sold at different levels of administration and to distinguish between officials working in government and those working within the party apparatus.[43] Not unexpectedly, the gain per position sold increases with the administrative (territorial) level: it is lowest at the county level and highest at the provincial level (Figure 3.8). This clearly says something about the net present value of income from the positions sold, but it also shows that people higher up in the hierarchy are able to make more money out of corruption. (The assumption is that people selling positions at a given level must themselves be at least at that level.)

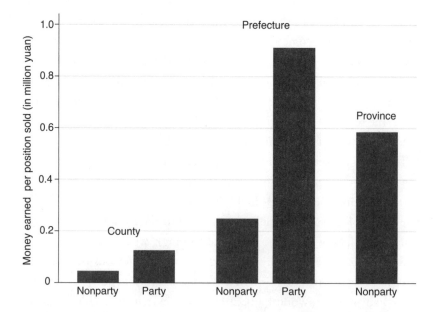

FIGURE 3.8. Money earned per position sold at different administrative levels (in millions of current yuan), for party officials and nonparty officials

Data source: Calculated from Pei (2016, appendix tables A1 and A2).

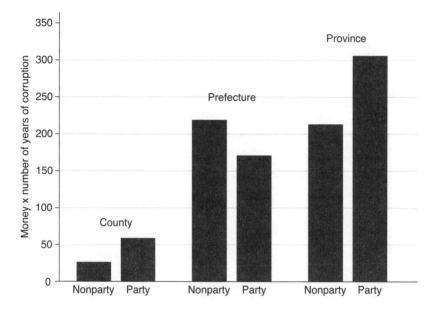

FIGURE 3.9. Money (in millions of current yuan) x number of years of corruption for cases involving multiple officials

Data source: Calculated from Pei (2016, appendix tables A1 and A2).

In addition to the variable of amount of money made per position sold, a second variable from Pei's data, the total amount of money made through corruption by officials at different administrative levels (again distinguished between those working within the party and those in government) shows exactly the same pattern of greater corruption as the administrative level goes up (results not shown here). Both results are thus consistent with my prior assertion that corruption increases inequality.

An interesting aspect revealed by the data is that the value per position sold is significantly greater (at a given administrative level) for positions sold by party officials than for those sold by officials working in government or in companies (Figure 3.8). At the prefecture level, positions sold by party officials are almost three times as valuable as positions sold by "mere" government officials. This presumably reflects party officials' ability to appoint people to more lucrative jobs. Whether party officials themselves are better off than other officials at the same administrative level is less clear. One might think so, if one were to conflate their ability to sell valuable offices with their own income (that is, if one assumed that the two were positively correlated), though it could also be that party officials are not well paid themselves but have access to powerful positions and thus use their sale of these positions to complement their income.[44]

Similar conclusions emerge from fifty more-elaborate cases of corruption that involved multiple individuals (and thus criminal networks). The chief perpetrators are, as before, distinguished by the administrative level at which they work and by whether they are party functionaries or not (the nonparty group now includes more businessmen than in the previous analysis). There are now several instances of provincial party officials engaged in corruption (there were none at that high level in the previous type of corruption), and the variable "money times duration of corruption" appears in their cases to be especially high (Figure 3.9). Party officials again earn more from corruption than nonparty officials at the provincial and county levels.

3.5 The Durability and Global Attractiveness of Political Capitalism

In the next two sections, I shall try—always a hazardous thing—to look into the future; first, to discuss the prospects for the durability of political capitalism in China itself, and then to look at the system's intrinsic attractiveness, along with China's willingness to promote and "export" it in the way that the United States has been "exporting" liberal capitalism since the time of Woodrow Wilson. We must keep in mind that the attractiveness of a system has to be discussed in terms of its own merits, regardless of the promoter. However, historically, the spread of any system has been helped significantly by the presence of a strong power that promoted it or imposed it on others. Whatever country Napoleon conquered, he broke the earlier feudal constraints, enacted anticlerical legislation, introduced the *Code civil*, created his own aristocracy, and, often, appointed rulers.

The US Constitution and tripartite division of power inspired practically all Latin American constitutions because the United States is a continental hegemon. After World War I the French created the *cordon sanitaire* of (unstable) parliamentary democracies in eastern Europe in order to thwart possible Sovietization of these countries. The Soviet Union, after World War II, simultaneously liberated and occupied some of these same countries by imposing its own economic and political system. Likewise, and on a much grander scale, the United States promoted and often imposed the capitalist system through coups and military actions. Is China ready to do the same?

But first we have to ask whether political capitalism, as defined by Deng Xiaoping, is likely to survive for a long time in China itself.

3.5a Will the Bourgeoisie Ever Rule the Chinese State?

China is not the West. But what exactly is the difference, in the long-term context, between the two? This is a huge question that has acquired additional importance in the past two decades due to the rise of China, the evident contrast between the organization of Chinese and Western economies, and (not least) the much improved historical data we now have. In order to answer that question and look at the prospects of political capitalism, it would be useful to consider an interesting approach suggested by Giovanni Arrighi in *Adam Smith in Beijing: Lineages of the Twenty-First Century* (2007).

Arrighi starts from a dichotomy that I think he was the first to have defined, in a series of articles, between what he calls a Smithian "natural" path of development of capitalism and a Marxian "unnatural" path. Smith's natural path, "the natural progress of opulence," in the terminology of *The Wealth of Nations,* is that of a market economy of small producers that grows, through division of labor, from agriculture into manufacturing and only later goes into domestic trade and eventually long-distance foreign trade. The path is "natural" because it follows our needs (from food to clothing to trade, from village to town to faraway lands) and thus does not

Smithian and Marxian capitalisms

jump over the stages. Throughout—Smith is careful to mention—the state lets the market economy and capitalists thrive, protects property, and imposes bearable taxes but does maintain its relative autonomy when it comes to economic and foreign policy. (This is why, in one part of *The Wealth of Nations,* Smith praises the Navigation Act, based entirely on the argument of national security, that is, state autonomy, even though in another part of the book, he implicitly savages it on the grounds of monopoly.)[45] Arrighi summarizes it thus: "The Smithian features . . . [are] the gradualism of reforms and state action aimed at expanding and upgrading social division of labor; the huge expansion of education; the subordination of capitalist interest to the national interest and the active encouragement of inter-capitalist competition" (2007, 361).

Marx's approach, in contrast, was to take what he observed in Europe in his time, a century after Smith, to be the "normal capitalist path of development" (what I have called the Western path of development). But what Marx thought of as "normal" was a system (1) that inverted the natural progress by developing commerce first and agriculture last, a system that was thus (in Arrighi's words) "unnatural and retrograde," and (2) where the state had lost its autonomy to the bourgeoisie.[46]

In fact, capitalist interests have been dominant in the running of Western states from Marx's time all the way to today, whether it comes to economics (think of the tax cuts under President Trump) or foreign policy (think of the profiteering that accompanied the Iraq War). Capitalists took over the state and, as Marx and Engels wrote in *The Communist Manifesto,* the government became "a committee for managing the common affairs of the whole bourgeoisie." Such a path inverted Smithian "natural" development by skipping the stages and going into long-distance trade and colonialism before local production had been laboriously and sufficiently developed. Most importantly, however, the Marxian path differs from the Smithian in that there is no state autonomy vis-à-vis the bourgeoisie. Since European capitalists thrived in conditions of conquest, slavery, and colonialism, they needed the state for such an "excentic" development, that is, for the projection of power abroad, and thus had to "conquer" the state. This made the European path aggressive and warlike.

Arrighi believes that what we hold today to be a standard capitalist path is the one described by Marx. Consistent with this idea, Peer Vries, in his excellent book *Escaping Poverty* (2013), defines capitalism as rational profit-seeking *plus* commodification of labor *plus* political collusion between the state and capitalists *plus* projection of power outside. The last two are obviously Marxian, not Smithian. But that path was specific to Europe and cannot be generalized or "deified." Arrighi argues that China followed an alternative path, much closer to the Smithian path, from the Song to the Qing dynasties. The market economy in China was more developed than in western Europe (probably until about 1500), but commercial interests were never able to organize themselves sufficiently to come even close to dictating state policy. The authoritarian state left rich merchants in peace as long as they did not threaten it—in a word, as long as they did not grow too big for their boots. But it always kept a wary eye on them.

As Jacques Gernet (1962) argued regarding Song China, many merchants did became rich, but they failed to create a "class," like the Third Estate in France or similar propertied classes elsewhere in western Europe, that managed first to win political representation and later to win power. In China, by contrast, there was a strong central government from the start that was able to check the power of merchants or anyone else. Debin Ma reprises a similar theme in his paper on the fiscal capacity of the Chinese state: "In China, the precocious rise of absolutism [centralized state based on hierarchically organized bureaucracy] with the absence of any representative institution ensured that the economic rents from the control of violence were firmly in the hands of political interest divorced from those of commercial and property interest" (2011, 26–27). It was surely not a government at the behest of the bourgeoisie.

Francis Fukuyama, in *The Origins of Political Order* (2011), explains the absence of a countervailing merchant class in China by the omnipotence of the state, which goes back to the formation of the Chinese state. Fukuyama argues that China was ahead of every other major power in building the state; it did so also before any other organized nonstate actors (independent bourgeoisie, free cities, clergy) were created. The state was thus far more powerful than anything else, and this "precocious state formation" continued to suffocate alternative centers of power from the Qin dynasty to Maoist China.

This leads us to present-day China. The current Communist Party–dominated government, and the distribution of political power between it and the already formed capitalist class, is reminiscent of this traditional pattern. The government is helpful to the interests of the bourgeoisie, but only as long as these interests do not run contrary to the objectives of the state (that is, of the elite that runs the state). Wang Hui (2003, 176) approvingly quotes Immanuel Wallerstein: "If anyone thinks that without state support or from a position of opposition to the state he can become a capitalist . . . this is an absurd presumption."

> *Unclear property rights and absence of rule of law are not anomalies*

The distinction between various property arrangements—whether state-owned, purely privately owned, or any of a myriad of ownership arrangements in between (for example, a state-owned corporation raising private capital on the stock exchange, communal property mixed with private property, state firms with foreign private participation)—is quite blurred in today's China and provides the right environment for the emergence of what I called earlier the politico-capitalist class, or what Hans Overbeek (2016, 320) calls the "cadre-capitalist" class.[47] The murkiness of various ownerships is not an "error," or something that is transitory or in need of "correction," but rather is the very basic condition for the existence of political capitalism. For example, Communist Party organizations ("cells") exist within fully privately owned companies. These organizations may be useful for capitalists to the extent that capitalists are able to co-opt them to lobby the party-state on their behalf. But the presence of Communist Party cells can also be enervating because they are yet another constituency to be pleased and bribed, or another body that could, if such were the political climate, turn against the capitalists. And these organizations could do that regardless of formal ownership structure and rights.

Even Chinese official statistics have difficulty dealing with the distinctions, so numerous are the forms of ownership and so many are the different rights of ownership, ranging from the ability to dispose and sell assets to usufruct only. This multitude of ownership and corporate structures was one of the main headaches for the unconditional partisans of the Washington Consensus, who insisted on the importance of clearly defined property rights for growth. It was impossible to fit China, with its scores of different property relationships, into the neoliberal straitjacket. Moreover, some of the most murky types of ownership, like township and village enterprises, registered the most spectacular rates of growth (see Weitzman and Xu 1993).

It may be useful at this point to draw a parallel between the multitude of ownership arrangements and the uneven application of the rule of law (the "zones of lawlessness" mentioned above). In the eyes of liberal capitalism, both are anomalies: ownership structure should be rectified so that is clear who owns what, and the law should apply equally to all. If neither of these anomalies is corrected, the system is regarded as somewhat imperfect. But this is not at all the case from the point of view of political capitalism. It is precisely the lack of clarity implicit in the multitude of ownership forms and arbitrariness in the application of the rules that allows for the creation of the politico-capitalist class. What appears to be a muddle is precisely the environment where political capitalism emerges and can prosper. In other words, what we are observing with regard to both property and law is not an abnormality but a defining feature of the system.

But will the Chinese capitalists who exist and thrive in this jungle of ownership types and uncertain property rights forever acquiesce to that particular role where their formal rights can be limited or revoked at any moment, and where they are under constant state tutorship? Or, as they become stronger and more numerous, will they organize, influence the state, and finally take it over, as happened in Europe and the United States? The European/American path as sketched by Marx seems in many respects to have a certain iron logic: economic power tends to emancipate itself and to look after, or impose, its own interests. If capitalists have economic power in their hands, how can they be stopped? But, on the other hand, the period of almost two millennia during which that uneasy and unequal partnership has existed between the Chinese state and Chinese business represents a formidable obstacle, knit of tradition and inertia, that might keep the state autonomous.

Democracy in China?

Thus, the question of the democratization of China needs to be posed in a very different fashion from the way it is usually done: the key question is whether Chinese capitalists will come to control the state and if, in order to do so, they will use representative democracy as their tool. In Europe and the United States, capitalists used that tool very carefully, administering it in homeopathic doses as the franchise expanded, often at a snail's pace, and retracting it whenever there was a potential threat to property-owning classes (as in England after the French Revolution, or in France after the Restoration, or in Hungary and somewhat less in Austria throughout the existence of the dual monarchy). But by 1918, it was politically impossible to continue with the imposition of literacy tests or income and tax censuses to exclude voters, and even the southern American states were ultimately pressured by the Civil Rights Act of 1965 to stop using a variety of means to disenfranchise voters. Chinese democracy, if it comes, would thus be similar to how it is in the rest of the world today, in the legal sense of one person, one vote. Yet given the weight of history and the precarious nature and still limited size of the propertied classes, it is not certain whether such a rule by the bourgeoisie could be maintained.[48] It failed in the first two decades of the twentieth century; could it be reestablished with greater success one hundred years later?

3.5b Will China "Export" Political Capitalism?

Political capitalism has manifest advantages for those who are in power: they are insulated from the immediate pressure of public opinion, they have the opportunity to parlay their political power into economic benefits, and they do not face institutionalized time limits to their rule. But political capitalism also conveys certain advantages to the population. If the system is associated with an efficient administration and tolerable corruption, it can more easily surmount the numerous legal and technical impediments that slow down growth in more democratic countries. The ability of the Chinese state to build roads and fast-train tracks through areas where such construction would take years, if not decades, of legal wrangling in a more democratic polity is an obvious advantage in social and economic terms—even if some people's rights might in the process be disregarded.

Long and often endless consultations on many aspects of public policy can eventually result in nothing being implemented. For sure, running roughshod over some objections may also lead to bad decisions, or to the selection of only those alternatives that are in the interest of a minority. But in many cases—and perhaps Chinese success in infrastructure projects is the best such example—they propel society forward.

Citizens themselves might prefer fast decisions to long consultations. In most successful capitalist societies, many people are too busy with their jobs and daily lives to pay close attention to political issues. They often lack a significant stake in these issues, so spending time on them is not rational, either. It is telling that in the United States, one of the oldest democracies in the world, the election of a person who, in many respects, has the prerogatives of an elected king is not judged of sufficient importance to bestir more than one half of the electorate to the polling booths.

It is wrong, I think, to argue that in today's circumstances people are still, as Aristotle described them, "political animals" who value involvement in civic matters as a general principle. This might have been the case in the agoras of Greek city-states, but even then, for only an affluent minority of free citizens. In today's commercialized and hectic world, citizens have neither the time nor the knowledge nor the desire to get involved in civic matters unless the issues directly concern them. The very "deepening" of capitalism through its undiluted emphasis on money-making and its expansion into the personal sphere (topics discussed in Chapter 5) leaves less time for broader political deliberations and cannot produce that ideal of the informed and concerned citizen that many democratic theories postulate. It can even be argued that such a citizen cannot coexist with hypercommercialized capitalism. Definitions of democracy that insist on citizens' participation are thus at odds with reality. Robert Dahl's and Joseph Schumpeter's much more technical definitions of polyarchy and democracy are more accurate. In the words of one of Dahl's critics, "Democracy and polyarchy are . . . [for Dahl] both purely instrumental devices for maximizing the satisfaction of prior, private wants [of citizens]—nothing more" (Krouse 1982, 449). But this is exactly true: and if liberal capitalism can satisfy those wants, so can political capitalism. Which one does it better is an empirical question.

I have argued above that political capitalism is indeed a society of built-in corruption. (This is exactly why it is so difficult to maintain an equilibrium between an efficient administration and intrinsic corruption, as the latter drives bureaucracy away from administrative neutrality.) But it is

Acceptance of moderate corruption

wrong to believe that people always view corruption, regardless of its level, as a scourge. Many societies have learned to live, or even thrive, with moderate to high levels of corruption that seep through the entire system and make the lives of many people easier than they would be in a purely "noncorrupt" system. In fact, many people who are used to functioning in a system where mutual favors are exchanged have a hard time adjusting to an entirely different, "clean" system. Bai, Hsieh, and Song (2014, 3) argue that decentralized local "crony capitalism" in China plays a role similar to the one that a multiplicity of European states played in the rise of capitalism: local administrations protect their own champions, but they cannot prevent other local administrations from favoring their own, perhaps more efficient, crony capitalists. Thus, cronyism joined with interlocal competition plays the role of Schumpeterian creative destruction.

We should not naïvely believe that the rankings of government transparency (based on "expert surveys" of perceived corruption) that place northern European countries on top mean that this kind of transparency can be easily applied elsewhere in the world, or that populations of other countries aspire to that level of "cleanliness" in government. In fact, many of them would find it hard to function in such an environment. The forces of what Fukuyama (2011) calls the "partimonialization" of the state are almost everywhere very strong. It is part of normal expectations in most societies that a cousin or a friend might suggest whom one should talk to in order to expedite a car registration, get a new ID, or avoid too frequent and intrusive fiscal controls of one's company. By not helping a relative or friend, one risks being ostracized by the community. Such corruption may not involve an actual transfer of money (although in-kind gifts are not really different from money), but it surely involves giving preferential treatment to some. Indeed, the difficulty many migrants face in adjusting to more anonymous and less favor-based systems, and thus their tendency to continue living within their own systems, is what some have argued represents a threat to the integrity of the Nordic welfare states. It comes under the rubric of cultural differences, but it often boils down in reality to the preference for personalized versus impersonalized application of the rules and administration of justice. Or, in other words, for a weaker rule of law.

Italy is an example of a country that has pervasive corruption spread across all layers of society, but where there is also a corruption equilibrium. Everyone might theoretically believe that getting rid of corruption would be desirable, but they also know that an attempt to do so individually would simply make their own position worse. This, however, should not be viewed simply as a problem of collective action, where if everyone could agree to remove corruption, all or most people would be better off. Many people would not know how to operate in that new system and might prefer to return to the old one. Capussela (2018, xxviii) quotes Italo Calvino's allegory of such equilibrium corruption:

> There once was a country founded on illegality. Not that laws lacked; and politics was based on principles that everyone more or less claimed to share. But the system, articulated into many power centres, required virtually limitless financial resources . . . and people could obtain them only illicitly, namely by asking for them from those who had them, in exchange for illicit favours. And those with money to trade for favours had usually gained it through favours that they had received previously; the resultant economic system was circular, in a way, and not without a certain harmony.

Thus the intrinsic advantages of political capitalism include autonomy for the rulers, the ability to cut through red tape and deliver faster economic growth, and widespread moderate corruption that fits with some or perhaps even many people's preferences. But the most important thing that the attractiveness of political capitalism depends on is economic success. And the fact that China has been by far the most economically successful country in the past half century places China in a position where other successful countries have been in the past: namely, where its economic and political institutions are imitated by others and where China can itself legitimately try to "export" them. But the question is whether China intends to do so.

The typical argument against China's desire to export its system is historical. It is based on ideas of Chinese self-centeredness and indifference toward the institutions and practices of "cooked" and "raw" barbarian nations.[49] The contrast between the great maritime expeditions conducted by Ming China in the fifteenth century and the comparatively trivially small expedition by Columbus is often used (including by the Chinese) to show the difference in approach. In one case,

China's aloofness

the objective was to enhance trade by making it safer (Zheng He's sailors fought pirates in several instances) but above everything else to showcase one's superiority to the rest of the world in a peaceful way. In the other case, the objective was also to trade but even more to exploit, conquer territory, and proceed to ideological conversions. One power, according to this interpretation, is basically aloof, peaceful, and indifferent; the other power is belligerent and hungry for gain and influence.[50]

This indifference has become, as the events of the nineteenth century showed, a debilitating factor in China's development, but it may still, despite the realization of its negative effects, dominate the thinking of Chinese elites. Martin Jacques, in *When China Rules the World* (2012), argues that China is likely to remain aloof because it views itself not as a nation-state but as a civilization-state, a fulcrum of Asia (and by extension of the world), while culturally often displaying deeply ingrained racism or an inability to comprehend "the other."[51] It is interesting to note that even in Maoist times China continued to manifest a degree of aloofness despite the fact that ideologically, by adopting Marxism, it became part of the West. Once it freed itself from Soviet tutelage, China consistently punched below its weight internationally (to invert the phrase coined to characterize British diplomacy in the second half of the twentieth century). China stayed away from the Non-Aligned Movement; it failed, despite professed Maoism in many quarters, to establish strong connections with, or provide help to, any such movements, and, most importantly, it failed to create a string of allies. This is particularly striking when compared with the United States and the Soviet Union, which each had a number of allies, satellites, or vassal states—whatever one wishes to call them. But China had no one except Albania, until even Albania broke with China when China became "revisionist" and engaged in Dengist reforms. Moreover, even today, save for

North Korea, China does not have a single ally. This is not behavior that one might expect from a would-be world hegemon.

In addition to the question of whether China is willing to "export" its model of political capitalism, a question worth asking is whether the model is transferable. As mentioned above, the key characteristics of political capitalism (technocratic bureaucracy, absence of the rule of law, and endemic corruption) can indeed be found in a number of different settings. But there are also some elements that seem largely specific to China and that are difficult to transplant elsewhere. In a series of influential articles and books, Xu Chenggang defines the Chinese political system as a "regionally decentralized authoritarian system."[52] The two essential features of the system are centralization (authoritarianism) and, though at first sight it seems paradoxical, decentralization. Regional decentralization, which in recent times Xu dates to the Great Leap Forward, allowed provincial and municipal governments to implement various economic policies and thus to discover what was best for them—as long as it was not in flagrant violation of the central rules and Communist Party ideology. (Although the disregard of the ideology was in reality accepted as long as it was well camouflaged and the policies were successful.)

> Transferability of Chinese political capitalism

Xu shows that all crucial developments, from the introduction of the household responsibility system (land reform) to the privatization of state-owned enterprises, started at the lower levels of government. They were not, as is sometimes believed, part of some grandiose plan of experimentation thought up at the top, but came about entirely through lower level–based initiatives.[53] If reforms were successful, their local promoters were able to get higher positions within the government and the party, to accede to central policy-making bodies (that's where the centralization part kicks in), and to try to apply the same recipe elsewhere. The key element was providing incentives to local leaders to improve the economic situation within their own regions while preserving social peace. The backbone of the system, however, is a centralized organization (the Chinese Communist Party) that rewards successful local leaders and punishes unsuccessful ones.

Note that the incentives are political: the concern is not with the incentives of individual actors (workers, peasants, or entrepreneurs at the local level) but with the incentives of administrative bosses, who must "produce" a successful region in order to move up in the hierarchy. Success is measured by some relatively easily measurable targets, like an increase of GDP or attractiveness to foreign investors. Local leaders can be seen as quasi-autonomous plenipotentiaries of the central authorities. It is a system not dissimilar to tax-farming, but where the duty of the local leaders is not just to provide revenues to the center but to ensure that the region advances economically.

This unique blend of political single-party centralization and significant discretion regarding regional economic policies is what, according to this view, explains China's success. It does, however, open up a number of issues, such as the inability to use multidimensional targeting to monitor the performance of leaders (e.g., if one's promotion depends on the regional growth rate, other goals, such as environmental protection and health of the population, will be sacrificed), or attempts to engage in protection of the local market (e.g., buying cars and trucks only from local producers), which result in segmentation of the Chinese market.

Now, leaving aside these other issues, which become more pressing after the economy has reached a certain level of development, the difficulty of implementing in other countries a model that calls for simultaneous centralization and decentralization is obvious. The Chinese model was built on a tradition of similar regional decentralization that existed during the imperial period, a tradition that most other countries lack. The model also requires a center that is strong enough to be able to reward or punish local leaders according to their performance and to draw back on some privileges of decentralization when needed, and yet is sufficiently far-sighted to allow experimentation. Finally, decentralization of decision-making makes much more sense in a vast and populous county like China than in a small or moderately sized country. An additional danger that many countries run (and that China itself is not immune from) is that broad decentralization can create strong regional power bases for local leaders and ultimately even lead to the break-up of the country. That danger was forestalled in China through a continuous process of rotating cadres (who almost never stay in any provincial governorship post for more than five years), but there is no guarantee that such policies will continue ad infinitum or that central political bodies in other countries will be able to implement them.

Thus, "regionally decentralized authoritarianism" fully adheres to the key characteristics of political capitalism, but it does so with features that are specific to China and may be difficult to transplant elsewhere. The weakness of the model of political capitalism appears clearly in this description because it highlights the absence of generalizable rules that in principle should be valid under most circumstances.[54]

Against the drawbacks of aloofness and the dearth of generalizable rules one has to set three factors. First, China is today, thanks to very large trade and foreign investment flows, much more integrated into the world economy than ever before in history. Aloofness is no longer a viable option, economically, politically, or even culturally. And indeed the number of foreign contacts, the omnipresence of the English language (even the *hukou* registration booklet has the cover page written in both Chinese and English), the number of Chinese people studying, working, or traveling abroad, and, increasingly, the number of foreigners living in China, make China an integral part of the world more than ever.[55]

Why China will have to engage with the world (more than now)

Second, historically, the most successful countries have tended to become emulated by others, which put them in a position where they took on global roles commensurate with their "objective" importance, whether they wanted to or not.

Third, China under Xi (and probably more broadly, because the policies associated with him have much broader resonance) seems ready to take on a more active international role and to "sell" its own success and experience worldwide. A number of recent initiatives make that apparent. The most important is the increasing role that China plays in Africa, and the overhaul of African development strategy that has resulted from it. It is not surprising that several of the countries with systems of political capitalism are in Africa, and that all of them have strong economic ties to China (see Table 3.1). It could even be argued that China proceeded for the first time to a successful and discreet overthrow of a foreign government when it engineered the removal of Robert Mugabe from power in Zimbabwe in 2017. It was a signal success because of the bloodless way in which it was done, the behind-the-scenes role of China, and the worldwide support for the move, given how unpopular Mugabe's regime had become both domestically and internationally. The success of that operation can be contrasted with the debacle of a similar Western operation in Libya, which resulted in a protracted civil war in the country and an almost total destruction of all accoutrements of modern society that shows no signs of abating or ending.

Another important, and even more ambitious, project is the Belt and Road Initiative (BRI), which is supposed to link several continents through improved, Chinese-financed infrastructure. Regular, large-scale deliveries of Chinese goods to continental Europe and the United Kingdom via the Eurasian land route (much faster than via sea) have already started to take place.[56] Not only does BRI represent an ideological challenge to the way the West has been handling economic development in the Global South, disregarding physical investments and focusing instead on "post-material" institution-building, but it will project Chinese influence far and wide and link BRI countries into what may be termed a Chinese sphere of influence. There are plans for any investment disputes that arise to be handled under the jurisdiction of a Chinese-created court (Economy 2018; Anthea Roberts, pers. comm.). This would be quite a reversal for a country whose "century of humiliations" was marked by foreigners in China not being subject to Chinese laws.

Many countries may welcome being part of BRI because of the tangible benefits that Chinese involvement will bring (roads, harbors, railways) and also because China is perceived as uninterested in influencing domestic politics and attaches no political strings to investments.[57] As Martin Jacques writes, unlike the United States, which emphasizes democracy within nations but imposes hierarchical relations internationally, China has no interest in the domestic policies of recipient nations; it does not practice what Joseph Schumpeter, in a critique of standard twentieth-century American policies, called "ethical imperialism."[58] Instead, China emphasizes democracy between nation-states, that is, it insists on formal equality of treatment of all countries.[59] For many in smaller countries, both sides of this equation (noninterference in domestic politics and formal equal treatment) are attractive.

Justin Lin, one of the ideologues of the Belt and Road Initiative, sees another potential advantage of BRI for poorer countries (Lin and Monga

2017). China will be gradually "vacating" manufacturing jobs that should "naturally" be taken over by less-developed countries. However, without a reasonably good infrastructure, they will not be able to do it. In fact, one of China's own development lessons has been that infrastructure is extremely important for attracting foreign investment, as the example of the special economic zones shows.

The difference in developmental emphasis (infrastructure versus institution-building) precisely matches the distinction between political and liberal capitalisms: through their preferred development strategies, both try to play to their strong suit. The strong selling point of political capitalism is state efficiency—the fact that it can bring private actors to build something that improves peoples' ordinary lives in tangible, material ways. The selling point of liberal capitalism is that the state is there to set the institutional framework within which private actors will decide on their own what (if anything) is the best thing to build. In the first case, the state is an active and direct actor; in the second case, the state is an "enabling" and passive actor. This reflects, of course, the ideal-typical role of the state in the two systems.

Finally, China, following again the same "constructivist" approach, has founded the Asian Infrastructure Investment Bank, which, as of mid-2018, has more than eighty countries as members and is headquartered in Beijing. Its obvious objective is the projection of Chinese economic power in its Asian near abroad. China's creation of new international economic institutions parallels what was done under US leadership after World War II, through the foundation of the World Bank and the International Monetary Fund.

There may be yet another (fourth) factor that might predispose China to be more active on the international stage. This factor links domestic and foreign policies. If China continues with a passive role where it does not advertise its own institutions, while the West continues advancing the values of liberal capitalism onto China, it is more likely that such Western institutions will become increasingly popular and supported by large swaths of the Chinese population. But if China is able to define what are the advantages of political capitalism, it will be able to resist foreign influence with some counter-influence of its own rather than with passivity. In that sense, being active internationally is a matter of domestic political survival and arises because of potential domestic weakness.

These are both the factors and the actual moves that seem to push China toward playing a much more active role in the "export" of political capitalism and the creation of a string of states with similar systems, even if it is difficult to see how such states may be linked in any formal alliance or arrangement with China. But it could also be that the informal influence may fit much better with Chinese history and preferences. Even with this kind of informal structure, China is bound to exercise increasing influence on world institutions that, in the past two centuries, have been built exclusively by Western states and were reflective of Western interests and history.[60] Now, this will no longer be the case. As Martin Jacques writes: "The emergence of China as a global power relativizes everything. The West is habituated to the idea that the world is *its* world; that the international community is *its* community, that international institutions are *its* institutions. . . . that universal values are *its* values. . . . This will no longer be the case" (2012, 560).

The viability of political capitalism as a successful model rests on (1) the ability to insulate politics from economics, which is intrinsically difficult because the state plays an important economic role, and (2) the ability to maintain a relatively uncorrupt centralized "backbone" that can enforce decisions that are in the national interest, not just in the narrow business interest. Point (2) is more easily realized in political regimes that have a revolutionary past and thus the required centralization, which is often a product of revolutionary struggle. But with the passage of time, maintaining an acceptable level of corruption becomes more difficult and can undo, or even overwhelm, the other advantages of the system. Note that both of the contradictions of the system identified in Section 3.3a have to do with corruption and corruption-generated inequality.

The bottom line: viability of political capitalism

The export potential of political capitalism is limited because we can expect points (1) and (2), insulation of politics and relatively uncorrupt administration, to hold in only very few countries. Or to put it another way, the system can be exported or copied, but in many cases it might fail to be economically successful. This, in turn, will undermine its global attractiveness.

CHAPTER 4

THE INTERACTION OF CAPITALISM AND GLOBALIZATION

In primitive history every invention had to be made daily anew and, in each locality independently. . . . Only when commerce has become world-commerce and has as its basis big industry, when all nations are drawn into the competitive struggle, is the permanence of acquired productive forces assured.

—Karl Marx, *The German Ideology*

In this chapter I look at the roles of capital and labor under globalization. The main feature that globalization imparts to both is mobility. Globalization has largely been synonymous with the movement of capital across borders. But labor, too, has recently become more mobile, and one of the reactions to that increasing mobility has been the erection of new obstacles at national borders. The mobility of labor is a response to the huge differences in returns to the same quality and quantity of labor across national jurisdictions. These gaps result in what I call "citizenship premium" and "citizenship penalty." Citizenship premium (or citizenship rent; the terms are used interchangeably), as I explain below, refers to the boost in income one receives simply from being a citizen of a rich country, while citizenship penalty is the reduction in income from being a citizen of a poor country. The value of this premium (or penalty) may be up to five to one or ten to one, even after adjusting for the lower price levels in poorer countries.

These income gaps are largely an inheritance of the nineteenth and twentieth centuries, during which Western countries, and a few others (Japan and more recently South Korea) have pulled ahead of the rest of the world in terms of per capita income. It would be surprising if such gaps did not produce movements of labor. This would be as strange as if a difference between an asset yielding 3 percent and another equally risky one yielding 30 percent did not lead capital owners to invest in the latter. Mobility of labor thus needs to be seen in the same way as mobility of capital—as part and parcel of globalization.

I begin this chapter with a discussion of labor under conditions of globalization. I then turn to capital, whose mobility, perhaps best reflected through so-called global value chains, accelerates the growth of poorer countries and, in the medium to long run, erodes the citizenship rents that motivate migration. Thus both cross-border movements, those of labor as well as of capital, are equilibrating movements whose ultimate outcome—probably never to be reached—would be a world of minimal differences in mean per capita income among nations.

Why do I single out global value chains as characteristic of globalization? I do so because of their twofold revolutionary impact. First, as I explain below, they make it possible for the first time in history to unbundle production from the management and control of that production. This has huge implications for the spatial distribution of economic activity. Second, they overturn the view held by structuralists and neo-Marxists that delinking from the Global North was the way to develop. To be clear, I do not argue against the idea that most Chinese economic growth can be explained in a more traditional way, as continuing along the same path of export-driven development with increasing degrees of sophistication that was taken decades ago by Japan and then South Korea and Taiwan. I focus on global value chains for the reasons just mentioned, not as an explanation of the totality of China's transformation.

Next I examine how the welfare state is affected by globalization, namely by the movement of capital and labor. And I end by looking at worldwide corruption. It might at first seem strange to include corruption on the same level as the movement of the two factors of production and the fate of the welfare state. This would be strange, however, only if we saw corruption as an anomaly. But that point of view is wrong. Corruption is linked to globalization no less than is the free movement of capital and labor. It is spurred by the ideology of money-making, which is the ideology that underlies capitalist globalization, and it is made possible thanks to the mobility of capital. But in addition, both political capitalism and the trend toward plutocratic rule in liberal capitalism "normalize" it. I have argued in Chapter 3 that corruption is an intrinsic part of political capitalism. The time has come to normalize corruption: we need to see corruption, in both types of capitalism, as a return (analogous to a rent) to a special factor of production, political power, which some individuals possess and others do not. Corruption is bound to increase with globalization, political capitalism, and plutocratic rule. Economists, who are not moralists, should treat corruption like any other type of income. This is what I do in the last part of the chapter.

4.1 Labor: Migration

4.1a Definition of the Citizenship Premium or Rent

The systematic differences in income between people who are equally educated, motivated, and make the same effort but are citizens of different countries can be called the "citizenship premium" or "citizenship penalty." For simplicity, I shall focus on the former. But although the existence of the premium seems factually clear, the really important question, from an economic point of view, is whether the citizenship premium can be likened to a rent, that is, to an income that is strictly speaking unnecessary to bring forth production. In other words, could one, in a mental experiment, replace people of a given skill level in an advanced economy with people from another, poorer country who have the same skill level and are identical in all other work-related respects, pay them lower wages, and end up with the same output?[1] The near equivalent of this mental experiment is to allow labor full freedom of circulation between countries.

Is the citizenship premium a rent? As our mental experiment shows, the answer seems to be yes. Since the higher-paid workers could be replaced by an identical group of workers who would be willing to work for a lower wage, the cost of production would be reduced, and the "national" or "global dividend" (i.e., net income) would increase. Citizenship rent exists, at the first approximation, because of the control of access to a given geographic portion of the world by the current residents. This, in turn, is associated with a high stream of lifetime income because of the high amounts of capital, advanced technology, and good institutions that exist there. The crucial element is control of land, although this is translated through control over an "ideal" share in citizenship. Citizenship gives to the holder the right to partake in the output produced in that part of the world to which the citizenship applies (and also, in some cases, to the output produced elsewhere by the citizens of the country).[2]

It thus seems, at first glance, that citizenship rent is similar to land or natural resource rent. This semblance stems from the fact that in both cases the element giving rise to rent is control over a piece of real estate. The analogy, however, is only partially correct. Land rent arises because of the differential productivity of various parcels of land. The price of the final product (corn or oil) is determined by the cost of production of the marginal (most expensive) producer for whose output there is still sufficient demand. Consequently, all inframarginal producers draw a rent. In the case of citizenship, which, as we shall see, is an "ideal" category and can be "degrounded," the link with the physical control of the land is more tenuous. Further, all citizens (as joint "owners") of every country partake in the citizenship rent, or in the case of the worst-placed country, they receive no rent. The second difference from land rent is that the object (land) that gives rise to the rent is marketable: it can be bought and sold. Citizenship, in principle, cannot (although we shall see that there are exceptions). Rent derived from citizenship is thus more similar to a monopoly rent obtained by associations such as guilds that act in restraint of trade. Just as in guilds, citizenship can be acquired by co-option, or by birth. The latter mode is similar to the situation of inherited occupations that are passed from parent to child.

Citizenship is an "ideal" category

Citizenship is still mostly "grounded," that is, it applies chiefly to people who live within the geographical boundaries of a particular country, with income needed to pay for the citizenship rent produced mostly in that country. But not only there. This can best be seen in the example of those citizens who do not live in their countries of citizenship (say, American expatriates). These people have access to the welfare benefits of their home countries, which form part of the citizenship premium; the resources that are used to produce the income needed to pay for the benefits are national, and mostly grounded in the country. An American citizen living in Italy will have access to US social security and other welfare benefits, but the money to pay for his or her benefits would have been earned mostly in the United States. With advancing globalization, these resources can become degrounded, however: we can imagine a world where an increasing share of US income could be produced outside the United States and would then return to the country through profits on capital invested abroad. A similar situation might be that of a Filipino citizen living abroad who lays claim to the benefits of Filipino citizenship while income needed to pay for these benefits comes from Filipino migrant workers' remittances.

Extending these trends into the future, we could imagine a situation where citizenship comes to be entirely degrounded: most citizens may not live in their country of citizenship, and most of the income of that country may be earned by labor or capital employed in other countries—yet the benefits of citizenship will continue to be received in the same way as they are now.

Citizenship is thus clearly seen to be an "ideal" category. It is not a formal property right in the same sense in which private property over a piece of land is. It is not even a joint property right over a part of the world surface by the people who live there. Citizenship is rather a legal construct that exists only in our minds (and is, in that sense, "ideal"). *In an economic sense, citizenship is a joint monopoly exercised by a group of people who share a given legal or political characteristic that gives rise to the citizenship rent.* Having a given citizenship is divorced from the need to live in one's country of citizenship, as we have seen here; moreover, income to pay for the citizenship premium need not be earned in the country of citizenship. Money used to pay for the benefits attached to citizenship need not be derived only from production realized in the particular locale that is formally attached to citizenship, or to be received by people who live there (because the country itself may contain foreigners who by the same token may be receiving their citizenship rent from another country). We thus see that citizenship as an economic asset can be, in principle, degrounded, or dematerialized, from the land to which it applies.

4.1b Citizenship as an Economic Asset

Like every rental income that is received over a period of time, citizenship rent can be transformed into an asset by discounting likely future yields. (In the case of citizenship, this period typically lasts until the death of the holder but in some cases, as with survivors' pensions, may last even longer.) If citizenship of country A brings x units of income per year more than citizenship of country B, then the value of the asset, citizenship of A, will be equal to the summation of all such x's (discounted by the appropriate discount rate) over the expected life of the holder. The gain from a given citizenship will vary in function of the citizenship that a person currently holds, her age, and many other circumstances that interest us less here, such as educational level. From an individual point of view, citizenship rent is estimated through a range of bilateral comparisons, where the value of one's current citizenship is compared with all other existing citizenships.[3] This value would be positive for some calculations and negative for others. That citizenship is an asset becomes very clear if we consider the age of the potential holder. Everything else being the same (including having and being concerned about one's children), citizenship as an asset will be more valuable to young than to old people. The stream of differential income that young people capture if they move to a "better" citizenship is greater.[4]

We need to consider now two additional issues that will bring our discussion closer to the real world: first, Can the asset of citizenship become an object of market transactions? and second, Are there differential categories of citizenship? Since the answer to both will be yes, the outcome will be to moderate the very sharp dichotomies drawn so far between (i) marketable assets and citizenship, and (ii) citizenship and noncitizenship.

Citizenship as a marketable asset

During the past twenty years, citizenship has become a legally marketable asset: the residence permits that lead to citizenship can be purchased in many countries, including Canada and the United Kingdom, by making a substantial private investment. The guild-like structure that protects citizenship has thus been somewhat relaxed, and citizenship has, in some cases, and on a very modest scale, become a marketable commodity. Governments have clearly realized that citizenship is indeed an asset and that it may be in the interest of current citizens for their government to sell it, assuming implicitly that the monetary gain from the sale of that asset will more than offset the loss of sharing citizenship with one more person. It is in the interest of current citizens to set the price of citizenship high. Citizenship is thus marketed only to rich individuals. The costs of acquiring it, either directly or through first obtaining a residency permit, are high: they range from €250,000 in Greece to £2 million in the United Kingdom. But these are hardly insuperable costs for high-net-worth individuals (people whose financial assets are between $1 million and $5 million): it is estimated that about one-third of these wealthy individuals, that is, about 10 million people worldwide, have a second passport or dual citizenship (Solimano 2018, 16, calculated from 2017 Credit Suisse Global Wealth Report).

To address the subject of citizenship as it exists in reality, we have to recognize that there are different categories (levels) of citizenship. Our concern here, of course, is with citizenship as an economic category: the right to a higher income stream. In most cases, citizenship is a bi- | *Subcitizenship* | nary category (0–1)—one is either a citizen or not—and a formal legal title to citizenship is needed to gain access to economic benefits. But other situations are more nuanced. There are also cases of what we might call "subcitizenship" that are associated with most but not all of the economic benefits that citizenship provides. The most well-known case is that of US permanent residents (green card holders), although similar arrangements exist in most European countries as well. Permanent residents have access to almost the entire set of benefits available to citizens, with the possible exception of some social transfers and voting rights (the exceptions vary by country in Europe and by state and province in the United States and Canada). But the existence of subcitizens is important because it shows how the rigid system of a binary distinction (citizen–noncitizen) can be made more flexible, mostly to respond to labor needs.

Subcitizenship is not limited to people who migrate in order to get hold of the citizenship rent and then find themselves for some time in the intermediate position of subcitizens. Until recently, individuals born in Germany of non-German parents did not have access to the full range of rights and benefits of citizenship, so they were also subcitizens. The situation of Arabs living in Israel is similar. Some remain permanently in resident status, without any hope of acceding to citizenship or passing permanent resident status on to their children. But Israeli citizens of Arab descent are in an even more unusual position. They are relieved of some duties, such as service in the army. They are thus in a paradoxical situation: if army duty is considered a cost (which it should be, for many good reasons including forgone income during service), their position is a mix of being subcitizens, on account of living in a country that is formally defined as a state of another people, and supercitizens, because they have the right to most of the benefits but are spared some of the costs. A number of other cases of such differentiated citizenship exist.[5]

4.1c Free Movement of the Factors of Production

As a historical reminder, it is worth noting that the current positions of rich and poor countries with respect to the free movement of the factors of production are the opposite of what they used to be. Rich

Changed attitudes toward free movement of factors of production

countries that were typically exporters of capital supported its free movement until very recently, when concerns over outsourcing emerged. They had no particular stance on migration, since there were minimal flows of people after cessation of the dislocations caused by World War II.[6] Poor countries, on the other hand, while at times welcoming foreign capital, were always wary of being exploited or marginalized. As discussed in the next section, this attitude has undergone a sea change with the advent of global value chains, which are now eagerly sought by emerging market economies. Poor countries were in favor of the free movement of people in the past, as they still are. This attitude was sometimes tempered by concerns about brain drain, but overall these concerns seemed minor compared with the advantages that many poor countries saw from reducing demographic pressure and gaining greater remittances. Thus, rich countries that used to be indifferent to or even in favor of migration (as Germany was during its *Wirtschaftswunder,* the economic "miracle" of the 1950s and 1960s) are now wary of more migration, whereas poor countries that used to be wary of foreign capital are now assiduously courting it.[7]

From an economic point of view, there is little doubt that preventing labor from moving among countries is inefficient. Mobility of each factor of production is considered to be superior to immobility because each factor of production will naturally tend to flow to the geographical area or line of business where its returns are the highest, and its returns are highest there because its contribution (the value of output produced) is greater than anywhere else. This general proposition applies with equal force to capital and to labor.

It is important to be clear about what the proposition does and does not imply. It implies that the factor that moves to a new location would be better off in its new location than before. This follows simply from the fact of its having two options—staying or moving—and choosing the latter. The proposition also implies that total output would be greater with the option of mobility than without it. But it does not imply that everything else concerned would be better off. The movement of labor or capital from its present location to another could disrupt, displace, or make labor and capital worse off in the original location, or it could make conditions worse for labor in the new one. This last element is a major source of friction and is probably one of the key reasons why the international mobility of labor is limited. In the political arena, this is often the reason rich countries adduce against immigration.

What is migration? For our purposes (i.e., under the conditions of globalization), we will define migration as *the movement of one factor of production (labor) when globalization takes place in conditions of uneven mean incomes between countries.* This may seem like a complicated definition, but each part in that definition is essential. First, labor is (from a strictly economic perspective) just a factor of production, no different from capital.

> *Migration under conditions of globalization*

In principle, we should not treat one factor of production differently from the other. For that reason the definition highlights that, at the first approximation, there is nothing special about labor.

Second, movement of people (again, like movement of capital) is made possible by globalization. If the world were not globalized and economies were autarkic, with strong controls on outflow and inflow of capital and labor, there would be no movement across borders of either factor.

Third, if globalization existed, but it occurred under conditions where incomes between different parts of the world were not vastly different, labor would have no systematic incentive to move. There would surely be some migration, since people would move either in search of somewhat better opportunities for specific skills they possessed or in search of a more pleasant climate or more congenial culture, but these movements would be small and idiosyncratic. Such flows of people are the ones that we observe within the United States, where, for example, software engineers are more likely to move to Silicon Valley and miners to South Dakota, or, within the EU15 (the fifteen pre-2004 members of the European Union), where English retirees move to Spain to enjoy better weather, or Germans buy villas in Tuscany. But these are different from the kinds of systematic movements that hold across the board—that is, when people of all ages and professions who live in a poorer country can gain in income by moving to a richer country.

When we look at migration within the context of present-day globalization, we can easily understand the origin and the logic of people's movements. It also becomes apparent that if both (i) globalization and (ii) big income differences between different parts of the world exist, workers will not remain where they were born. To believe they would goes against the elementary economic proposition that people desire to improve their standard of living. If we believe, however, that people should not move among countries (which is a value statement), we can logically argue either that globalization should be reversed (that is, that obstacles to the free movement of both capital and labor be introduced), or that a massive effort be made so that income convergence between poor and rich countries could be accelerated. While the former approach would cut off migration immediately, the latter would take decades to slow it down—but eventually it would.[8]

The fact that there are only two possible approaches, and only one of them works quickly, explains why opponents of migration have only one logically consistent proposal. This is to make countries less globalized, which means to erect barriers to the movement of both capital and labor.

While consistent, the proposal runs into several problems. Such a dramatic reversal of globalization is possible to imagine but is unlikely to be realized because of the extremely complex organizational structure supporting globalization that has been erected over the past seventy years. Even if some countries were to opt out of globalization, a majority would not. Additional barriers to the free movement of capital and labor would also lead to the reduction of incomes globally, including in the countries that opted out. The proof for that can be provided by an argument from the contrary: if one argued that national income would be unaffected by border barriers, then one should argue as well that income would be unaffected by within-nation barriers to the movement of capital and labor. One would then have to argue that it does not matter whether people or capital move or not, for example, between New York and California or any two places in the United States. Continuing to ever smaller geographical units, one would soon reach the conclusion that mobility of labor (whether geographically or by occupation) has no effect on total income—a manifestly false proposition.[9] The absurdity of such a position reveals that the same position held with respect to the free movement of people between countries is equally absurd.

The inadequacy of this argument leaves the adversaries of migration in a cul-de-sac where they need to defend antimigration policies despite these policies' negative effects on global welfare and on the welfare of the country they contend they are trying to protect. This is indeed a very difficult position to argue, and very few people who have undertaken the logical exercise sketched above would take it.

It thus seems that, as for trade in goods or cross-border movement of capital, the best policy regarding labor would be the fully free and unimpeded movement of people from one country to another. Where the effects on specific groups of workers might be negative, such effects should be addressed by specific policies directed toward those groups, in the same way as is normally done (at least in theory) to mitigate the deleterious effects of imports on select categories of domestic workers.

So, have we solved the problem of migration? Unfortunately, no.

The reason that we have not yet solved the problem of migration is that the opponents of migration have an additional card to play which so far we have ignored. It is the belief that labor and capital, while both factors of production and thus in an abstract sense the same, are fundamentally different. Capital, in that view, can enter societies without producing dramatic changes within them, whereas labor cannot. Proponents of such a view may argue that a foreign company can invest in a country, introduce a new way to organize labor, perhaps even replace some types of workers and employ different ones, but it will not—no matter how many such foreign companies arrive—disturb the key cultural or institutional features of the society. This position, however, can be contested. What new technology does is often socially very disruptive: not only are some skills made redundant, but even a change that seems to be for the better will have many side effects, some of which may be negative. Foreign companies may, for example, be less hierarchical or more open to hiring and not discriminating against women or gay people. While many would regard such developments as desirable, the native population might regard them as disturbing the way of life they lead and value. The point here is to remind those who ascribe socially disruptive effects to migrant labor only that similarly disruptive effects can be produced by migrant capital.

Why labor is different from capital

But it could still be true that movement of labor is *more* disruptive. This is indeed the final and key defense mounted by the opponents of migration. Large inflows of foreign laborers whose cultural norms, language, behavior, and trust toward outsiders, for example, are very different from the values of the native population can lead to dissatisfaction on both sides (native and migrant), social conflict, loss of trust, and ultimately even civil war.

George Borjas (2015) argues that migrants from poor countries carry within themselves the value systems of their countries. These value systems have, by and large, been inimical to development (that's why their countries are poor), and by entering a richer country and bringing these inferior modes of behavior with them, the migrants undermine institutions in the rich country that are necessary for growth. Migrants, in that view, are like termites; they destroy stable and sturdy frameworks, and it would thus be reasonable to stop them from doing so. Note that Borjas's position completely contradicts the American historical experience, both factually and in terms of its ethos of "Give me your tired, your poor, your huddled masses yearning to breathe free." By Borjas's logic these "tired and poor" masses should long ago have subverted American prosperity.

There are, however, historical examples that support the view of people like Borjas. When the Goths found themselves under the onslaught of the Huns in the early fourth century, they implored the Romans to allow them to cross the *limes,* the military frontier, at the Danube and to settle in today's Balkans. After some deliberation, the Romans agreed. But while allowing the Goths in, they decided to profit from their helplessness and performed a number of outrages—taking away the Goths' children, abducting the women, and enslaving the men. What seemed a wise and generous move to the leaders at the center of the empire who made the decision turned into its very opposite on the ground. The outcome was that the "rescued" Goths who had been allowed in nursed an implacable hatred for the Roman Empire that led first to their rebellion and later to numerous battles, including the one that witnessed the first death of a Roman emperor on the battlefield and eventually to the sack of Rome by the Gothic leader Alaric in 410 (although Rome by then was no longer the capital). Large-scale migration and mixing of populations proved in this case disastrous. Similar examples may be adduced almost ad infinitum, especially if we consider (as we should) the European conquest of the Americas as an example of migration, that is, of the movement of people looking for a better life. The conquest was a catastrophe for the indigenous populations, who had started their encounter with the European migrants by being, in many cases, very welcoming.

These kinds of arguments against migration do have some validity. The large-scale mixing of peoples of different cultures might, rather than leading to higher income for all, produce clashes and wars that could make everyone worse off. A very pessimistic view of human nature that sees the cultural overlay of one's own group as fundamental and often incompatible with the cultural overlay of another group of people would thus militate in favor of limited or zero migration—even if migration would, in a purely economic sense, be a net positive for the native population. But, in the longer term, according to such views, allowing migration could prove to be disastrous.

4.1d Reconciling Concerns of Natives with Desires of Migrants

It is the acknowledgment of some validity contained in the point of view that migration is culturally disruptive, or if one wishes to qualify the statement further, the acceptance that this point of view—whether valid or not—is held implicitly or explicitly by many people, that leads me to propose an alternative (and sure to be controversial) approach to migration where—to repeat—migration occurs in an environment of uneven mean incomes between countries and, thus, significant citizenship premiums enjoyed by the people living in rich countries.

The chief feature of my approach, on which it survives or falls, is the following proposition: *The native population is more likely to accept migrants the less likely the migrants are to permanently remain in the country and use all the benefits of citizenship.* This proposi-

The proposal on migration

tion introduces a negative relationship between (i) willingness to accept migrants and (ii) extension of migrants' rights. Let us look at it in more detail by first considering its opposite. A positive relationship between (i) and (ii) is unlikely. It would imply that the more rights natives conceded to migrants, ultimately equalizing them entirely in terms of their status with the rest of the citizenry, the more keen the natives would be to receive additional migrants. It is not impossible to believe that natives might be keen to integrate foreigners as much as possible, but it is, I think, quite unlikely that as natives fully granted rights to migrants they would want to let in even more of them. One could imagine this condition to hold only where greater population was desperately needed, say, because of an external threat, or where migrants came from a group that the ruling class believed was useful to expand. (The latter was the case in some Latin American and Caribbean countries that encouraged migrants from Europe in order to reduce the share of indigenous or black populations.) But, by and large, a positive relationship between the two seems very unlikely—and, except for some specific cases where a given type of migrant plays a preassigned role, not even the most open countries have ever exhibited it. So the best case that we could hope for is that the natives might simply have a strong view on how many migrants they wished to accept regardless of how many rights the migrants were given.

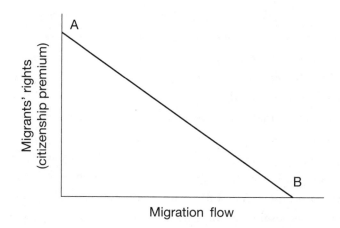

FIGURE 4.1. Trade-off between number of migrants and rights granted to migrants

The graph shows that if very few rights are granted to migrants, natives may be more willing to accept greater numbers of them.

In that case, factors (i) and (ii) would be orthogonal to each other; we would be dealing with the "lump of migrants" situation: a fixed number of migrants—which could be zero—that the natives are willing to accept no matter what.

But short of holding the "lump of migrants" view (such that no amount of incentives will change natives' views on migration), it seems reasonable to believe that there is a kind of demand curve for migrants, where the demand is less when the cost of migrants, in terms of the rights and sharing of the citizenship premium they can claim, is greater. This relationship is shown in Figure 4.1.

Consider now the two polar cases of that relationship. In one, all migrants are given, on arrival, exactly the same rights and duties as citizens. Imagine that they are handed IDs and passports, access to welfare payments, social transfers, job protection, voting rights, health care, housing, and free education as soon as they set foot on the soil of the new country. We can assume that, if such were the policy, natives would tend to accept very few migrants. This is why a position of close to zero desired migration by the natives corresponds to the position of full and extensive rights (Figure 4.1, point A). The opposite extreme is when migrants are given very few rights: they may not have access to free education, welfare, and social security, or the right to bring their families, or they may even, as Richard Freeman (2006) suggested, be subject to higher taxation than the natives (since their benefits from migration are crystal clear). I posit that at this extreme the natives would be willing to accept more migrants than in the first extreme case, that is, that the value on the horizontal axis in Figure 4.1 (point B) would be greater.

These two cases illustrate my proposition of a negative relationship between willingness to accept migrants and the extension of migrants' rights. The two polar points (A and B) are, in effect, sufficient for the presence of a negative relationship (assuming the relationship is continuous and monotonic). We can just draw a line (the "demand" curve) connecting the two points. Depending on an individual country's circumstances, the extensiveness of the bundle of rights it provides, its history of dealing with migrants, or the generosity of the local population, the downward sloping curve that connects the two points might take different shapes. It could be steeper or flatter; there could be some portions where it may be almost flat and others where it goes down steeply. But the crucial relationship of the negative slope is established, and it would be up to each individual country to find which point on the demand curve it wished to select.

The relationship suggested here can accommodate a wide variety of outcomes measured in terms of treatment of migrants and their inflows. Under the least advantageous treatment for migrants, one could imagine a system of circular migration where a migrant would be allowed to stay for only one term of, for example, four or five years, without his or her family, and would be allowed to work for only one employer. All job-related rights of migrants would be the same as the rights of domestic labor (wages, accident and health protection, union membership, and the like), but the migrants would have no other civic rights. They would be denied non-job-related social benefits and would have no right to vote. They would, in short, receive a very diluted citizenship premium. Under that worse-case scenario for migrants, the system would be similar, absent mistreatment and threats of violence, to that which presently exists in the Gulf Cooperation Council countries and in Singapore, and on certain visas in the United Kingdom and the United States. One could also move along the demand curve and offer more rights; at the extreme, the offer would be of full equality with the domestic citizenry.

The advantage of thinking about migration within such a context is not only that it allows flexibility regarding the choice of the best migration strategy, but more important, that it preempts, through the provision of flexibility, the choice of the worst option of zero migration. I describe zero migration as the worst option advisedly since, compared with any other alternative, it would be worse for the migrants, for large segments of the native population (those *Advantages of the proposal* whose skills are complementary with those of the migrants or who would benefit from lower costs of production of goods and services produced by migrants), and for global poverty and inequality. Giving differential rights to different categories of residents is a way to combat the worst-case scenario. It is not an ideal solution. If the world were organized differently (e.g., not in nation-states), or if peoples' cultures were homogeneous, or if the gaps between countries' mean incomes were small, or if people were always nice and peaceful, it could, no doubt, be improved upon. But since none of that is the case, we need a realistic solution that takes the world and people's opinions as they are and, within such constraints, develops a viable solution.

Treating different categories of residents differently is already, as I mentioned above, a reality in many countries. Residence permits allow people to live and work in recipient countries without enjoying a full gamut of civic rights. In the United States, the system of rights and duties is already segmented. Subcitizens such as undocumented migrants, whose numbers are estimated at more than 10 million, or about 3 to 4 percent of the US population, have no rights to social benefits and often face hurdles to free education or are simply denied it in some states or some state schools; they have a very limited choice of jobs (only those where full documentation is not required); and they live under the permanent threat of deportation. They cannot travel outside the United States (which makes their position similar to that of citizens of the former Eastern bloc countries). They do, however, accept these severe limitations on their rights and freedoms, as well as a lower social status compared with the native population, because of large income gains, less violence, and better treatment compared with what they would experience in their home countries, as well as in the expectation that their children's rights will not be as constrained as theirs. Higher categories above that of undocumented immigrants include people on different types of temporary visas, who are allowed to stay in the United States for only a certain number of years and to work for a specific employer. Green card holders are, in terms of job possibilities and also taxation, equivalent to citizens, but they do not have the right to vote (and hence cannot determine taxation or any other national policy). We thus see in this example that there are already variable conditions, some having crept in surreptitiously, and degrees of belonging in an area that, theoretically, should admit only of a binary distinction between citizens and noncitizens. Many of these approaches represent accommodations with globalization and the world of nonautarky, where the kind of sharp division between citizens and noncitizens that existed in the twentieth century is no longer tenable.

Flexibility as to the choice of the point on the demand curve does not mean flexibility as to the application of the rules. The very reverse is true. For the system of circular migration to function, legal channels of migration have to be kept open. But at the same time, all illegal channels of migration have to be closed off. If they are not, the well-considered choice of the optimal point on the demand curve will become immaterial, and the actual level of migration may far exceed the optimal one that has been chosen. Then the danger of backlash would be severe. If a country is shown to be unable to enforce the rules, domestic voters might decide that the only sensible solution is zero migration. For the system to work, flexibility in the choice of optimal levels of migration must coexist with at times ruthless cracking down on excess migration.

But such proposals calling for de facto discriminatory treatment of migrants have their disadvantages, too. The most serious is probably the creation of an underclass that, even if not always composed of

Disadvantages of the proposal

the same individuals (in the case of circular migration), would exist without ever being absorbed into the native community. It is possible to think that this would lead to the development of local ghettoes, high crime, and a general feeling of alienation from the native population (and vice versa). The problem of ghettoization may be less severe than it seems at first sight, as more skilled and well-paid migrants would mix more easily with native populations, but it is unlikely that the stigma and the problems of exclusion would ever be entirely eliminated. It would also require robust and possibly violent enforcement of exits when the time was up, and big changes in countries that do not have national ID cards.

This concern brings up the problem of how to ensure social stability in such a diverse and somewhat disarticulated society where migrants might be a class apart. To the extent that migrants were more diverse in education and income, they would be less likely to be perceived as a class apart— perhaps like green card holders in today's United States, who are not seen to form a distinct group precisely because they are individuals with diverse educational levels, skills, and cultures. Differences in skills, type of job, and income mean that they will not live in separate geographical areas (away from natives), and differences in ethnic background mean that they will not be a physically recognizable group or have much in common with each other.

Moreover, when we weigh the disadvantages of the proposed solution we must not simply look at the sum of all such disadvantages. We have to weigh them against the alternatives, for example, that greater aid by the rich countries could be one way to stave off migration. But against that one should note that aid so far has borne very little fruit and that even if this were to change, it would take a very long time for this approach to solve the essential problem of vast differences in income levels, and thus an unstoppable incentive to migrate.[10] Therefore, the alternative to the flexible menu of citizenship rights would turn out again to be a solution of zero migration, which would mean Fortress Europe and Fortress America and many more deaths along the borders between these two rich areas and their poorer southern neighbors. Not a desirable outcome in any way.

We move next to capital mobility under conditions of globalization.

4.2 Capital: Global Value Chains

The global value chain, a way of organizing production such that different stages of production are located in different countries, is probably the most important organizational innovation in this era of globalization. Global value chains were made possible both by the technological ability to control production processes effectively from distant locations and by global respect for property rights.

In the past, the lack of these two elements limited the expansion of foreign capital. Adam Smith noted almost two hundred and fifty years ago that owners of capital prefer to invest near to where they live so they can keep an eye on production and on the way the company is managed (*Wealth of Nations*, book 4, chap. 2). Before the information and communication technology (ICT) revolution enabled people thousands of miles away to keep close control over the process of production, Smith's dismissal of the possibility of globalized capital held true.

The global protection of property rights is the second important change. The first era of globalization, which can be broadly dated from 1870 to 1914, was hampered by the lack of a guarantee that one's property would be safe from abuse or nationalization in foreign locales. The "solution" was found in imperialism and colonialism. Capital-exporting nations either conquered other countries or made sure that they controlled the economic policy of quasi-colonies so that places like China, Egypt, Tunisia, and Venezuela had no choice but to protect the property rights of foreigners.[11] The same role that colonialism played then, more brutally, is played today by the International Monetary Fund (IMF), the Multilateral Investment Guarantee Agency, hundreds of bilateral investment treaties, and other global governance bodies: they are the guardians against nationalization and the abuse of foreign property. In that respect, globalization has created its own governance structure.

Global value chains have redefined economic development. It was argued in the past that the participation of developing countries in the international division of labor was inimical to their development in at least three ways and would lead to the "development of underdevelopment," as André Gunder Frank termed it in an influential article published in 1966.

First, according to the *dependencia* (or theory of dependency) school of thought, linkages with the Global North involved only a limited number of exporting sectors and failed to develop internal backward or forward linkages to push developing countries onto the path of sustained development.

This view was complemented by a second argument, called "export pessimism," which predicted that the Global South would indefinitely remain an exporter of raw materials, with deteriorating long-term terms of trade.

Finally, Robert Allen (2011) has recently argued that technological progress always takes place at the capital-labor ratio of the country that is the most developed at the time. For example, Britain, the most advanced economy in 1870, had an interest in introducing new ways of producing output at the capital-labor (K/L) ratio it faced then; similarly, the United States, as the most advanced economy today, has an incentive to innovate for those production techniques that use very high K/L ratios. In general, advanced economies do not have an incentive to innovate at the K/L ratios at which they do not produce. (No one in the United States, for example, would spend money to find a better way to build a car using manual labor rather than robots.) The implication is that poor countries today face the same technologically backward, two-centuries-old production function because no one in the rich world has an incentive to improve the efficiency of production at their K/L ratios. In other words, technologically advanced countries do not have an interest in finding more efficient ways of production at the K/L ratios they do not themselves experience, and poor countries do not possess the know-how to do it. Poor countries are thus caught in a poverty trap: in order to develop they need to upgrade their production, but technologies that exist at their K/L ratios are old-fashioned and inefficient.

All of this Global South pessimism was upended by the rise of global value chains. Today, for a country to develop, it must be included in Western supply chains rather than trying to delink from the rich world. A key reason for this is that foreign investors see global value chains as integral parts of their own production processes: they no longer have to be "begged" to bring in the most advanced or the most appropriate technology. They now have the incentive to introduce technological development at the level of the wage rate and the K/L ratio they face in poor countries, thus doing away with the poverty trap that Allen identified. The importance of this change, both for real life and for what it tells us about the ideological justification of globalization as a way forward for the development of poorer countries, cannot be overestimated.

These matters are very ably analyzed in Richard Baldwin's book *The Great Convergence* (2016). Baldwin argues that only those countries that

Globalization as unbundling

have been able to insert themselves into global supply (or value) chains have succeeded in accelerating their development. These countries are, according to Baldwin, China, South Korea, India, Indonesia, Thailand, and Poland; several others (Bangladesh, Ethiopia, Burma, Vietnam, Romania) could be added to the list. However, to understand why they have benefited so much from globalization, we need to understand the technical ways in which today's globalization differs from the previous globalization in addition to much better protection of property rights (thanks to international treaties and mechanisms of enforcement). It is these novel and specific features of globalization that have made global value chains of such importance.

Baldwin defines three eras of globalization that are characterized by the reduced cost of transporting, successively, (1) goods, (2) information, and (3) people. The first two eras correspond to the two globalizations I have already mentioned, while the third lies in the future. The argument goes as follows: When the transportation of goods was perilous and expensive, production and consumption had to coincide geographically—communities consumed whatever they produced. In even the most developed premodern societies, such as ancient Rome, the bulk of trade consisted of luxury items and wheat. But Rome was an exception; in most premodern societies, trade was minimal.

Then came the Industrial Revolution, which lowered the transportation cost of goods. This made shipment of goods to faraway destinations possible and created the first globalization, or the "first unbundling," as Baldwin calls it: goods were produced "here" and consumed "there." This also gave economics practically all the concepts and the intellectual toolkit that we still use today. The first unbundling produced a new concern with national trade balances and thus introduced mercantilism. It also led to a focus on national production of goods through all their stages and a view of trade as consisting of nation A exporting a good to nation B (but not of company A selling goods to company B, or of company A selling things to its subsidiary, which then sells them to company B). Finally, it gave us a theory of growth that sees nations advancing from the production of food to the production of manufactures and further on to services. Practically all the tools of modern economics are still rooted in the way the first unbundling occurred.[12] The main features of the first unbundling were (i) trade of goods, (ii) direct foreign investment (which, absent any other means of securing property rights in distant locations, led to colonialism), and (iii) nation-states.

Today, in what Baldwin identifies as the second unbundling (and the second globalization), all three main actors have changed. Now, the control and coordination of production is done "here," but the actual production of goods is done "there." Notice the difference: first you unbundle production and consumption, then you unbundle the production itself.[13] The unbundling of production was made possible by the ICT revolution, which allowed companies to design and control processes from the center while spreading the production to hundreds of units or to subcontractors dispersed around the world. The reduced cost of transporting information (basically, the ability to coordinate and control regardless of distance) is for the second unbundling what the reduced cost of shipping was for the first. Now, the main players are (i) information and control (instead of goods), (ii) global coercive institutions (instead of colonialism), and (iii) companies (instead of nations).

> *The second globalization*

A couple of other things are distinctive about the second unbundling. First, the importance of institutions has increased. When globalization involved only the export of goods, institutions in the country to which the goods were exported did not matter much; whether institutions "there" were good or bad, exporters were paid about the same.[14] This is not the case with the second unbundling. When production is delocalized, the quality of the institutions, infrastructure, and politics in the recipient country matters enormously to the center. If designs are stolen, goods are impounded, or the travel of people between the center and the offshore location is made difficult, the entire production structure of the company collapses. For the center, the quality of institutions in the offshore location becomes almost as important as the quality of institutions locally. This means that institutions in the periphery now either have to hew as closely as possible to the institutions that exist in the center or to be as integrated as possible, which is exactly the opposite of what the *dependencia* school taught.

Second, technological progress in the offshore locations now has an entirely different hue than in the past. Whereas in the past developing countries had to try hard to induce foreign investors to share their know-how, now a company based in the center (the mother company) has incentives to make sure the best technology is used in the offshore location, which has become an integral part of the center's production chain. This is an enormous change: rather than poor countries trying to incentivize foreign companies to transfer technology, now the owner of that technology is keen to transfer to the offshore location as much of it as possible.

The tables, in some sense, have turned: it is now the nation where the mother company is located that tries to prevent the company from transferring its best technology to the periphery. Innovation rents, received by the leaders in new technologies, are being dissipated away from the center. This is one of the key reasons why people in the rich world often complain about outsourcing (or offshoring). They criticize it not only because domestic jobs are affected but because innovation rents are shared more often with foreign than with domestic labor. The gains from new technology accrue to the entrepreneurs and capitalists in the center but also to the workers in the less-developed areas to which the production is outsourced. An indication of that process is that offshoring has been particularly strong in high-tech industries. In a study of eight advanced economies (Japan, Denmark, Finland, Germany, Italy, the Netherlands, the United Kingdom, and the United States), Bournakis, Vecchi, and Venturini (2018) found that high-tech offshoring increased from 14 percent of the value added in the late 1990s (the level at which it has been since the beginning of that decade) to about 18 percent by 2006. Offshoring in low-tech industries has remained stable at around 8 percent of the value added. The people who are cut out from the benefits are workers in the rich countries. This change is also one of the main reasons why today's globalization is accompanied by labor's loss of bargaining power in rich countries and the stagnation of wages for less-skilled workers (or at least those who can easily be replaced by foreigners). This also explains recent attempts to roll back globalization in the developed world. And most importantly, it is at the origin of a tacit coalition that has been formed, at the global level, between rich people in rich countries and poor people in poor countries.

The second unbundling also fundamentally changes our view that development goes through orderly, predetermined stages. The old-fashioned view, following upon the way England, and later the United States and Japan, developed, was that countries went through an import-substitution stage with significant tariff protection, then developed exports of simple manufactures, and later gradually moved into more sophisticated products with higher value added. This was the idea that underlay most

> *The second globalization introduces global capitalism*

of development policy between the 1950s and the 1980s. South Korea, Brazil, and Turkey were the best examples of countries following such policies. In the 1990s, with the second globalization, things changed. What has become crucial for the success of developing countries is no longer to develop through various predetermined stages using their own economic policies, but to become part of the global supply chains organized by the center (the Global North). And moreover, not merely to go into higher value-added stages by copying what richer countries are doing, but, as China is doing now, to become technological leaders themselves. The second unbundling has made it possible to skip the stages that were earlier thought necessary. As recently as the 1980s, it was unthinkable that countries that were overwhelmingly rural and poor, like India and China, would within two or three generations become technological leaders, or at least come close to the production possibility frontier in some areas. Thanks to their insertion into global supply chains, it became a reality.

The way to interpret Asia's success in the current era is not by seeing China, India, Indonesia, Thailand, and so on as the latest versions of South Korea. They are the trailblazers of a new road to development which, through integrating one's economy to the developed world, leapfrogs over several technological and institutional stages. The most successful countries in the second globalization are those that, because of institutional factors, the skill and cost of their labor, and their geographical proximity to the North, are able to become an integral part of the Northern economy. This pattern inverts the old *dependencia* paradigm, which held that delinking was the way to develop. On the contrary, becoming linked is what allowed Asia to travel the road from absolute poverty to middle-income status in a remarkably short span of time. *This technological and institutional linking is at the origin of capitalism's spread to the rest of the world and its current universal dominance.* The second globalization and the dominance of capitalism thus go together.

What will the third globalization be, according to Baldwin? The ultimate unbundling (at least from today's perspective) will come with the ability of labor to move seamlessly. This will happen when the costs of moving labor or telecommuting become low. For operations that require the physical presence of a person, the cost of temporarily moving that person to a different location is still high. But if the need for the physical presence of a worker is solved through remote control, as we already see with doctors performing surgeries remotely using robots, then labor may become globalized, too. The third unbundling, that of labor (as an input in the production process) from its physical location will make us think of migration and labor markets very differently: if tasks that now require the physical presence of a worker will be able to be done remotely by a person at any point on the globe, then migration of labor may become of much smaller importance. As a result of the third unbundling, we may achieve a global labor market that will mimic how the world would look if migration were completely unrestricted—but with no actual movement of people.[15]

Perhaps the most important insight yielded by Baldwin's view of globalizations as successive unbundlings is that it allows us to see the economic progress of the past two centuries as a continuum driven by the successive facilitations of movement of goods, information, and ultimately people. It also provides a glimpse of a utopia (or perhaps a dystopia) where everything could be almost instantly and seamlessly moved around the globe. It would be the ultimate victory over the constraints of place and time.

But the third big unbundling has not yet arrived, and so we are still living in a world where labor has to physically move to the place where the work is performed, and returns to the same unit of labor continue to vary widely depending on where that labor is located. In other words, we are still dealing with a world where, as shown in the previous section, incentives to migrate are huge, and the migration of labor is a big issue.

We shall look next at what movements of capital and labor imply for the viability of the welfare state—thus extending the discussion from Chapter 2.

4.3 The Welfare State: Survival

The existence of the citizenship rent, and accordingly the fact that citizenship is an asset, derives from three key economic advantages that citizenship gives to the holder: (a) a much greater set of economic opportunities, best reflected in higher wages and more interesting jobs, (b) a claim over the stream of valuable social benefits, and (c) certain nonfinancial rights linked to existing institutions (e.g., the right to a fair trial and to nondiscrimination). Element (a) is not new, although it has become more salient. Since the beginning of recorded history, communities have differed in the wages and opportunities they offered their citizens. For example, Rome and Alexandria were full of non-natives who had come there for more remunerative jobs and better prospects of upward mobility. However, the gap between rich and poor societies has never been as wide as it is now. Element (c) is not new either: when threatened by torture, the Christian apostle Paul exclaimed "Ego sum Romanus ciis" (I am a Roman citizen), which in principle protected him from such treatment—as indeed it did in Paul's case.

But element (b)—economic gains that derive from the existence of the welfare state—is new, because the welfare state itself is a modern construct. Since the welfare state was explicitly based on the idea of citizenship, partly as a way to transcend the internal conflict between capital and labor, it is quite normal that citizenship became the key criterion for receiving social transfers dispensed by the state. The nation-state, the welfare state, and citizenship thus became inextricably linked. Moreover, the welfare state, especially in Scandinavia, was erected on the premise of cultural, and often ethnic, homogeneity. Homogeneity had two functions: it guaranteed that norms of behavior, which are crucial for the sustainability of the welfare state, would be the same across most sectors of the population, and it emphasized the idea of national unity and thus blunted the edge of class conflict.

In our globalized age, a clear conflict has emerged between the welfare state, access to which is based on citizenship, and the free movement of labor. The fact that there is a welfare state with benefits assigned to citizens only and thus forming part of their citizenship rent (in some cases a substantial part) cannot but be in tension with the free movement of labor. If migrants are more or less automatically granted citizenship, this implies dilution of the rent received by the current citizens. The existence of the welfare state is not, in the longer run, compatible with full-scale globalization that includes the free movement of labor. As we have seen, the citizenship rent emerges because of a de facto restraint on migration exercised by the current citizens (akin to restraint on trade exercised by the monopolist). This restraint is imposed in order to preserve element (a) of the rent (higher wages), but also element (b)—welfare benefits. Element (c), being a public good, is, from the point of view of the existing citizens, probably less important because it can be shared with others at relatively little cost.

The great differences among nations in all three elements (a, b, and c) lead to high citizenship premiums or penalties, and in turn to more restrictive policies regarding free movement of labor. The divergence of countries' mean incomes throughout most of the twentieth century (i.e., when rich countries were growing, on a per capita basis, faster than poor countries) and the existence of the welfare state are both responsible for much less tolerant attitudes toward mobility of labor in receiving countries. A large citizenship premium and anti-immigration policies are two sides of the same coin. One does not exist without the other. This leads us to the conclusion (already discussed in Section 4.1) that for the globalization of labor to become less of a political issue, either gaps between national incomes must be reduced (poorer countries catching up with the rich), or the existing welfare states in the rich world must be severely reduced or dismantled, or migrants must be granted considerably fewer rights than natives. If we consider that free mobility of labor is desirable because it increases global income and the incomes of migrants, thus reducing world poverty, we must conclude, following the same reasoning, that one of the major obstacles to these favorable developments is the welfare state in rich countries. But, to continue this reasoning further, if the welfare state is unlikely to be reduced or dismantled because its dismantlement would be politically resisted, since it would erase most of social progress realized by citizens and workers of the rich countries, one is led to the proposal that curtails the economic rights of migrants.[16]

One of the political consequences of the close linkage between the welfare state and citizenship is the antiglobalization stance of certain left-wing parties (such as La France Insoumise in France, and the Social Democrats in Denmark, Austria, the Netherlands, and Sweden). These parties are against both capital outflows (because outsourcing and investments in poorer countries destroy jobs in rich countries, even if they might create many more jobs elsewhere) and migration. These left-wing parties, which played a crucial role in the creation of the welfare state, are thus placed in the seemingly paradoxical position of being both nationalist and anti-internationalist, breaking with a long tradition of internationalist socialism. This change in attitude stems from a change in the underlying economic conditions that has taken place during the past one hundred and fifty years: a movement away from uniformity in economic conditions among poor people regardless of nation, and the construction of complex and comprehensive welfare states in the rich world. The change in policy of left-wing parties is thus not accidental but is a response to long-term trends. Left-wing or social democratic parties have relatively well-defined constituencies of workers in the industrial and public sectors, whose jobs are threatened by the free movement of both capital and labor. By effectively abandoning the tradition of internationalism, these parties have become more similar, and politically closer, to the right-wing parties with which they often (as in France) now share the political space and voters. The residual of internationalism can still be seen, however, in left-wing parties' antidiscrimination policies, whose main beneficiaries are migrants already living in the countries of reception. These parties' voters thus display a somewhat schizophrenic attitude of being supportive of the rights of the migrants who have managed to make it into the country, while being against more migrants coming in, and against more capital going out to give employment to people poorer than themselves.

> *Left-wing parties and the welfare state*

I conclude this section with a more philosophic problem that underlies the discussion of migration. The existence of the citizenship rent implies manifest inequality of opportunity on a global scale: two identical individuals, one born in a poor country and one in a rich country, will have rights to very unequal income streams over their lifetimes. This is an obvious fact, but its implications have not been fully drawn out. If we contrast the situation of these two individuals born in two different countries with two identical individuals born of poor and rich parents in the same country, we notice that in the latter case there would be some concern with inequality of opportunity and an often shared belief among most citizens of the country that such inequalities in starting position ought to be leveled out. But no such concerns appear to exist in the former case. John Rawls's work provides a perfect example of this discrepancy, or inconsistency. In his book *A Theory of Justice,* he accords within-nation inequalities a place of highest importance and argues that inequalities between people born to rich and poor parents need to be alleviated or eliminated. But when he turns to the international arena in *The Law of Peoples,* he completely ignores inequalities between people born in rich and poor countries. Yet in the words of Josiah Stamp (1926), written almost a century ago, "While we may focus on individual inheritance, it cannot be wholly dissociated from the communal aspects. When [a person] comes into the world, he has, as an economic unit, to associate with two types of assistance, i.e. what he individually inherits from his parents, and what he socially inherits from previous society, and in both of these the principle of individual inheritance has been present."

Global inequality of opportunity

Global inequality of opportunity is not generally considered a problem at all, much less a problem in need of a solution. Within nation-states, many people regard the intergenerational transmission of family-acquired wealth as rather objectionable; but among nations, the intergenerational transmission of collectively acquired wealth is not considered an object of concern. This is interesting because individuals' links to their family are closer than their links to an entire community, and one might think that the transmission of family wealth across generations could be viewed as less objectionable than the transmission of societal wealth across generations of unrelated individuals. The reason that it is not seems to lie in one crucial difference, namely that in the first case, where the intergenerational transmission of wealth takes place within the same community, individuals can easily compare their positions with each other, and they resent injustice; in the other case, inequality is international, and individuals cannot easily compare themselves or perhaps they do not care to do so (or at least, the rich do not). Distance, as Aristotle noted, often makes people indifferent to the lot of others, perhaps because they do not see them as peers with whom they compare their income or wealth.[17] Formal belonging to a community (citizenship) is key to explaining these differences. The basic issue was defined with utmost clarity by Adam Smith in *Theory of Moral Sentiments:* "In the great society of mankind . . . the prosperity of France [because of a larger number of inhabitants] should appear to be an object of much greater importance than that of Great Britain. The British subject, however, who upon that account, should prefer upon all occasions the prosperity of the former to that of the latter country, would not be thought a good citizen of Great Britain" (part 6, chap. 2).

By our long custom of "methodological nationalism," where we essentially study certain phenomena within the confines of a nation, we are led to the position that equality of opportunity seems to apply, and to be studied, only within the nation-state. Global inequality of opportunity is forgotten or ignored. This may have been, philosophically and practically, a reasonable position in the past, when knowledge of differences among nations was vague and inequality of opportunity was not addressed even at home. But it may not be a reasonable position now. Cosmopolitans and statists will no doubt differ on that question. But we need to put the issue on the table in economic terms, too, and discuss it with respect to migration, which is its most visible manifestation.

4.4 Worldwide Corruption

There is, I think, a general feeling that in most countries, corruption is greater today than it was thirty years ago.[18] If we measure corruption by the number of cases of corruption that are unveiled, however, that impression could prove to be misleading. It could be that the ability to control corruption and punish criminals is on the increase, rather than corruption itself. Or, alternatively, it could be that our sense of rising corruption worldwide is driven by the fact that we have much more information now than we did in the past, not only about local corruption but also about corruption in many different parts of the world. Neither possibility can be easily dismissed. Regarding the first, we have no reliable data over time on enforcement, and even if we did, a rise in the number of prosecuted cases of corruption could not tell us anything about the magnitude of corruption or about the strength of law enforcement. This is because the extent of corruption (the denominator that we wish to have when judging whether enforcement has improved or not) is by definition unknown. We would know only of the cases of corruption brought to court, not the true extent of corruption.

This lack of knowledge can be remedied to some extent through indicators based on surveys that ask various experts for their opinion about the prevalence of corruption, such as the Transparency International Corruption Perception Index and the World Bank's Worldwide Governance Indicators. These are not surveys of corruption as such but rather of the perception of corruption.[19] But they did not begin until the mid-1990s, when globalization was already in full swing. More importantly, such indicators allow for only relative comparisons of corruption (Was Russia more corrupt than Denmark in a certain year?), not the evolution of corruption over time (Is Russia more corrupt in 2018 than it was in 2010?) or cardinal comparisons (Is Russia more corrupt compared with Denmark this year than it was last year?). This is because the indicators simply rank countries each year; they do not compare values from one year to another. We also cannot say much about whether people's perceptions themselves may be influenced by greater reporting of cases of corruption, more open media, and greater knowledge of corruption outside their own small circles.

For more information, we may turn to recent estimates of the amount of funds held in tax havens. The use of these havens is not a neat indicator of corruption, but the two are related. Of course, money made through corruption need not be held in tax havens; it can be "converted" into legitimate activities or, for example, used to buy real estate in London or New

York. Thus, assessing the size of tax havens alone could underestimate corruption. But it could also overestimate it, since money earned legally can also be placed in tax havens, simply for the purpose of avoiding taxation. In either case, however, most of the money held in tax havens is extra legal in that it is corrupt either in origin or in intention (to evade taxes).[20] Using data on anomalies in assets positions across countries, Gabriel Zucman (2013, 1322) estimated that in 2008, about $5.9 trillion—8 percent of global household financial wealth, or 10 percent of global GDP—was held in tax havens (three-quarters of it unrecorded). That number has been stable from 2000, when Zucman made the first estimates, to 2015.[21] By definition, it includes only financial wealth and does not account for many other forms (real estate, jewelry, works of art) in which stolen assets, or legally acquired assets that are protected from taxation, can be stored.

Another way to assess corruption is to look at the global net errors and omissions, a category in each country's balance of payments that reflects, in part, genuine errors, and in part capital flight that may be related to domestic corrupt activities such as underinvoicing of exports or overinvoicing of imports (so that the resulting difference is kept abroad), and other illicit transactions. Data from the International Monetary Fund (IMF) show that global net errors and omissions, while never exceeding $100 billion annually before the 2008 global financial crisis, have since, in the five years for which data are available, amounted to an average of more than $200 billion per year.[22]

Another approach to quantifying corruption or, more exactly, to quantifying a proxy for wealth that is acquired through political connections, was used by Caroline Freund in her pathbreaking book *Rich People Poor Countries: The Rise of Emerging Market Tycoons and Their Mega Firms* (2016). Freund classified billionaires around the world according to whether the main source of their wealth was self-made or inherited. Within the former category, Freund separated out a group of billionaires whose wealth derives from natural resources, privatizations, or other connections to the government.[23] Figure 4.2 shows the percentage of billionaires (not the percentage of their total wealth) estimated as falling into that group. In advanced economies, the share is about 4 percent (with an increase for Anglo countries and Western Europe between 2001 and 2014). In emerging market

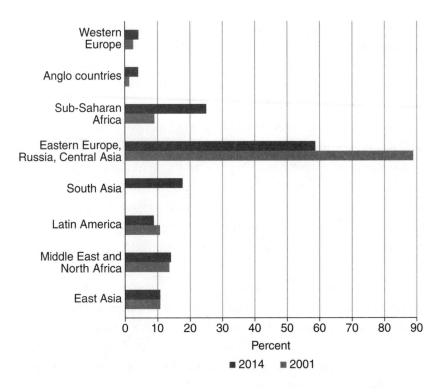

FIGURE 4.2. Percentage of billionaires whose wealth is estimated to derive from natural resources, privatization, or other connections to the government, 2001 and 2014

The Anglo countries are Australia, Canada, New Zealand, and the United States. Developed East Asia is omitted because the share in both years is zero. *Data source:* Based on Freund (2016, table 2.4, pp. 37–38).

economies, the share is between 10 percent and 20 percent, with the exception of an extraordinarily high share in the group composed of Eastern Europe, Russia, and Central Asia, driven by billionaires from the republics of the former Soviet Union. Other than in this last region (which may be considered by far the most corrupt) and Latin America, the percentage of billionaires that owe their wealth to political connections is on the rise in all regions. The increase is particularly strong in sub-Saharan Africa and South Asia (mostly due to India). The worldwide share of total billionaires' wealth estimated to have been acquired through government connections increased from 3.8 percent in 2001 to 10.2 percent in 2014, with, predictably, the highest share in Eastern Europe, Russia, and Central Asia

(73 percent), the Middle East and North Africa (22 percent), and Latin America (15 percent).[24]

4.4a Three Grounds for Corruption in the Age of Globalization

Despite the impossibility of direct measurement of corruption and our reliance on proxies, there are strong theoretical grounds to believe that worldwide corruption is greater now than it was twenty or thirty years ago, and possibly that it will keep on rising. I see at least three such grounds: (i) hypercommercialized and globalized capitalism, where life success is measured only by financial success (discussed in greater detail in Chapter 5), (ii) open capital accounts, which make it easier to move money between jurisdictions and thus to launder stolen money or evade taxes, and (iii) the demonstration effect of globalization, whereby people (especially bureaucrats) in middle-income and poor countries believe they deserve the level of consumption available to people in similar positions in rich countries, a level that they, with their low official salaries, can attain only if they engage in corruption. Point (i) is fundamentally ideological and general (that is, it applies anywhere in the world and in principle to everybody); point (iii) is more narrow, applying only to select groups of people; and point (ii) is an enabling condition, a factor that facilitates worldwide corruption.

I briefly discuss each of these points in turn.

Here I take as granted an argument that I develop at greater length in Chapter 5: hyperglobalization requires as its intellectual superstructure an ideology that justifies money-making (of any kind) and in which financial success dominates all other objectives and creates a society of fundamental amorality. Amorality implies that society and individuals are indifferent about the way wealth is acquired as long as things are done on the verge of legality (even if unethically), or beyond legality but without being discovered, or in a way that is illegal in one jurisdiction but can be presented as legal in another. Under these conditions, it directly follows that there will be strong incentives to engage in corrupt behavior.[25] The objective will be to engage in "optimal" or "smart"

> *Limits on corruption in countries not integrated into the capitalist world economy*

corruption that may be ethically unacceptable but is difficult to detect or even to classify as corruption. Even if such activities would be widely regarded as corrupt, that does not mean that they would be legally classified as such and pursued by authorities, as, for example, in the United States, where lobbying always teeters on the edge between legality and illegality.[26] Corruption is further helped by the creation of an entire apparatus of lawyers whose interest is to advise clients how best to achieve their corrupt objectives without openly breaking the law, or by breaking the law in a minimal fashion. London, for example, is the host to a legal industry that has worked hard to make it possible for corrupt individuals from Russia, China, Nigeria, and many other countries to launder their money in England or to use London as the hub through which to launder it elsewhere.

The spread of globalization to all parts of the world has been very important in facilitating corruption. In his seminal books on corruption in China, Minxin Pei explained why corruption was almost nonexistent in Maoist China (Pei 2006, 147–148). He identified several reasons: the ability of people to monitor the spending patterns of local officials, who lived close to their constituents and were exposed to periodic purges (if suspected of corruption[27] or disloyalty); poverty and a lack of attractive goods that severely limited what corrupt officials could buy with their money; and China's isolation from the rest of the world, which made it impossible for officials to transfer money abroad. The last element was probably the most important.

The way in which a different economic system as well as autarky or isolation from capitalism limited corruption is indeed best seen in the case of communist countries. Most money transactions in those countries occurred between state-owned enterprises and entirely circumvented household flows of money. Such enterprise moneys were often just accounting units that circulated within the enterprise sector and could not be used for household purchases. Perhaps the simplest way to visualize it is to imagine a situation where all business transactions between companies are conducted in an electronic currency that cannot be used to pay for wages or for privately purchased goods.[28] A furniture-producing company can sell furniture for electronic money only to another state company. Now, the head of the latter company could physically steal the delivered furniture, but that would be both difficult (received furniture would be entered in the books) and rather open and clumsy. In other words, there was only a small chance that goods bought through enterprise money would end up illicitly in the hands of individuals.

Special advantages and premiums received by top state and party officials or enterprise bosses were almost always in-kind—the use of state-owned cars, or access to better goods or larger apartments. They could not be monetized, saved, or transmitted to the next generation. Moreover, they could be taken away at will; in fact, as a rule, they would be withdrawn as soon as an official lost the job that provided the privileges. They were strictly ex officio privileges. This was not an accident. Such privileges are supposed to guarantee obedience precisely because they can be withdrawn so easily. A privilege that can be monetized, transmitted to one's heirs, or in general be inalienable creates a sphere of independence for the individual. Granting such independence is incompatible with authoritarian or totalitarian regimes. But on the positive side, this lack of independence limited corruption.

Another important factor limiting corruption was lack of full integration into the international (capitalist) economy. That was true even for rich capitalist countries, many of which in the 1960s and 1970s had currency controls that limited the amount of cash one could take abroad, whether on vacation or business trips.[29] The constraints were even greater in developing countries with nonconvertible currencies. And they were the severest again in socialist or quasi-socialist countries (such as the Soviet Union, Eastern European countries, China, India, Algeria, Vietnam, and Tanzania) that were not integrated into the world economy. Even if officials somehow got hold of money (and if they were able to convert it into foreign exchange—a big "if"), the knowledge of how to transfer that money abroad was lacking. Relying on the help of other people who might have such knowledge would open an official up to the charge not only of corruption but also of treason, since most of those with the knowledge of how capitalist economies operated and how to make investments were typically people who had emigrated from the communist countries and were thus considered class enemies.

I remember one case from the mid-1980s, when the communist regimes in Europe were already at the stage of disintegration, party control was noticeably weakening, and the idea of officials stealing money and hiding it abroad began to be seen as a possibility, even if, I think, it was almost never a reality—at that time. (One had to wait for the collapse of the communist regimes and privatization of state-owned assets to make it into a reality.) A rumor was going around that the Yugoslav prime minister had bought an apartment in Paris. I discussed the rumor with my friends and argued that it was unlikely to be true. I pointed out that, first, it was difficult to see where he could get so much money in foreign exchange without this being noticed by the secret police. Perhaps, while rising to the top, he helped a foreign firm get a particularly advantageous contract, which might have been the only activity where he could hope to "earn" a sizeable amount of money. But even then it was not obvious how he could have been paid for this "service." It was illegal to own accounts in foreign countries, and opening an account, whether in his own name or in that of a relative, was an exceedingly dangerous move that, if discovered, would have ended his career long before he became prime minister. Opening a foreign account later, when he was in a position of high authority, would have been equally dangerous and difficult. When visiting foreign countries, officials at such high levels were never left alone. It was inconceivable that the prime minister would have been able to just walk into a Parisian bank office and open an account. (Leaving aside for the moment that, in those years when capital controls existed in leading market economies as well, it would have been hard for him to do so, since he would not have been able to provide a local address and an ID.) Asking someone else to do it for him would have been dangerous, too, opening him up to the possibility of blackmail but also of political downfall if such activity were revealed to the "competent organs." Finally, my argument went, even if he had somehow overcome all these obstacles, I just could not see how he could technically buy an apartment abroad, as he most certainly did not know anything about where to get information about the apartments for sale, their prices, or how to do the required legal paperwork. (He surely could not hire a foreign lawyer.) Note that even officials in noncommunist countries that were not an integral part of the capitalist world (India, Turkey) often lacked knowledge and contacts to transfer money abroad.

The inability to do anything meaningful with illicitly earned money surely made engaging in corrupt activities much less attractive. Thus it is not only that opportunities to make money through corruption were fewer in less "integrated" countries, but perhaps equally important, the ability to use illegally obtained money to acquire desirable things was much more limited. It is unclear what corrupt officials from a nonintegrated country could do with that money. We saw that they would not be able to buy a foreign apartment, or even to transfer money abroad. They certainly could not dream of retiring to the French Riviera, either. Or, say that they wanted to use such black money to finance foreign education for their children. This was impossible, too, because sending children to capitalist countries for education was seen as a betrayal of socialism and socialist education. Any official of a communist country whose children were sent to the United States for education (other than during the time of his foreign posting) would have been promptly demoted and investigated as to the origin of the funds. In other words, the official would have to be prepared to go to prison. It is thus not surprising that only private entrepreneurs (who had to be sufficiently rich), or people who were somewhat independent from political power (say, doctors or engineers) and had relatives abroad could even imagine providing a foreign education to their children.

This difference between countries that were integrated into the capitalist system and those that were not (as well as between millionaires and "ordinary" people) struck me very strongly when I read an autobiographical article by José Piñera, son of one of the richest men in Chile and himself later, under Augusto Pinochet, minister of labor and social security.[30] He somewhat nonchalantly mentioned how he attended Harvard. I found this nonchalance, as in many similar cases that I have observed among rich people, mostly from Latin America, extraordinary. Leaving aside how someone who is not a son of a very rich person would get into one of the exclusive prep schools that serve as feeders for top universities, practice expensive sports, or find the time to pursue unusual activities (parachuting, playing in an orchestra) that might help him or her qualify for Harvard or similar top schools, the money necessary for tuition and daily expenses is such that no one living in a non-English-speaking country with a middling level of income and moderate inequality and without convertible currency could even entertain the idea of studying at Harvard. Of course, I have here in mind the situation as it existed in the 1960s and 1970s (when indeed Piñera studied abroad).

In a nonintegrated world, which would later, after it became integrated, provide through Russia and China the bulk of international corruption, corruption was thus limited in a systemic fashion.

The second ground for believing that corruption has been increasing has to do with the enabling framework. I have already touched upon it by showing how currency controls, which were common across the world including in advanced economies, as well as nonconvertible currencies, limited the ability to transfer money abroad. In addition, there was not much of a framework in place to enable corruption in countries that were potential recipients of money.

Enablers of worldwide corruption in recipient countries

The growth of banks that specialize in high-net-worth individuals and of legal offices whose main role is to facilitate transfers of illegally acquired money happened in tandem with globalization. Greater opportunities for corruption, or in this case an increased "supply" of parties interested in hiding or investing their money abroad, called forth greater "demand" for such funds, as reflected in the creation of new occupations that specialize in helping illegally acquired money find a new home. It is thus no accident that supply and demand grew jointly and that growth of the enabling banking and legal sectors was stimulated by capital flight out of Russia and China. According to Novokmet, Piketty, and Zucman (2017), about half of Russian capital is held abroad, courtesy of foreign enablers, and much of it is used to invest in Russian company shares. This finding highlights one of the novel aspects of globalization, where domestic capital is held offshore to benefit from lower taxes and better property protection, but is then invested in the country of origin in the guise of foreign investment to benefit from better conditions afforded to foreign investors—and also to exploit local connections, including language, customs, and knowledge of whom and how to bribe. The Russian case is just an extreme instance of this general phenomenon; another example is that about 40 percent of Indian foreign investments come from Mauritius (the largest investor in India!) and Singapore.[31] These funds are, of course, just camouflaged Indian funds, many illegally acquired domestically and then transferred overseas, whence they re-emerge in India as "foreign investments." This is something that would have been as difficult to imagine in the India of the 1970s as in the Soviet Union of the same era, but that has become a somewhat banal technique in the age of globalization.

Here one needs to consider more carefully the enabling role of the global financial centers and tax havens. The latter have been extensively discussed—especially those in Switzerland and Luxembourg—by Gabriel Zucman in *The Hidden Wealth of Nations* (2015). The role of tax havens has also been starkly documented by the release of the Panama Papers and the Paradise Papers, and in Brooke Harrington's book *Capital without Borders* (2016). But the role of large financial centers like London, New York, and Singapore has attracted less attention. Without the creation of entire batteries of banking and legal services to serve and help it, corruption on a global scale would not have been possible. The domestic theft of money is meaningful only if that money can be internationally laundered, and this requires the support of the main global financial centers. These financial centers have thus worked directly against the establishment, or reinforcement, of the rule of law in Russia, China, Ukraine, Angola, Nigeria, and elsewhere—simply because they are the main beneficiaries of those countries' lawlessness. They have provided a safe haven for all stolen assets. It is ironic that areas with good rule of law (and, of course, where there is indifference as to how foreign money has been acquired) have been the greatest enablers of worldwide corruption. They have been instrumental in laundering stolen money at much greater rates than any traditional money-laundering business (such as opening a loss-making restaurant or movie house) could have achieved.

Next to that apparatus of banks and law offices stand universities, think tanks, NGOs, art galleries, and other worthy causes. While banks have been engaged in financial laundering, these organizations have offered what we might call "moral" money laundering. They do so by providing safe havens where corrupt individuals, by donating a small portion of their stolen assets, can present themselves as socially responsible businesspeople, establish important contacts, and gain entry into the more rarified social circles of the countries where they have transferred their money.[32] A good example is the Russian businessman Mikhail Khodorkovsky, who, thanks to his political connections in Russia, bought assets at a fraction of their value, allegedly misappropriated an estimated $4.4 billion of government funds, and then destroyed the evidence by running a truck into a river.[33] Khodorkovsky and others like him have now reemerged as "responsible donors" in the West. Khodorkovsky deserves special mention because he was an innovator in the art of moral laundering. He realized early on (as early as the turn of the twenty-first century) that to help both his worldwide and Russian businesses, the most profitable investment he could make would be to offer campaign contributions to American politicians and make donations to Washington think tanks. The approach has since become more common.

Although for Khodorkovsky himself the strategy did not work well (he was arrested and jailed by Putin), in the era of globalization, where many key decisions are made in political centers like Washington or Brussels, this strategy is probably correct in the long term. Other foreign businesses, not least Saudi ones, have adopted the same approach. Some other oligarchs—for example, Leonid Blavatnik, who made his fortune during the "Wild East" years of privatization in the Russia of the 1990s—thought that investing in an eponymous business school or art gallery might work better than making campaign contributions as a means of moral laundering.[34] In a private communication, an administrator at a university in India mentioned to me that it is very difficult to get donations from the Indian super-rich, even though they give tens of millions of dollars to Ivy League universities. This is, he said, because they want to look like they are good citizens in the United States when legislators start to ask awkward questions about the number of Indian visa workers they employ instead of Americans. They would not get a comparable benefit from donating to an Indian university.

Imitation of the consumption pattern of rich countries

The third reason for increased corruption in the era of globalization is the demonstration effect, otherwise known as keeping up with the Joneses. Now, the demonstration effect is not a new phenomenon. The structuralists in Latin

America have been arguing since the 1960s that one of the reasons why the savings rate in Latin American countries is low is that the rich are unwilling to save lest their consumption pattern be seen as falling below that of their (richer) North American counterparts. Thorstein Veblen made a similar point in his writings about conspicuous consumption of luxury goods—that the wastefulness of consumption deflected the funds from more productive uses, but that wastefulness itself was the objective sought after.[35] Much further back, Machiavelli zeroed in on the same idea, namely, that relations with richer neighbors stimulate corruption:

> The goodness is the more to be admired in these days in that it is so rare. Indeed, it seems to survive only in this [German] province. This is due to two things. In the first place the towns have but little intercourse with their neighbors, who seldom go to visit them, or are visited by them, since they are content with the goods, live on the food, and are clothed with the wool which they produce. The occasion for intercourse, and with it the initial step on the road to corruption, is thus removed, since they have no chance of taking up customs either of the French, the Spaniards or the Italian, nations which, taken together, are the source of world-wide corruption (1983, book 1:55, p. 245).

The contribution of the structuralists was that they saw imitation of rich people's consumption patterns crossing national borders. In that sense, the structuralists were precursors of the demonstration effect during globalization. But today, the demonstration effect, I argue, not only feeds into greater consumption but also motivates corruption—that is, it elicits the need for higher income regardless of its legality.

One important facet of globalization is that people have much better knowledge than they did in the past of ways of life in places far from where they live. Another is more frequent interactions and work collaborations with people from different countries. When people with similar levels of education and ability work together but come from different countries and receive different incomes per unit of skill, the outcome, whether we put it under the heading of envy, jealousy, or fair pay, or a just resentment of inequity, is that people from poor countries, not unreasonably, feel cheated and think that they deserve the same income. This realization is especially strong where people work closely together and are able to find out directly what their skills are and also how differently they are paid. Perhaps nowhere is this more obvious than in the case of government officials from poor or middle-income countries who are often badly paid and yet, in their various capacities in ministries (development, finance, energy, and so on), interact with rich foreign businesspeople and bureaucrats.[36]

The feeling of what to these individuals from poorer countries seems to be injustice provides internal justification for bribe-taking, since the bribe is then seen merely as compensation for an unfairly low salary, or even for the unfair lot of having been born in a poor country and having to work there. It is indeed very challenging for those who have to make decisions on contracts worth dozens or hundreds of millions of dollars while being paid only several hundred dollars per month and, in addition, interacting with people who are paid several thousands of dollars per day, to remain supine in the face of such income differences. It is absolutely unexceptional that in such a situation, corruption would be seen as a step toward the leveling of life injustices. (Some might say that civil servants should properly compare their lot with much poorer people from their own countries. But this is not realistic: we all tend to compare our position with that of our peers, and in this case, the peers—people with whom they often interact—are foreigners.)

The role played by differential pay for identical work, and the effect that it has on corruption, is also easy to see in the case of native citizens from poorer countries who work in their own countries while being paid by international organizations. Whether they take government positions (subsidized by foreign donors) or work in universities, think tanks, or NGOs, their salaries exceed by an order of magnitude those of their fellow citizens who are paid at domestic rates. It is not surprising that such foreign-paid but locally born bureaucrats and academics rarely engage in corruption: they are paid very well and have their own international reputations to worry about. But it is also unsurprising that the much higher salaries they earn for the same job are discouraging and enervating for domestically paid civil servants, and that the latter may complement their income through bribery.

If one disregards this aspect (working on the same job alongside people who are paid many times more), it is very easy to blame local culture for corruption. The reality is more complex: corruption is seen as an income that is, in some sense, owed to those who are born with a citizenship penalty. Migration is, as we have seen, one of the ways to convert one's citizenship penalty into premium; corruption is just another.[37]

4.4b Why Almost Nothing Will Be Done to Control Corruption

How, then, should we deal with corruption at this time of hypercommercialized global capitalism? It is worth going back to the three grounds for increased corruption that I identified at the outset of this section. The first, ideological, comes from the very nature of the system that places money-making of any kind at the pedestal of its values. Incentives for corruption are inherent in the system, and there is nothing one can do, short of changing the system of values, to affect it.

The second ground, the enabling of corruption, is linked with the openness of capital accounts and the battery of services, located either in rich countries or in tax havens, whose main objective is to attract thieves from poorer countries or tax evaders from rich countries by promising them, respectively, immunity from legal pursuit if they bring their money to the countries where the rule of law holds, or shelter from taxes. Here there are lots of things that can be done. Cracking down on tax havens would be relatively easy if important countries that themselves are big losers because their own citizens evade taxes decided to do so. Some recent examples show that big countries, if and when they decide to act, have the power to crack down on corruption: the United States successfully challenged Swiss banking secrecy laws, the European Union ruled against zero corporate tax rates in Ireland and Luxembourg, Germany took severe measures against tax evasion encouraged by Lichtenstein, and the British parliament required that wealth registers be introduced in British-ruled tax havens like the Cayman Islands and the British Virgin Islands. But these kinds of efforts would keep in check only one part of corruption—that which affects the rich countries themselves, which are losing income because of the tax evasion of their citizens.

It is much more difficult to deal with the other aspect of corruption in which rich countries are direct beneficiaries, that is, where their banking and legal systems encourage corruption in poor countries by promising immunity from prosecution. In that case, the policies of the rich countries will have to be directed against strong vested interests within their own nations: bankers and lawyers who directly profit from corruption; real estate agents and developers who make money off corrupt foreigners; and politicians, universities, NGOs, and think tanks that participate in moral money laundering. Simply listing all of the groups that have an interest in the continuation of Third World corruption is sufficient to give us pause as to the likelihood that any serious anticorruption measures will be effected.

The situation with this type of corruption is similar to the situation encountered in the drug trade and prostitution. Attempts to remedy corruption and to reduce drug use and prostitution target the supply side only—by telling countries like Ukraine and Nigeria to control their corruption, Colombia and Afghanistan to cut their production of cocaine, or sex workers to change professions. In none of these areas is the policy directed toward the demand side, that is, against the beneficiaries of corruption in rich countries, against the consumers of drugs in Europe and the United States, or against the users of sex workers' services. The reason why this is so is not that the antisupply approach is more efficient; in fact, there are strong arguments that it is less efficient. The reason is that going after the demand side is politically much more difficult. One must therefore be skeptical that this political calculus, as far as corruption is concerned, will change any time soon.

The last ground for globalization-related corruption is the demonstration effect. It is also very hard to see how that could change, since very large, and broadly known, income differences among countries (and thus the existence of large citizenship premiums or penalties) will persist for the foreseeable future, while collaborations between people from different countries who are paid different amounts for the same job will become even more common. If anything, we can expect this kind of self-justificatory corruption to increase.

Combating the type of corruption that directly affects powerful countries through their loss of tax revenues can be expected to garner sufficient political support, and perhaps such corruption may be reduced. All of the others are hardwired into the type of globalization that we have; we should become used to increased corruption and treat it as a logical (almost normal) source of income in the age of globalization. By its very nature it will never become legal—except possibly in some of its manifestations like political lobbying—but it has already become normalized, and it will become even more so. We should also recognize our hypocrisy and stop moralizing about corruption and browbeating poor countries: many people in rich countries benefit from corruption, and the type of globalization that we have makes this inevitable.

CHAPTER 5

THE FUTURE OF GLOBAL CAPITALISM

With mortals, gold outweighs a thousand arguments.

—Euripides, *Medea*

5.1 The Inevitable Amorality of Hypercommercialized Capitalism

5.1a Max Weber's Capitalism

Capitalism has a side of lightness and a side of darkness.

Observations about the bright side go back at least to Montesquieu's "doux commerce" and are echoed, in similar form, by authors as different as Adam Smith, Joseph Schumpeter, Friedrich Hayek, and John Rawls.[1] The general idea is that because in commercial societies success (that is, money-making) depends on pleasing others, offering them something they are willing to buy or trade for, the trait of niceness pervades all human behavior and spreads from business deals into personal interactions. The light side, the "adoucissement des moeurs" (softening of manners), becomes even stronger with the commodification of people's ordinary lives. In developed capitalist societies, many of our daily transactions do have an ulterior, mercenary motive. And while this is something that at times empties such transactions of their traditional meaning (and thus might present

176

the dark side of commercialized societies), it also makes us behave toward others with consideration and respect. As the sphere of transactionary relations expands, so does the sphere of niceness—compromise and awareness of other people's preferences and interests. In a commercialized society, we are interdependent: we cannot satisfy our interests without also satisfying those of other people. Adam Smith's baker cannot sell his loaf of bread unless he convinces his customer that it is better than other loaves. All of this makes us more polite and cognizant of other people and their needs.

Purely commercial societies are by definition societies where hierarchies, or distinctions among people, are not based on extra-economic criteria like one's family background or membership in a social order (e.g., the aristocracy or clergy), or even the type of work one does (which, for example, in Hinduism is used to stratify the population). Hierarchy is based simply on monetary success, and such success is in principle open to everyone. As I argued in Chapter 2, it is not equally open to everyone in practice, but ideologically it is. Nothing would disqualify those who started at the bottom of the social pyramid and had managed to become rich from receiving as much respect from their peers as if they had started in the middle or at the top. They might even receive more recognition because of the difficulties they had overcome. Money is a great equalizer, and commercial societies provide the best examples of its power.

The gradual equalization of opportunity for people of different genders, sexual preferences, disabilities, and races additionally makes it possible for members of these formerly disadvantaged groups to attain top positions. Even more important for our purposes, these individuals do not carry over any stigma from their earlier disadvantaged position: once they have become rich they are as good as anyone else. This, I think, is at its most obvious in the United States, where it is sometimes said that wealth acts as a form of cleansing. Money "launders" all previous "sins."

When hierarchy is determined only by wealth, it naturally leads people to focus on acquiring wealth. As Rawls writes: "The social system shapes the wants and aspirations that its citizens come to have. It determines in part the sort of persons they want to be as well as the sort of persons they are" (1971, 229). Systematic rational pursuit of wealth has been, since Max Weber defined it as such, one of the key sociological characteristics of capitalism. Even the "pursuit of happiness," a famous addition to the US Declaration of Independence (which Jefferson introduced in place of property in the more common expression "life, liberty, and the protection of property"), could be seen as a call to the untrammeled pursuit of wealth—untrammeled by the old-fashioned feudal entrapments of rank and birth—because wealth is, not unreasonably, seen as a proxy (or a key requirement) for happiness.[2] That such a pursuit of wealth would dissolve the extra-economic hierarchy among people was noticed early on by Adam Smith in *The Theory of Moral Sentiments*. Smith also noted, in the same work, that there is a danger that this single-minded pursuit of wealth might end in encouragement of amoral behavior. This is why Smith vehemently, but not altogether persuasively, disagreed with Bernard Mandeville's view of economics, aptly summarized in the title of his book as "private vices, publick benefits"—without denying that the system of "Dr. Mandeville . . . in some respects bordered upon the truth."[3]

And this leads us to the dark side.

For in reality, Mandeville noticed very early on and very well what was the distinguishing feature of the new commercialized societies. Success de-

"*Private vices, public virtue*"

pended on stimulating in individuals the most selfish and greedy behavior—behavior that was "mollified" and concealed through the need to be pleasant to others, but which tended to produce falsehood and hypocrisy. Thus greed and hypocrisy went hand in hand. Smith saw the danger, worrying that such a literal reading of the spirit of capitalism might lead to moral turpitude or moral equivalence regarding the way wealth is acquired—which for a moral philosopher like Smith was abhorrent. He tried to disprove Mandeville. But I am not sure he succeeded—not only because he lacked good arguments, but because (I think) Smith himself, at least when he was wearing his economist's hat in *The Wealth of Nations,* did not entirely believe that Mandeville's key insight was erroneous (see also the discussion in Appendix B).[4]

For Marx, greed is the product of a "particular social development"; it is historical, not natural. It is inextricably linked with the existence of money. The remarkable paragraph from *Grundrisse* in which Marx defines greed as "abstract hedonism" is worth quoting in full:

Greed as such, as a particular form of a drive, i.e., as distinct from a craving for a particular form of wealth, e.g. for clothes, weapons, jewels, women, wine is possible only when general wealth . . . has become individualized in a particular thing . . . money. Money is therefore not only the object but the fountainhead of greed. The mania for possession is possible without money; but greed itself is a product of a particular social development, not natural, as opposed to historical. . . . Hedonism in its general form and miserliness are the two particular forms of monetary greed. Hedonism in the abstract presupposed an object which possesses all pleasures in potentiality. Abstract hedonism realizes that function of money in which it is the material representative of wealth. . . . In order to maintain it as such, it must sacrifice all relationship to the objects of particular needs, must abstain, in order to satisfy the need of greed for money as such. (Marx 1973, 222–223)

There is little doubt, I think, that Marx would regard greed as a necessary concomitant of the increasing commodification of life.

An alternative that would preserve the acquisitive spirit needed for the flourishing of commercialized societies but would keep that spirit in check was to internalize certain forms of acceptable behavior through religion. This is why Protestantism, in Weber's reading of it, not only was correlated with capitalist success but was indispensable for maintaining the otherwise incomprehensible efforts of capitalists (their working and acquiring wealth without consuming it), the decorum of the upper classes, and the acceptance of unequal outcomes by the masses.[5] It eschewed ostentation and the crude behavior that characterized earlier elites. It was austere: it limited the consumption of the elites and imposed bounds on how much wealth was to be displayed. It internalized the sumptuary laws of the past.[6] As John Maynard Keynes observed in *The Economic Consequences of the Peace* (1919), nineteenth-century capitalism in Britain ensured sufficient popular acceptance of the landlord-capitalist-worker hierarchy that the society did not explode in a revolution of the kind that engulfed, one after another, feudal societies in France, China, Russia, the Habsburg Empire, and the Ottoman Empire.[7] As long as capitalists used most of their surplus income to invest rather than to consume, the social contract held.[8] The internalization of desirable behavior, that behavior which, in John

Rawls's words, reaffirms in its daily actions the main beliefs of a society, was possible thanks to the constraints of religion and the tacit social contract. It is not clear if societies so dedicated to the acquisition of wealth, by practically any means, would not explode into chaos were it not for these constraints.[9]

5.1b Outsourcing Morality

Neither of these two constraints (religion and a tacit social contract) holds in today's globalized capitalism.

It is not the objective of this book to explain why the world has become less religious, at least as far as economic behavior is concerned, nor do I have enough knowledge to do so. But there is no doubt that it has. In most advanced countries, attendance at Christian churches has fallen steadily, and the number of people who say they have no religion has increased.[10] This is not to say that attendance at church would itself guarantee ethical behavior, not least because religions today say relatively little about what constitutes correct economic behavior. Some ministers, such as Billy Graham, even extol greed as a virtue.[11] The American preacher Pat Robertson remarked in the wake of the gruesome murder of the Saudi journalist Jamal Khashoggi in 2018 that one should not be too tough on the Saudi regime (the presumed murderers) because "we've got an arms deal that everybody wanted a piece of . . . it'll be a lot of jobs, a lot of money coming to our coffers. It's not something you want to blow up willy-nilly."[12] This example is so extreme because the call to ignore murder is made on behalf of greater earnings from the sale of weapons. But it is representative of a religion that places money-making, by any means, among its top values.

It is difficult to see how, even theoretically, the constraints of religion and a social contract would work in a globalized setting, not only because religions are diverse and many have internalized the objectives of hyper-commercialized capitalism, but also because individuals are unmoored from their social settings.

Our actions are no longer "monitored" by the people among whom we live. Adam Smith's baker's immoral business actions would have been observed by his neighbors. But the immoral actions of people who work in one place and live in an entirely different one—with the world of coworkers and that of neighbors and friends never interacting—are unobservable. In his book *Capital: The Eruption of Delhi* (2015), Rana Dasgupta tells the story of a respectable Indian-born doctor who lives in a middle-class neighborhood in Toronto, complete with a nice garden and a two-car garage—but whose main income comes from overseeing the forcible harvesting of organs from poor slum dwellers living thousands of miles away near Delhi. The doctor can be seen as an upstanding member of the community, quite rightly, from what his neighbors know of him, while in reality he is a criminal.

As the internal mechanisms of constraint have atrophied or died or do not work in a globalized setting, they have been replaced by external constraints, in the form of rules and laws. I do not mean that laws did not exist before. But while internalized constraints on behavior mattered, both laws and self-imposed limits affected people's behavior. The present situation is characterized by the disappearance of the latter. In cases where we cannot expect the rich to behave ethically or with sufficient discretion so as not to inflame the passions in those who have less, reinforcement of laws is obviously a good thing.[13] In a 2017 lecture, the political historian Pierre Rosenvallon proposed that countries should introduce a modernized version of sumptuary laws that would either heavily tax or ban certain types of behavior and consumption. The problem is that instead of two handrails to help keep the actions of the rich (or anyone, for that matter) on the right path, we now have only one—laws. Morality, having been gutted out internally, has become fully externalized. It has been outsourced from ourselves to society at large.

The drawback of outsourcing morality is that it exacerbates the original problem of the absence of internal inhibitions or constraints. Everyone either will try to walk the fine line between legality and illegality (doing things that are unethical but technically legal) or will break the law while trying not

> *No internalized rules of conduct*

to be caught. Breaking the law is not unique to today's commercialized societies. But what is unique is for people to claim that they have done everything in the most ethical manner possible if they have remained just barely on the right side of the law, or, if they have strayed into illegality, that it is the business of others to catch them and prove they have broken the law. Internal checks, stemming from one's own belief in what is moral and what is not, seem to play no role whatsoever.

This is perhaps most obvious in commercialized sports, where the old-fashioned notions of fair play, which internalized acceptable conduct, have all but disappeared and have been replaced by behavior that in some cases openly breaks the rules. Such behavior is fully accepted and even encouraged, since people believe that it is up to the referees alone to enforce the rules. Take the 2009 example of the famous soccer goal marked by hand by Thierry Henry, which allowed the French national team to qualify for the World Cup and sent the Irish team home. No one, from Henry to the last French supporter, denies that the goal was scored by hand, that it was illegal, and that it should not have been allowed to stand. But they would not draw the obvious consequences. In everyone's opinion the matter was not to be decided by Henry (say, by his telling the referee that the goal was illegal) or by his teammates (doing the same thing), but solely by the referee. Once the referee, not having seen how the goal was scored, has accepted it, the goal is as legal as can be, and there is no shame in celebrating it. Or even bragging about it.

The conflict between what is legal and what is ethical is nicely illustrated in a story told by Cicero, and recently retold by Nassim Taleb in *Skin in the Game* (2018). It concerns Diogenes of Babylon and his pupil Antipater of Tarsus, who disagreed on the following matter: Should the merchant who is bringing grain to Rhodes at a time of scarcity and high prices reveal that another ship from Alexandria, also carrying grain, is just about to arrive in Rhodes? From a purely legal point of view, defended by Diogenes, it is fully acceptable not to reveal private information—moreover, information that no one could prove the person possessed. But from an ethical point of view, defended by Antipater, it is not. There is, I think, little doubt that the former position would be taken by everyone in today's business world. Even if they might verbally claim that they would follow Antipater, they would in fact behave like Diogenes. And behavior is all that counts, not what we say about how we would have behaved.

Outsourcing morality through reliance solely on the law or on rule enforcers means that everyone tries to game the system. Any laws that are introduced to punish new forms of unethical or amoral behavior will always stay one step behind those who are able to find ways around them. Financial deregulation and tax evasion provide excellent examples. There is no internal moral rule, as we have amply seen, that would check the behavior of top banks and hedge funds, or of companies like Apple, Amazon, and Starbucks, when it comes to tax evasion or tax avoidance; or that of the rich, who hide their wealth from tax authorities, in part legally and in part illegally, in the Caribbean or the Channel Islands. Their objective is to play the game as close to the rules as possible, and if the rules need to be bent or ignored, to try to avoid being caught. And if caught, to try, by using a phalanx of lawyers, to find the most recondite and specious explanations for this behavior. And if that fails, then to settle.

Financial settlements spread amorality further afield: the aggrieved party has to choose between, on the one hand, the pleasure of righteous anger and satisfaction in punishing the villain, and, on the other hand, swallowing their pride and accepting a monetary compensation that makes them to some extent accomplices in the wrongful behavior. This is the standard procedure whereby those accused of sexual harassment, tax evasion, unlawful lobbying, and a number of other crimes "solve" their problems— that is, if they ever get to the stage where some form of punishment threatens to be exacted. Buying off the injured party, often by buying their silence, is an option that is difficult for those to whom it is offered to reject. For what is the choice: moral satisfaction that within days will be forgotten, or having more money? Moreover, settling is not socially frowned upon: it is regarded as a rational move, as we would expect in a commercialized society.

I have met people who have gladly accepted being "fired"—whether because they created problems for their employer or were too visible to be dismissed outright—with the provision that they would be paid off handsomely and would never reveal the details of the deal. There are few things more annoying than when a friend tells an obvious lie about the reasons why and conditions under which he left his job; yet he has no choice but to lie because the settlement requires him to be mum about what happened. Or when a person writes an entire book savaging one institution but not another very similar one for which she worked, because she was paid a settlement that forbade her from discussing anything regarding her previous job.

But it is wrong to criticize such behavior in soccer players, banks, hedge funds, rich individuals, or even ourselves by claiming that those who engage in it are morally defective. What people making such a critique fail to see is that they are criticizing the symptom and not the disease. In reality, such amoral behavior is necessary for survival in a world where everyone is trying to acquire as much money as possible and to climb higher in the social pyramid. Any alternative behavior seems self-defeating.

When money becomes established as the sole criterion by which success is judged (as is the case in hypercommercialized societies), other hierarchical markers vanish (which is in general a good thing), but the society also sends the message that "being rich is glorious," and that the means used to achieve glory are largely immaterial—as long as one is not caught doing something illegal. Thus, criticizing the rich or the banks for what they are doing is futile and naïve. Futile because they will not change their behavior, since doing so would risk losing their wealth. Naïve because the origin of the problem is systemic and not individual. A bank might become a most ethical and careful actor, but it would then lose the commercial race with its competitors. Soon its financial results would worsen, nobody would want to buy its shares, its best people would leave for jobs elsewhere, and it would ultimately go bankrupt. The bank's shareholders, who in their ordinary lives might see themselves as the most ethical people, would nevertheless sell their shares or try to change the management of the bank.

It is, of course, possible to impose strong ethical constraints on oneself, but only if one plans to drop out of society, or move to some tiny community outside the globalized and commercialized world. Anyone who remains inside the globalized and commercialized world has to fight for survival using the same means and the same (amoral) tools as everyone else.

5.1c "There Is No Alternative"

One might agree with the analysis so far and then argue as follows: Isn't this state of affairs a plea for change in the socioeconomic system? Doesn't it follow that we should ditch the world of hypercommercialized capitalism in favor of an alternative system? The problem with this otherwise sensible argument is that we lack any viable alternative to hypercommercialized capitalism. The alternatives the world has tried have proved worse—some of them much worse. On top of that, discarding the competitive and acquisitive spirit that is hardwired into capitalism would lead to a decline in our incomes, increased poverty, deceleration or reversion of technological progress, and the loss of other advantages (such as goods and services that have become an integral part of our lives) that hypercommercialized capitalism provides. One cannot hope to maintain these while destroying the acquisitive spirit or dislodging wealth as the sole marker of success. They go together. This may be, perhaps, one of the key features of the human condition: that we cannot improve our material way of life without giving full play to some of the most unpleasant traits of our nature. This is, in essence, the truth that Bernard Mandeville gleaned more than three hundred years ago.

The attempt to come up with a viable alternative is where many of the recent proposals to mitigate the supposed dark features of commercialized capitalism err. The idea that more leisure would make our world a better place is one of these seemingly reasonable but utterly wrong ideas (see Raworth 2018; Bregman 2017). It assumes that if somehow we could convince a sufficient number of people that they would be better off by working less, the hypercompetitive features of capitalism would be remedied. We

> *Withdrawing from the system is not a realistic option*

would live lives of pleasure, visiting art exhibits and sitting in cafés discussing the most recent theatrical productions. But people who decided to follow this more relaxed way of life would soon run out of money to pursue it (unless they had a sufficient amount of previously acquired wealth). Their children would be angry at them for preferring to lead lives of leisure and idleness rather than making sure that the children had all the gadgets that their peers enjoyed and attended the best and most expensive schools. This is why parents cannot stop climbing ever higher and trying to transmit to their children all the privileges that, as we saw in Chapter 2, lead to the creation of a self-perpetuating upper class in liberal capitalism. This is why Barack Obama, despite all of the rhetorical embellishments about public education in his speeches, sent both of his daughters to an elite private high school and later to the most expensive private universities. Again, we find that a life of leisure is possible only for those who have inherited significant wealth or are willing to retire to communities that are self-contained and largely self-sufficient. Withdrawals from hypercommercialized capitalism are indeed possible, but we can be assured that they will remain very rare.

Let us imagine that those who argue for a gentler alternative somehow succeed in convincing an entire nation to change its ways. For example, residents of a rich country in Europe might decide that the level of welfare they enjoy now is exactly sufficient and that it can be maintained thanks to technological progress with a much smaller labor input. They might decide to work only fifteen hours per week, the number of hours that John Maynard Keynes, in "The Economic Possibilities for Our Grandchildren" (1930), believed would be sufficient to "satisfy old Adam in most of us." But very soon such a country and its population would discover that they had been overtaken by others. Perhaps, happy in their comfortable lifestyle, they would not worry too much about global economic rankings at first. But people from more successful and increasingly rich countries would start buying properties in that country, moving to the most attractive locations, eating in the best restaurants, and gradually displacing the local population. That this is not a fantasy can be seen in today's Italy. Cities like Venice and Florence may, in some not too distant future, be almost entirely peopled by rich members of other nationalities, whether German, American, or Chinese. (This is already largely the case in central Venice and parts of Tuscany.) In a fully globalized and commercialized world, if Italian incomes continued to fall relative to incomes in other countries and regions, the beauty of Italy would no longer be enjoyed by its original inhabitants. And there is no reason why it should be. Everything has a price in a commercialized world. If a Chinese person can pay more for a view of the Grand Canal than its current Italian owner can, he or she should have access to that view.

We thus reach the conclusion again that the only way to defy the commercialized world is by withdrawing from it altogether, either through personal exile in a secluded community, or, in the case of larger groups like nations, by embracing autarky. But it is an impossible task to convince sufficiently large numbers of people to withdraw from this world, give up on the amenities of commercialization, and accept a much lower standard of living, if they have been socialized in the acquisitive spirit and have internalized all of its goals. There are some communities, such as the Pennsylvania Dutch and Israeli kibbutzim (both of which are in decline), that may not be enervated by the presence of much greater wealth in their neighborhood, but very few other groups evince an urgent desire to imitate them.

People who write about the need for more leisure do not realize that societies the world over are structured in such a way as to glorify success and power, that success and power in a commercialized society are expressed in money only, and that money is obtained through work, ownership of assets, and, not least, corruption. This is also why corruption is an integral component of globalized capitalism.

5.2 Atomization and Commodification

5.2a Decreased Usefulness of Family

Modern capitalist societies include two features that represent two sides of the same coin: (a) atomization and (b) commodification.

Atomization refers to the fact that families have largely lost their economic advantage as an increasing number of goods and services that used to be produced at home, outside the market and not subject to pecuniary exchange, can now be purchased or rented on the market. Activities like preparing food, cleaning, gardening, and taking care of babies and sick and elderly people were provided "free" at home in traditional societies and, until very recently, in modern societies (unless one was very rich). It was certainly one of the main reasons marriage existed at all. But with increasing wealth we can purchase almost all of these services externally, and we have less and less of a need to share our lives with others. It is not an accident that the richest societies today tend toward a family size of one. Norway,

Denmark, and Sweden are already almost there, with average household sizes between 2.2 and 2.4. In contrast, the poorest societies in central Africa have an average household size of 8 or 9.[14] It is not necessarily because people in poorer countries love being together, but because they cannot afford to live alone. Living together "internalizes" these activities (cooking, cleaning, and so on) and also provides economies of scale in everything from cooking oil to electricity (that is, utilities and cooking expenses are lower for two people living together than for each of them living alone multiplied by two).[15] But in rich societies, all of these activities can now be outsourced. Taken to a dystopian conclusion, the world would consist of individuals living and often working alone (other than for the period when they are taking care of children), who would have no permanent links or relations to other people and whose needs would all be supplied by markets, in the same way that most people today do not make their own shoes but buy them in a store. There is similarly no reason why anyone (except for the very poorest) would have to wash their own dishes or prepare their own food.

Atomization (which, taken to the extreme, implies the end of the family) is also accelerated by growing legal intrusions into family life. The reason

Legal intrusion into family life furthers atomization

why the family has been the unit that takes care of the old and the young, and exchanges goods and services among its members regardless of who is a net "winner" or "loser," is because the rules existing within families are different from those holding outside. The family and the rest of the world are, in a moral and even physical sense, two distinct worlds (or rather, used to be two distinct worlds). In Rana Dasgupta's (2015) book about modern Delhi, this moral and physical duality is illustrated by the cloistered life that mothers and grandmothers lead (and expect from their daughters-in-law) and whose objective is to minimize contact with anyone who is not a member of the family. Physically, the division between the two worlds is expressed in changing shoes several times before entering the home, lest some particle of the outside world (dust? grass?) might penetrate the sanctum of the home.

While this extreme separation between family and nonfamily might seem bizarre to many today, it was something that most societies in the world entertained until recently. And it was only because of such a separation between "us" and "them" that many home activities—both chores and pleasures—could be shared by members of the household. In other words, sharing was predicated on excluding.[16]

Today's commercialized model lies at the other extreme. The external world is allowed to break inside not only in the form of the delivery of dinners and cleaning services but also in the form of legal intrusion. These intrusions—such as prenuptial agreements, and the ability of the courts to take away children and to control the behavior of spouses toward each other—while in many cases desirable developments (e.g., in preventing spousal abuse), further hollow out the internal tacit compact that held families together. This legal intrusion of society into family life is just another instance of outsourcing. The internal family "legal code" is simply outsourced to society at large, the same way that cooking a meal is outsourced to the nearby restaurant. Both types of outsourcing cannot but raise the ultimate question: What is the advantage of family or of cohabitation in a rich, commercialized world where every service can be purchased?

One can identify three historical types of interactions between the private and public (economic) spheres. The first is the precapitalist one, where production is carried out within the household. As we saw in Chapter 3, this "household mode of production" was long characteristic of China, all the way into the nineteenth century, when western Europe had already moved to the much more prevalent use of wage labor that defines the second historical type.[17] This second type involves the use of wage labor outside the home (that is, not the putting-out system in which people do piece labor for others inside their own home). It is part of a typical capitalist mode of production with a sharp distinction between the production and family spheres—a distinction that Weber thought was absolutely fundamental for capitalism. Finally, the new hypercommercialized capitalism again unifies production and family but does so by folding the household into the capitalist mode of production. We can see this as a logical outcome in the development of capitalism, as capitalism moves to "conquer" new spheres and to commodify new goods and services. This stage also implies substantial improvements in the productivity of labor because only sufficiently wealthy societies can afford to fully commodify all of the personal relations that have traditionally been left out of the market.

5.2b Private Life as Daily Capitalism

The reverse side of atomization is commodification. In atomization, we become alone because all of our needs can be satisfied by what we buy from others, in the market. In a state of full commodification, we become that

| *Creation of new commodities* |

other: we satisfy the needs of people through maximum commodification of our assets, including our free time.[18]

What global capitalism does is to give us, as consumers, the ability to purchase activities that used to be provided in kind by family, friends, or community. But to us as producers, it also offers a wide field of activities (precisely the same ones) that we can supply to others. Thus, atomization and commodification go together.

The most obvious case is the commodification of activities that used to be conducted within extended families and then, as people became richer, within nuclear families. Cooking has now become outsourced, and families often do not eat meals together. Cleaning, repairs, gardening, and child-rearing have become more commercialized than before or perhaps than ever. Writing homework essays, which used to be "outsourced" to parents, can now be outsourced to commercial companies.

The growth of the gig economy commercializes our free time and things that we own but have not used for commercial purposes before. Uber was created precisely on the idea of making better use of free time. Limousine drivers used to have extra time between jobs; instead of wasting that time, they began to drive people around to make money. Now anybody who has some free time can "sell" it by working for a ride-share company or delivering pizza. A portion of leisure time that we could not commercialize (simply because jobs were "lumpy" and could not be squeezed into very short bits of free time) has become marketable. Likewise, a private car that was "dead capital" becomes real capital if used to drive for Lyft or Uber. Keeping the car idle in a garage or parking lot has a clear opportunity cost. Similarly, homes that in the past might have been lent out for a week without compensation to family and friends have now become assets that are rented out to travelers for a fee. As soon as this happens, such goods become commodities; they acquire a market price. Not using them is a clear waste of resources. Whereas in the past their opportunity cost was zero, now it is positive.

This does not mean that everyone will use every free moment to do a gig, or will rent out their home every day that it is empty. Similarly we do not use every minute of our lives to try to earn money. However, once the opportunity cost of the hitherto free activities becomes positive, we are ultimately led to think of these activities as commercial goods or services. It then requires greater effort of the will to let opportunities go and not succumb to benefiting from them.

Just as there is a logic in the way hypercommercialized capitalism obliterates the divide between the production and family spheres, so is there a certain historical logic in the progression of what becomes commodified. First, agriculture was commodified through the commercialization of surplus production, that is, through a movement out of subsistence agriculture. Then came the commodification of manufacturing activities, especially clothing production. New markets emerged as the goods that had traditionally been produced by households started to be produced commercially. At the origin of the Industrial (and industrious) Revolution in Europe was wage work outside the home and, together with it, the practice of using the wages thus earned to purchase commodities that had previously been produced within the household by these same workers (with productivity much higher under the new system).[19] This is exactly the same process that we observe today with respect to services. The commodification of services, and ultimately of free time, is just an additional logical step on the road to development. Personal services are more difficult to commodify because productivity increases are slower than in the production of goods (so the advantages of commodification are less obvious), and the gains from the division of labor are less: the advantage of a delivered meal compared with a home-cooked one is not as clear as the advantage of buying mass-produced shoes compared with making them at home.

The commodification of what had previously been noncommercial tends to make every person do many jobs and even, as in the renting of apartments, to transform them into daily capitalists. But saying that workers do many jobs is the same thing as saying that workers do not hold durably individual jobs and that the labor market is fully "flexible," with people getting in and out of jobs at a very high rate. As Max Weber remarked, "Irregular work, which the ordinary laborer is often forced to have, is often unavoidable, but always an unwelcome state of transition. A man without a calling thus lacks the systematic, methodical character."[20] In other words, the type of work that is likely to exist in the twenty-first century is not the kind of work that Weber would view as desirable because it lacks a sense of calling, or dedication, to a profession.

Thus workers indeed become, from the point of view of the employers, fully interchangeable "agents." Each one stays in a job for a few weeks or months: everyone is about as good or bad as everyone else. We are coming close to the dream world of neoclassical economics where individuals, with their unique characteristics, no longer exist; they have been replaced by agents—interchangeable avatars that might at most differ in terms of some general characteristic like educational level, age, or sex. Once these characteristics are taken into account, individuals, lacking any personal features, are fully interchangeable.

It thus becomes apparent that these three developments are interrelated: (i) the change in family formation (atomization), (ii) the expansion of commodification to new activities, and (iii) the emergence of fully flexible labor markets with temporary jobs. If we have one, we cannot but have all three.

The problem with this kind of commodification and "flexibilization" is that it undermines the human relations and trust that are needed for the

The downside of commodification market economy to function smoothly. If people stay in the same job for a long period, they try to establish relationships of trust with the people they interact with frequently. That is, they engage in what economists call "repeated games." But if everyone moves from one place to another with high frequency and changes jobs every couple of months, then there are no repeated games because everyone is always interacting with different people. If there are no repeated games, people adjust their behavior to reflect the expectation that they will play just a single game, have a single interaction. And this new behavior is very different.

After being away from New York for a couple of months, I came back to discover that many of the people with whom I thought I was playing repeated games, in restaurants I frequent and in the apartment building where I live, had simply changed. New people had appeared who treated me (understandably) as a complete stranger. When this happens, you do not have much of an incentive to behave "nicely," to send signals of cooperative behavior, because you know that these new people too will soon change. Investing in being nice is costly; the effort it takes is justified by the expectation that this niceness will be reciprocated. But if the person with whom you interact will not be there in a month, what is the point of being nice? It is just a waste of effort. The same reasoning, of course, is made by the other side: why should that person care about you if they are already eyeing their next gig?

The numerous reviews now available of both providers and users of services are a way to try to ensure "niceness" despite the lack of durable relationships. This is indeed an improvement compared to not having any review system. But the system can be gamed. And the point is that in a globalized world with a flexible labor force, durable business relations would be very rare; personal knowledge of the other and responsibility toward that person are replaced by a points system, which, although in some ways providing more information, is impersonal.

Why do we change our behavior when our interactions are commodified? I cannot do better than cite a friend's comment: "Because we are reduced to economic agency, because we cannot think any other way, because being nice is an investment, because the logic of being nice goes beyond market logic." Since commodification has entered our personal sphere, we can think of hardly anything that exists and that is beyond or outside it.[21]

The spread of commodification does away with alienation. In order to be alienated, we need to be aware of a dichotomy between ourselves as ontological beings and ourselves as economic agents. But when economic agency is within ourselves, the order of things is internalized in such a way that there is nothing jarring anymore.

The transformation of ourselves into objects of management and maximization was very well captured by the law professor Daniel Markovits in his address to the 2015 graduating class of Yale Law School: "Your own talents, training and skills—your self-same persons—today constitute your greatest assets, the overwhelmingly dominant source of your wealth and status. . . . [You have had] to act as asset-managers whose portfolio con-tains *yourselves*."[22]

The increasing commodification of many activities along with the rise of the gig economy and of a radically flexible labor market are all part of the same evolution; they should be seen as movements toward a more ra-tional, but ultimately more depersonalized, economy where most interac-tions will be one-off contacts. At some level, as in Montesquieu's "doux commerce," complete commercialization should make people act nicer toward each other. But on the other hand, the shortness of interactions makes investing in cooperative behavior prohibitively expensive. This is why hypercommercialization may not move us toward a society where people act nicer. Niceness is being eroded from two directions: atomization hol-lows out family life, and shortness of interactions reduces the potentially "sweet" behavior praised by Montesquieu. And all of this is taking place against a background of fundamental amorality.

The ultimate success of capitalism is to have transformed human na-ture such that everyone has become an excellent calculator of pain and plea-

People as capitalist centers of production

sure, gain and loss—so much so that even if capitalist fac-tory production were to disappear today we would still be selling each other services for money; eventually we shall become companies ourselves. Imagine an economy (sim-ilar externally to a very primitive one) where all production was conducted at home or within the extended family. This would seem to be a perfect model of an autarkic nonmarket economy. But if we had such an economy today, it would be fully capitalistic because we would be selling all these goods and services to each other: a neighbor will not keep an eye on your children for free, no one will share food with you without payment, you will make your spouse pay for sex, and so forth. This is the world we are moving toward, and the field of capitalistic operations is thus likely to be-come unlimited because it will include each of us and our mostly mundane daily activities. To quote from Paul Mason's book *Postcapitalism* on the capitalism of the new "weightless" economy, "The 'factory' in cognitive capitalism is the whole of society" (2016, 139).

Mason argues that commodification was imposed on us by companies that want to find new sources of profits. But this is wrong. The truth is that we are willingly, even eagerly, participating in commodification because, through long socialization in capitalism, people have become capitalistic calculating machines. We have each become a small center of capitalist production, assigning implicit prices to our time, our emotions, and our family relations.

Other authors also note the increasing commodification that is "descending," as Nancy Fraser puts it, "all the way down" into our personal sphere. They, too, for different reasons than Mason, see commodification as leading to a crisis of capitalism, or even its end: "the result [of commodification] can only be intensified crisis" (Fraser 2012, 10). Fraser does see the good sides of commodification of labor, and indeed criticizes Karl Polanyi for ignoring "the billions of slaves, serfs, peasants, racialized peoples and inhabitants of slums and shanty-towns for whom a wage [marketization of previously unpaid activities] promised liberation from slavery, feudal subjection, racial subordination, social exclusion, and imperial domination, as well as from sexism and patriarchy" (Fraser 2012, 9). Nevertheless, she believes that the current commodification of the personal sphere is an unnatural development that presages the crisis of capitalism.

This view, in my opinion, is wrong. Rather, the exact opposite is true. Commodification "all the way down" is a commodification process in which individuals participate freely, and, moreover, it is something that they often find liberating and meaningful. Some may see this as shallow (Does the ability to drive your own car for profit or to deliver pizza at any hour that suits you give meaning to your life?), but it dovetails perfectly with the system of values that sustains hypercommercialized capitalism and that individuals have internalized. This system, as I mentioned before, places the acquisition of money on a pedestal. The ability to trade one's own personal space and time for profit is thus seen both as a form of empowerment and as a step toward the ultimate objective of acquiring wealth. It therefore represents the triumph of capitalism.[23]

Commodification of the private sphere is the apogee of hypercommercialized capitalism. It does not presage a crisis of capitalism. A crisis would result only if the commodification of the private sphere were seen as intruding into areas that individuals wanted to protect from commercialization, and as putting pressure on them to engage in activities in which they did not want to participate. But most people perceive it as the opposite: a step toward enrichment and freedom.

We can make the following conclusions. First, on a purely factual side, there is no serious argument disputing that as societies grow richer, the sphere of commodification expands.[24]

Second, while greater commodification has made our lives better in many cases and responds to a definite choice by people, it has also often weakened personal ties and sometimes made us more callous, because our knowledge that any pesky little problem can be solved by throwing money at it has made us less concerned about our neighbors and family.

Therefore, as we live in an increasingly commodified environment where interactions are transitory and discrete, the space where we can exercise "nice" cooperative behavior shrinks. When we get to the point where we have all become just agents in one-off deals, there will no longer be any place for freely given niceness. That end point would be both a utopia of wealth and a dystopia of personal relations.

Capitalism has successfully transformed humans into calculating machines endowed with limitless needs. What David Landes, in *The Wealth and Poverty of Nations* (1998), saw as one of the main contributions of capitalism, that it encourages better use of time and the ability to express everything in terms of abstract purchasing power, has now moved into our private lives. To live in capitalism, we do not need the capitalist mode of production in factories if we have all become capitalistic centers ourselves.

5.2c The Dominion of Capitalism

The domination of capitalism as the best, or rather the only, way to organize production and distribution seems absolute. No challenger appears in sight. Capitalism gained this position thanks to its ability, through the appeal to self-interest and desire to own property, to organize people so that they managed, in a decentralized fashion, to create wealth and increase the standard of living of an average human being on the planet by many times—something that only a century ago was considered almost utopian.

But this economic success made more acute the discrepancy between the ability to live better and longer lives and the lack of a commensurate increase in morality, or even happiness. The greater material abundance did make people's manners and behavior to each other better: since elementary needs, and much more than that, were satisfied, people no longer needed to engage in a Hobbesian struggle of all against all. Manners became more polished, people more considerate.

But this external polish was achieved at the cost of people being increasingly driven by self-interest alone, even in many ordinary and personal affairs. The capitalist spirit, a testimony to the generalized success of capitalism, penetrated deeply into people's individual lives. Since extending capitalism to family and intimate life was antithetical to centuries-old views about sacrifice, hospitality, friendship, family ties, and the like, it was not easy to openly accept that all such norms had become superseded by self-interest. This unease created a huge area where hypocrisy reigned. Thus, ultimately, the material success of capitalism came to be associated with a reign of half-truths in our private lives.

5.3 Unfounded Fear of Technological Progress

5.3a Lump of Labor Fallacy and Our Inability to Visualize the Future

We have two hundred years of experience with the introduction of machines that replace human labor. Every time large-scale automation of activities previously performed by humans has taken place or loomed on the horizon, there have been fears of massive unemployment, social dislocation, and, in a word, doom and gloom. And every time, these fears have been considered unique and absolutely novel. And every time, after the shock is past, it turns out that they have been exaggerated.

Recent discussions about the advent of robots focus on the threat of robots replacing humans as something truly novel that could fundamentally change our civilization and way of life. But such a development would be nothing new. Machines have been replacing repetitive (and sometimes creative) labor on a significant scale since the beginning of the Industrial Revolution. Robots are no different from any other machine.

Robots and fascination with anthropomorphism

The obsession with, or fear of, robots has to do with our fascination with their anthropomorphism. Some people speak of great profits that would be reaped by "owners of robots," as if these owners were slaveholders (see, for example, Freeman 2014 and Rotman 2015). But there are no owners of robots; there are only companies that invest in and implement these technological innovations, and it is these companies that will reap the benefits. It could happen that increasing automation would cause the capital share in national income to increase further, with all the consequences on interpersonal inequality that were discussed in Chapter 2, but again this is not different from the effects of the introduction of new machines that replace labor—a thing which has been with us for at least two centuries.

Robotics leads us to face squarely three fallacies.

The first is the fallacy of the lump of labor doctrine, which holds that the total number of jobs is fixed and that as the new machines take over jobs they will cause many workers to face permanent unemployment. The shorter our time horizon, the more that proposition seems reasonable. This is because in the short term, the number of jobs is indeed limited; so if more jobs are done by machines, fewer jobs will be left for people. But as soon as we extend our gaze toward longer time horizons, the number of jobs is no longer fixed; we do not know how many jobs will be lost or how many new jobs will be created. We cannot pinpoint what new jobs, or how many of them, there may be because we do not know what new technologies will bring.[25] But the experience of two centuries of technological progress can help us. We know that similar fears have always existed and have never been realized. New technologies ended up creating enough new jobs, and actually more and better jobs than those that were lost. This does not mean that no one loses as a result of automation. The new machines (called "robots") will replace some workers, and some people's wages will be reduced. But however tragic these losses may be for the individuals involved, they do not affect society as a whole.

Estimates of the proportion of jobs under threat from automation vary widely, both among countries and within countries, depending on the methodology used. For the United States, estimates of the proportion of jobs at risk vary between 7 and 47 percent; for Japan, between 6 and 55 percent.[26] The high values are obtained when occupations are deemed by more than 70 percent of "experts" as likely to be affected by automation; but when the same exercise is conducted looking at the more granular distinction between tasks within occupations, the percentages are much smaller, ranging between 6 and 12 percent for OECD countries (Hallward-Driemeier and Nayyar 2018). These figures estimate only job losses; they do not include (nor could they) the unknown number of new jobs that will be created by the same technologies that have displaced workers in the first place and created new needs.

Hence the second "lump" fallacy: human needs are limited. The second fallacy is linked with the first—namely, our inability to pinpoint what new technology will bring—because our needs are, in turn, determined by the available and known technology. The "needs" that current technology cannot satisfy are not, in an economic sense, real needs. If we feel today the need to fly to Pluto, that need cannot be satisfied and has no economic importance. Likewise, the need of a Roman senator to record his speech—if anyone at the time did indeed experience such a need—could not have been satisfied and did not matter. But today it matters.

These two fallacies are related in the following way: we tend to imagine that human needs are limited to what we know exists today and what people aspire to today, and we cannot see what new needs will arise with new technologies (because the technologies themselves are unknown). Consequently, we cannot imagine what new jobs will be required to satisfy the newly created needs. Again, history comes to the rescue. As recently as fifteen years ago we could not imagine the need for a smart cellphone (because we could not imagine its existence), and thus we could not imagine the new jobs created by smart phone applications: from Uber to applications that sell airplane tickets or connect dog owners with available dog-walkers. Forty years ago, we could not imagine the need to have a computer in our own house, and we could not imagine the millions of new jobs created by the personal computer. Some hundred years ago, we could not imagine the need for a personal motor car, and thus we could not imagine Detroit and Ford and GM and Toyota and even things like the Michelin restaurant guide. Some two hundred years ago, Jean-Baptiste Say, one of the most renowned early economists, claimed that "no machine will ever be able to perform what even the worst horses can—the service of carrying people and goods through the bustle and throng of a great city."[27]

Other famous economists, like David Ricardo and John Maynard Keynes (in "The Economic Possibilities for Our Grandchildren"), thought that human needs were limited. We should know better today: our needs are unlimited, and because we cannot forecast exact movements in technology, we cannot forecast what particular form such new needs will take.

The third "lump" fallacy is the "lump of raw materials and energy" fallacy, the idea of the so-called carrying capacity of the earth. There are of course ultimate geological limits to the supply of raw materials, simply because the earth is finite. (Note however that the cosmos, at least from our small, human perspective is indeed unlimited.) But experience teaches us that the terrestrial limits are much wider than we generally think at any one time because our knowledge of what the earth contains, and how it can be used for our needs, is itself limited by our current level of technology. The better our technology, the more reserves of everything we discover, and the more efficient we are in using them. Accepting that X is an exhaustible energy source or raw material, and that at the current rate of utilization it will run out in Y years, is only part of the story. It omits the fact that as X becomes scarce and rises in price, incentives will increase to create substitutes (as the inventions of beet sugar, synthetic rubber, and fracking show) or to use different combinations of inputs to produce the final goods that now require X as the input. The cost of the final good may go up, but this is just a change in relative price, not a cataclysmic event. The concept of carrying capacity, which does not include development of technology and pricing in its equation, is just another "lump" fallacy.

Some prominent economists, like Stanley Jevons, who collected tons of paper in the nineteenth century in the expectation that trees would run out, entertained the same illogical fears.[28] Not only did it turn out that, with many thousand (or million?) times greater use of paper, the world did not run out of trees, but in addition, Jevons, understandably, could not imagine that technology would enable the recycling of paper and the efficient replanting of forests, or that electronic communications would cut back on our need for paper in the first place. We are no smarter than Jevons. We, too, cannot imagine what might replace fuel oil or magnesium or iron ore. But we should be able to understand the process whereby substitutions come about and to reason by analogy.

Fears of robotics and technology arise, I think, from two human frailties. One is cognitive: we simply do not know what future technological change will be and thus cannot tell what new jobs will be created, what our future needs will be, or how raw materials will be used. The second is psychological: we get a thrill from fear of the unknown—in this case, the scary and yet alluring prospect of metallic robots replacing flesh-and-blood workers on the factory floor. This desire for a thrill responds to the same need that makes us watch scary movies and to what Keynes called our "readiness to be alarmed and excited." We like to scare ourselves with thoughts of the exhaustion of natural resources, limits to growth, and replacement of people by robots. It may be fun, or perhaps it makes us feel virtuous for not being naïve and anticipating the worst, but history teaches us that the world of robotic workers is not something we should rationally fear.

5.3b Problems with Universal Basic Income

Reaction to such fears of massive unemployment has given sudden prominence to the concept of universal basic income (UBI).[29] The UBI has four features: it is universal, that is, it would provide an income to each citizen; it is unconditional, that is, it is given to everyone with no requirements; it is disbursed in cash; and it is an income source, that is, a constant flow rather than a one-off grant. (A grant can also have the first three features but would be paid to an individual only once.) The idea of a UBI has become popular on the left because it seems generous and, if set at a sufficiently high level, would reduce poverty and possibly inequality. It seems to tackle the problem of inequality from the bottom up: rather than limiting the highest incomes, it raises the lowest incomes. And if the lowest incomes are made sufficiently high, it also implies relatively high taxation of the rich (to fund UBI), which, in a circuitous way, then reduces income inequality. The concept also appeals to the right for precisely the opposite reasons. It seems to be a way to get rid of endless complaints about excessively high incomes and of attempts to limit them, and to dispense once and for all with incessant tinkering with the tax and transfer system. Once the rich agree to provide everyone, regardless of their merits or demerits, with an income that is sufficient for decent living, subsequent inequality can be whatever the market and monopolistic competition allow it to be. The right therefore views UBI as a device to maximize high incomes while giving them an aura of social acceptability.

Clearly, if something appeals to two constituencies whose objectives are exactly the opposite, it is bound to disappoint at least one of the two, or perhaps both. But while UBI is being debated, each side might believe that it will ultimately be proven right, which means that the political attractiveness of the concept may not diminish for either side. This is precisely the situation we are in now.

But, whatever its political appeal, UBI has significant problems that make its application difficult.

First, we have almost no experience with it. The 2019 World Bank's World Development Report, which is largely dedicated to issues of automation and UBI, lists only two nationwide experiences with UBI. One was in Mongolia, where a UBI equal to $16.50 a month lasted for two years, until the money from which it was financed (a high world price for rare minerals) ran out. The other was in Iran, where energy subsidies were replaced by a cash transfer paid to 96 percent of the population. The amount was $45 per month per person, and the program lasted for one year.[30] That is all.

Other similar programs are pathetically small. Finland had a trial that involved two thousand unemployed citizens, and Oakland, California, experimented with just one hundred families. Note, in addition, that the money in the Finnish case was disbursed only to the unemployed; thus the program was neither universal nor unconditional. The State of Alaska distributes annual grants to all citizens from the proceeds of a natural resource fund. But this is a windfall grant that varies with the fortunes of the fund and is not a guaranteed monthly income, supposed in principle to defray living expenses. When one puts all these experiences together, they amount to practically nothing—and come nowhere close to what a real UBI, according to its supporters, should be: that is, a universal and sustainable program providing, by itself, an "acceptable" minimal income, and being paid monthly ad infinitum (from the society's point of view) or until death (from the individual's point of view).

Now, it could be argued that just because something has not been tried does not mean that it cannot work. That is a valid point—but it is also true that we have, as of now, no experience showing how UBI would actually work.

The second problem is the cost. Here the situation is a bit more complex. It is obvious that UBI cannot be assumed, for financial reasons, to run alongside all other existing programs, from child benefits to disability insurance. So the question becomes: If UBI is going to be fiscally neutral, what other programs would be cut and by how much? It is clearly possible to make UBI fiscally neutral by dropping or curtailing existing programs and setting the cash amount paid out by UBI at an appropriate equivalent level. The question is then whether such a level would be considered sufficient for a "decent" standard of living. Those on the left would not be deterred if it were not sufficient; they would simply advocate greater taxes. Fiscal neutrality is not necessarily something they are concerned about. It is not obvious, however, that the right would be at all comfortable with such a costly program and the high taxes it would imply.

The UBI would have to have a built-in mechanism whereby not only would its amount increase with inflation, but there would be some link between its level and real GDP growth. For example, every two or three years, UBI could be increased by the same (or perhaps a lower?) percentage than the percentage that GDP per capita had gone up. Or it could be reduced when GDP per capita dropped.

The third problem is philosophical. The welfare system as it exists in rich countries has been created around the idea of social insurance. Offer and Söderberg (2016) argue that the social insurance principle is the backbone of social democracy. It insures individuals (and in some cases, only those who are employed) against predictable contingencies that result in the inability to work and to maintain one's standard of living. It insures

> *UBI implies a new philosophy of the welfare state*

people against sickness and disability, against loss of income due to childbearing, against old age, and against job loss. It needs to be "social," that is, universal, in order to avoid the sort of self-selection that would render the system financially unmanageable: if those who thought that their risk of unemployment was low could decide not to contribute, then only the high-risk cases would remain and the premiums would be excessively high. This is why universalism and redistribution are integral to the system. In addition, for those who fall between the cracks and still have no acceptable income despite these social insurance programs, the system introduces social assistance benefits that are means-tested and whose objective, unlike social insurance, is straightforward poverty prevention.

The philosophy underlying the welfare state would be overhauled by introduction of a system of universal basic income. UBI does not insure against risks; it completely ignores them. It distributes money to everyone equally, though money received by well-off individuals is later clawed back through taxation. This is not necessarily a dispositive argument against UBI. The philosophy on which a welfare system is based can, and perhaps should, be changed. It nevertheless reminds us that moving from the current system to UBI would not only be a technical and financial change; it would entail an overall change in the philosophy that has dominated the welfare state for more than a century.

The fourth problem is also philosophical but concerns the broader question of what kind of society the introduction of UBI would encourage. The left and the right, as we have seen, seem to visualize two very different societies that would result: the left believes that UBI would introduce limits on the highest incomes and would curb inequality; the right believes that it would do the opposite. In addition, we do not know what effect UBI would have on people's propensity to look for jobs and to work. On the one hand, a lump-sum regular transfer like UBI should not affect decisions about work (the substitution effect as between leisure and work should be zero, since UBI is received either way, and at sufficiently low levels of income it might not be clawed back by taxation). On the other hand, the higher income that people would get, as compared with no income at all or social assistance at much lower levels, might predispose them to consume more leisure, that is to work less.

It is possible that on balance the effect of UBI on work would be small; but it is also possible that society might become very polarized, with, say, some 20 percent of the working-age population choosing not to work at all. To those who would choose not to work because they found UBI sufficient we should add those who might not need to work because of the high capital incomes they inherited (as discussed in Section 2.4). This would give us a tripartite society where those at the bottom and many of those at the top would not work at all, while the middle class would. Would such a society, where work is not treated as something intrinsically good and desirable and where perhaps one-third of young people would routinely be outside the labor force, be considered a good society?

These are the questions that ought to be addressed before we decide to be in favor of UBI or against it. None of the objections that I have raised is by itself sufficient to shoot the idea down; each of them could be either solved, finessed, or perhaps dismissed as unlikely. But all of them taken together raise questions as to the advisability of moving rapidly toward UBI.

5.4 Luxe et Volupté

5.4a The Two Scenarios: War and Peace

When we chart the further evolution of global capitalism, we have to seriously take into account the possibility of a global nuclear war that, if it did not destroy all life on the planet, would radically change the future of the world compared with what it would be under more peaceful circumstances. There would be, to say the least, a sharp discontinuity in development—although we should not fall prey to viewing such a war as exogenous to the capitalist system. An analogy with World War I would be helpful. The Great War significantly changed the trajectory of world history, compared with any reasonable counterfactual. It directly caused the communist revolution of 1917 and thus led to the establishment of an alternative socioeconomic system that represented, for the better part of the twentieth century, a serious and credible challenge to capitalism. It also produced—with a delay of some twenty years, in its continuation known as World War II—a diminution in the global importance of Europe and the rise of the United States to the position of a global hegemon. And it almost certainly accelerated the process of decolonization, in part by weakening European colonial powers and in part by delegitimizing their rule.

World War I did not just come out of the blue: its seeds were contained in conditions prevailing before the war. As John Hobson (1902) originally argued, the European imperialism that ultimately led to the war arose because of high domestic inequality in income and wealth generated by globalized capitalism. Lots of income in the hands of the rich (whose average propensity to consume is low) caused a disproportion between the (high) amount of savings and the availability of profitable domestic investments. The rich thus turned to foreign investments as the best use for their savings. These new fields of action for global capitalism could be made safe for capital either by colonial conquest or by de facto political control. Several major states all sought to expand their reach in this way at the same time, and imperialist competition ensued. This situation, when translated into European politics, produced the war.[31]

There was thus a strong link between the economic conditions prevailing before the war and the "necessity" of the war. As I argued in Chapter 3, World War I represents perhaps the strongest possible rebuttal of the thesis that capitalism needs peace (or promotes peace) because of the strong economic interdependence that it creates among nations. Everyone thought so before 1914: it was common wisdom that a war would have devastating effects on all parties, and yet, when the final decisions had to be made, everyone went over the precipice with their eyes closed.

The same logic applies today. Everyone is aware that a war between the major powers would have a cataclysmic effect on all states involved, with only slightly less of an effect on the others. During the twentieth century, the most murderous in history, an estimated 231 million people died as a result of wars; this represents about 2.6 percent of the approximately 8.9 billion people who were born during the century.[32] A war in the twenty-first century could be much more murderous in absolute numbers, and possibly in relative numbers as well. The melancholy thought is that capitalism at its previous highest point of global spread and power generated the most devastating conflict in history up to that time; and there is a more than negligible chance that similar internal mechanisms might lead to another such conflict.

Such a war, if it did not lead to the extinction of humankind, would not negate all of the technological advancements that have been made during the past several hundred years. The reason is that globalization has spread the knowledge of technology far and wide. Even if North America, Europe, and Russia were more or less obliterated and made uninhabitable (with resulting drastic decreases in income per capita and probably massive emigration of the surviving population to Latin America, Africa, and Asia), technological knowledge—from the production of cars and computers to genetically modified food—would not be lost. The relative powers of different states would be fundamentally altered (as after the two world wars of the twentieth century), but, although technological progress would suffer a huge setback, it would not be halted. It is thanks to globalized capitalism that technological developments have spread to the whole world, and it would be (ironically) thanks to globalized capitalism that they would be preserved even following a massive holocaust.[33] Under this gloomy scenario global capitalism would be both a cause of devastation and the savior of civilization. In other words, Einstein's supposed quip that the Fourth World War would be fought with rocks would not be proven true. Even if half of humankind were destroyed, technological knowledge would not be wiped out.

In conclusion, the problem of a global war revolves around the question of whether humankind has achieved sufficient maturity to realize that such a calamity would make a mockery of the concept of "winners" and "losers," or if it will take a practical demonstration for humans to come to this realization.

If a global war does not happen, what trajectory might global capitalism follow in the decades to come? This question leads us to consider the competition between the two types of capitalism that I have considered in this book.

5.4b Political Capitalism versus Liberal Capitalism

I discussed in Chapters 2 and 3 the roles that the United States and China play as the leading exponents of, respectively, liberal and political capitalism. At the more abstract level, we should consider the advantages of the two types of capitalism independently from their main promoters. The advantage of liberal capitalism resides in its political system of democracy. Many people (but not all) regard democracy as a "primary good"—desirable in itself and thus not in need of justification by its effects on, say, economic growth or life expectancy. This is one advantage. But there is also an instrumental advantage of democracy. By requiring constant consultation of the population, democracy does also provide a very powerful corrective to economic and social trends that may be detrimental to the populace's welfare. Even if people's decisions sometimes result in policies that reduce the rate of economic growth, increase pollution, or reduce life expectancy, democratic decision-making should, within a relatively limited time period, reverse them. To believe that democracy does not matter as a check on detrimental developments, one would have to argue that the majority of the people will be consistently making wrong (or irrational) choices for a long time. This seems unlikely.

Against these advantages of liberal capitalism, political capitalism promises much more efficient management of the economy and higher growth rates. This is not a small advantage, especially if high income and wealth are ranked as the ultimate objectives—a ranking not only ideologically rooted in the very idea of global capitalism, but also expressed daily in the actions of virtually all participants in economic globalization (which means practically the entire globe). Rawls argued that primary goods (basic liberties and income) are lexicographically ordered: people give absolute priority to basic liberties over wealth and income and thus do not accept a trade-off.[34] But everyday experience seems to show that many people are willing to trade parts of democratic decision-making for greater income. One need simply observe that within companies production is generally organized in the most hierarchical fashion, not the most democratic. Workers do not vote on the products they would like to produce or on how they would like to produce them (say, with or without machines). The reason seems to be that hierarchy results in higher efficiency and higher wages. As Jacques Ellul (1963, 209) put it more than half a century ago, "Technique is the boundary of democracy. What technique wins, democracy loses. If we had engineers who were popular with the

Trade-off between income and political freedom

workers, they would be ignorant of machinery." The same analogy can be extended to society as a whole: other democratic rights can be (and have been) given up willingly for higher incomes. It is on such grounds that political capitalism asserts its superiority.

The problem, however, is that in order to prove its superiority and ward off a liberal challenge (that is, to be selected by people in preference to liberal capitalism), political capitalism needs to constantly deliver high rates of growth. So while liberal capitalism's advantages are "natural," or to put it differently, are built into the setup of the system, the advantages of political capitalism are instrumental: they have to be constantly demonstrated. Political capitalism thus starts with a handicap. It needs to prove its superiority empirically. In addition, it faces two further problems: (i) the difficulty of changing course if a wrong direction has been chosen because of the absence of democratic checks, and (ii) an inherent tendency toward corruption because of the absence of the rule of law. Relative to liberal capitalism, political capitalism has a greater tendency to generate bad policies and bad social outcomes that cannot be reversed because those in power do not have an incentive to change course. It can also, quite easily, engender popular dissatisfaction due to its systemic corruption. Both of these "scourges" are less important in liberal capitalism.

Political capitalism therefore needs to sell itself on the grounds of providing better societal management, higher rates of growth, and more efficient administration (including administration of justice). Unlike liberal capitalism, which can take a more relaxed attitude toward temporary problems, political capitalism, if it is to succeed, must be permanently on its toes. This may, however, be seen as an advantage from a social Darwinist point of view: because of constant pressure to deliver more to its constituents, political capitalism might hone its ability to manage the economic sphere well and to keep on delivering, year in year out, more goods and services than its liberal counterpart. Thus, what appear at first as a defect may prove to be an advantage.

In their book *Democracy and Capitalism,* published in 1986, Samuel Bowles and Herbert Gintis foresaw three possible directions in which globalization might evolve. The first was neoliberal, dictated by the West and centered around liberal meritocratic capitalism.

Three scenarios

The second was neo-Hobbesian, defined as "expansion of the terrain over which property rights reign, the contraction of the domain of personal rights, and the construction of unaccountable state institutions" (198–199). This variant is very much like what I define as political capitalism. Bowles and Gintis furthermore described this variant as "Burkean in its acceptance of traditional values, [but also] more akin to the forward-looking social engineering of [Henri de] Saint-Simon" (198). Neo-Hobbesian capitalism combines relatively conservative social values, expansion of property rights in many domains (what I refer to as increased commodification) and attempts to "improve" society through social engineering. These are all characteristics of successful political capitalism.

The third variant that Bowles and Gintis consider consists of a society of rentiers who lease or lend their capital to democratically organized companies. This type of capitalism does not currently exist anywhere, although it is not impossible to imagine that with greater abundance of capital and a halt to the increase of population, we could see societies where the process of hiring between the factors of production could be reversed: that is, where labor would hire capital instead of vice versa. This reversal has not happened so far not only because of the stronger bargaining position of capital owners (i.e., the relative scarcity of capital compared with labor), but also because of coordination problems among workers. It is easier to coordinate the interests of a couple of capitalists than of thousands of workers—a fact that Adam Smith had already noted. Another obstacle is the absence of collateral among workers, which makes capitalists wary of lending them money. Furthermore, a democratically organized company would not be, by definition, under the control of the providers of capital, which is another reason capitalists would be leery of lending their funds.[35] Still, despite all these problems, one cannot rule out that a change in the relative bargaining power between labor and capital might occur during the twenty-first century (as more capital is being accumulated and the global population stops growing) and that a democratically organized workplace might appear as an alternative to liberal and political capitalism. It would remain capitalist in the sense that the private ownership of the means of production would be retained, but there would be no wage labor. Using the standard definition of capitalism that requires both to be present, it is not obvious that we could call such a society "capitalist" anymore.

5.4c Global Inequality and Geopolitical Changes

Throughout the earlier chapters, I have shown the effects of the economic and geopolitical changes that have dramatically reduced income gaps between a resurgent Asia and the West. If these trends continue, which we can quite reasonably expect, they will bring income levels in China and later other Asian countries such as Thailand, Indonesia, Vietnam, and India, close to those of Western countries. This convergence will return the world to the relative parity of income levels that existed before the Industrial Revolution, when China's and India's incomes were similar to that of western Europe. This pattern can be seen in Figure 5.1, which shows Chinese and Indian GDP per capita as a percentage of British GDP per capita, beginning in 1820 for China and 1870 for India and then focusing on four crucial points in time: (i) the early 1910s, just before World War I, (ii) the late 1940s, at the time of the communist revolution in China and independence in India, (iii) the late 1970s, when Chinese reforms began, and finally (iv) today. The figure also shows Indonesia compared in the same way, and at similar points in time, to the Netherlands. In all three cases, the pattern is the same. At the time of the Industrial Revolution, per capita income in Asian countries was about 40 percent of that in Britain (by then the most developed country in Europe). Asian relative income levels then dropped rapidly, so much so that from the middle of the twentieth century all the way to the late 1970s and early 1980s, per capita income of Asian countries was less than one-tenth that of Britain or the Netherlands. But in the past forty years, the situation has drastically changed, especially for China, which is now back to almost the same relative income level that it had in the early nineteenth century. We are in a sense witnessing the undoing of the effects of the first Industrial Revolution. Figure 5.1 illustrates the story of the past two centuries in a nutshell.

This convergence in income is also responsible for the first sustained drop in global income inequality since 1820 (see Figure 1.1).[36] In the last two decades of the twentieth century, the underlying increase in global inequality

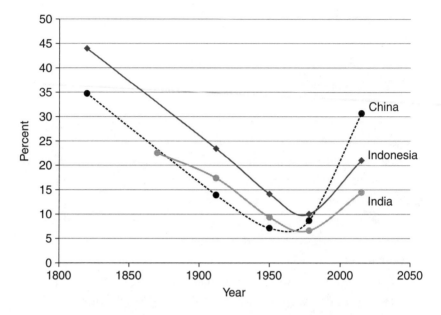

FIGURE 5.1. GDP per capita for China and India as a percentage of British GDP, and for Indonesia as a percentage of Dutch GDP, from the Industrial Revolution to today

Data source: Calculated from the Maddison Project (2018); all GDP per capita data in 2011 PPPs (variable cgdppc, which is the real GDP variable used for cross-country comparisons at a given point in time).

was checked entirely thanks to Chinese growth (Milanovic 2012). In that period, growth in China alone not only prevented global inequality from rising, but it also accounted for more than 95 percent of the reduction in the number of the people in the world living below the absolute poverty line (Chen and Ravallion 2007). Around the turn of the twenty-first century, China was joined in that role by India, which, because of its large population, relative poverty, and high growth rate, now also contributes significantly to a decline in both global income inequality and global poverty.

The importance of reduced global inequality does not reside in a decrease in a single number (the Gini coefficient of inequality), but rather in the convergence in real incomes across vast groups of people. We can thus, for perhaps the first time in history, speak of the emergence of a global middle class. It is unclear, though, what the political consequences of this development will be. In individual nations, a large middle class has been considered important for protection of property rights and political stability (since this class has tended to protect its property from being confiscated by the poor and to prevent the rich from claiming monopoly on governance); but it is not at all clear whether that particular role can be played by the global middle class, given the lack of a global government. It is more likely that income convergence and the emergence of a global middle class will simply mean that more people will share similar patterns of behavior and consumption—something that we can easily observe already but that will become much more common and include many more people, as incomes in other populous Asian countries catch up with those in Europe and North America. As an indicator of how far that convergence has already progressed, note that in 2017, in terms of real GDP per capita (adjusted for the differences in price levels), China was only 10 percent below Bulgaria, the poorest country in the European Union, and was at 41 percent of the population-weighted EU GDP per capita. However, with a conservative assumption of Chinese GDP per capita growth of 6 percent per year versus an EU-wide growth of 2 percent, it will take China only about one generation (twenty-four years) to reach the EU-wide average GDP per capita. Thus, by 2040, the world's entire Northern Hemisphere, including North America, Europe (except for Russia), Japan, Korea, and China may have approximately the same income, while South and Southeast Asia will not be far behind. It will be an epochal change.

One big unknown concerning global inequality is what will happen in Africa. Africa is important for two reasons. First, Africa has, so far, shown very few signs of being able to start the process of convergence in a sustained way, that is, to exhibit in most countries per capita income growth rates that are higher than Western growth rates over a long time period (say, twenty years). Second, Africa has by far the greatest expected increase in population of any continent. If Africa fails to catch up with the rich world (in per capita terms, it must be emphasized) and if its population continues to grow in absolute numbers and at a higher rate than in the rest of the world, it is not impossible to envisage a scenario under which the trend toward a decline in global income inequality first stalls and then reverses. This would be an unfortunate development. It could be that we would then have to wait for a third, African, episode of remarkable regional growth (the first being Western and the second Asian) to create a world-wide convergence of mean country incomes.

In conclusion, during the next few decades we can expect convergence of incomes across wide swaths of Eurasia and North America, the regions that currently include more than half of the world population. It remains unknown whether sub-Saharan Africa, which currently accounts for about 14 percent of world population but is likely to represent 20 percent by 2040, will join that convergence or not.[37]

It is in this context that we should address the role that China might play in Africa's economic development. If the Chinese approach to Africa, which puts an emphasis on infrastructural investment, land development, and increased production of food and natural resources, does lead to faster growth in important African countries, the worldwide convergence of incomes will be accelerated. In addition, faster growth in African countries might reduce the migration of Africans whose desired destination is the rich countries of Europe. The success of China's economic strategy in Africa would signally help Europe, which is, as I pointed out in Chapter 4, the region of the world in greatest need of foreign labor yet the most reluctant to open itself to further large flows of migrants. We thus see empirically the growing interdependence of various parts of the world: the success of China and India is not only good for their populations and for the global middle class but could also jump-start the development of Africa and relieve the immediate migratory pressures on Europe.

The convergence of worldwide incomes might also decrease the risk of a disastrous global war. Having noticed that Europeans' superior force in the eighteenth century allowed them to commit all kinds of injustices, Adam Smith thought that greater equality in wealth and power between different parts of the world might, through mutual fear, preserve the peace: "The natives of those countries may grow stronger, or those of Europe may grow weaker, and the inhabitants of all the different quarters of the world may arrive at that equality of courage and force which, by inspiring mutual fear, can alone overawe the injustice of independent nations into some sort of respect for the rights of one another."[38]

5.4d Concluding Notes on the Social System toward
Which This Book Might Lead

Let me conclude by summarizing the past development of Western capitalist societies and speculating on what the future holds. I first outline the three types of existing liberal capitalism (defined in Chapter 2) and two other hypothetical types, people's capitalism and egalitarian capitalism, which have never existed in reality. I then set out policies that might help us attain one of these two types.

- *Classical capitalism.* Workers have income from labor only, capitalists have income from capital only, and all capitalists are richer than all workers, that is, the income distributions of workers and capitalists do not overlap. There is only very minimal redistribution via taxes and transfers. Interpersonal inequality is high. Advantages of wealth are transmitted across generations. This form is also called Ricardo-Marx capitalism.

- *Social-democratic capitalism.* Workers have income from labor only and capitalists have income from capital only, but not all capitalists are richer than all workers. There is significant redistribution through the tax and transfer system, including free or accessible public health care and education. Interpersonal inequality is moderate. Relatively equal access to education allows intergenerational income mobility.

- *Liberal meritocratic capitalism.* Most people have some income from both labor and capital. The share of capital income increases with income level, such that the extremely rich have mostly capital income. But the most affluent (say, the top 5 percent) also have substantial labor income. The increase in the capital share as societies get richer, and the association of high capital and labor incomes in the same individuals, translate into greater interpersonal inequality. The tax and transfer system redistributes a significant part of total income, but social separatism, whereby the rich prefer to invest in private education and health systems, becomes more important. Intergenerational mobility is less than in social-democratic capitalism.

- *People's capitalism.* Everyone has approximately equal *shares* of capital and labor income. People's incomes still differ; some have more of both capital and labor income. Increased capital share does not translate into greater interpersonal inequality, so inequality does not have a tendency to rise. Direct redistribution is limited, but free health care and education help intergenerational income mobility.
- *Egalitarian capitalism.* Everyone has approximately equal *amounts* of both capital and labor income, such that a large increase in the capital share does not translate into greater inequality. Interpersonal inequality is low. The role of the state in redistribution is limited to social insurance. Relative equality of incomes ensures equality of opportunity. Libertarianism, capitalism, and socialism come close to each other.

In a very abstract way, the question of how capitalism will evolve depends on whether liberal meritocratic capitalism will be able to move toward a more advanced stage, that of people's capitalism, where (1) the concentration of capital incomes (and the concentration of ownership of wealth) would be less, (2) income inequality would be lower, and (3) intergenerational income mobility would be greater. The last point would also prevent the formation of a durable elite. In order to move there—if it is found that such a move is desirable—it is not sufficient to have incremental policies, however well meaning and well designed they are. It is important to have a clear and measurable goal in mind. If either people's or egalitarian capitalism is the goal, the measurement of progress toward that goal becomes relatively simple and could be done using knowledge and techniques we possess today. The two most important goalposts for monitoring progress are whether concentration of wealth and income from capital is being reduced, and whether intergenerational (relative) income mobility is improving. Both are longer-term indicators, so annual changes might not mean much. But it would be possible to set a goal in this way and to measure at several-year intervals whether progress is being made.

The policies that would lead to progress toward that goal, all of which I have discussed in earlier chapters, are relatively simple and can be summarized under four headings:

Incremental vs.
non-incremental.
(Idea of non-Revolution.)

1. Tax advantages for the middle class, especially in the areas of access to financial and housing wealth, and a corresponding increase in the taxation of the rich; plus, the return to high taxation of inheritance. The objective is to reduce concentration of wealth in the hands of the rich.

2. A significant increase in funding for and improvement in the quality of public schools, whose cost must be low enough to be accessible not only to the middle class but also to those in the bottom three deciles of the income distribution. The objective is to reduce transmission of advantages across generations and make equality of opportunity more real.

3. "Citizenship light," which would entail the end of a strictly binary division between citizens and noncitizens. The objective is to allow migration without provoking nationalist backlash.

4. Strictly limited and exclusively public funding of political campaigns. The objective is to reduce the ability of the rich to control the political process and form a durable upper class.

Or convergence of liberal and political capitalisms? An altogether different evolution of liberal capitalism would be a movement toward a plutocratic and ultimately political capitalism. This scenario is also possible—and the stronger the plutocratic features in today's liberal capitalism become, the more likely such an evolution is. It would be an evolution to a large extent compatible with the interests of the new elite that is being formed under liberal capitalism. It would enable the elite to be much more autonomous from the rest of society. In fact, as shown in Chapter 2, the preservation of the elite requires its control of the political domain, what I called "tying up the knot on wealth and power." The more economic and political power in liberal capitalism become united, the more liberal capitalism becomes plutocratic and comes to resemble political capitalism. In the latter, political control is the way to acquire economic benefits; in plutocratic, formerly liberal, capitalism, economic power is used to conquer politics. The end point of the two systems becomes the same: unification and persistence of the elites.

Elites may also believe that they are able to run society more effectively by using the technocratic toolkit of political capitalism. A transition toward political capitalism could be boosted if young people became increasingly disenchanted by mainstream parties that follow more or less the same policies, and consequently lost hope that democratic processes could lead to meaningful change. The objective of political capitalism is to take politics out of people's minds, which can be more easily done when disenchantment and lack of interest in democratic politics are high.

If liberal capitalism were to evolve toward political capitalism, it would display all or most of the features that I discussed in Chapter 3. A very effective management of the economy would be required to produce the relatively high growth rates that would keep the population satisfied; an efficient bureaucracy would be needed to implement such measures; and there would be an increase in intrinsic corruption that can always, in the long term, present a threat to the survival of a regime.

APPENDIXES

NOTES

REFERENCES

ACKNOWLEDGMENTS

INDEX

THE PLACE OF COMMUNISM
IN GLOBAL HISTORY

The view I put forth in Chapter 3 about the place of communism in global history has two major implications for how to interpret the history of the twentieth century, and, perhaps, that of the twenty-first century as well.

Point 1. My conclusion implies, in many substantive ways, a vindication of the Marxist view that capitalism leads to imperialist competition that generates war. World War I stands as clear proof of that. The view that the autonomous role of the state is often circumscribed and that, domestically, capitalists often control the political process was also vindicated.

Point 2. I explained that the Marxist view was seriously wanting in two important respects. First, it did not sufficiently take into account the ability of capitalism to transform itself and create a social-democratic variant, which, as described in Chapter 2, is one of the three variants of modern twentieth- and twenty-first-century capitalism. That variant has provided substantial increases in income for the lower and middle classes, enabled the spread of education and social protection, and generally allowed the countries that practiced it to reach the highest levels of prosperity and political freedom ever enjoyed by any group of people in history.

Second, Marxist theory entirely misjudged the historical role of communism or, to stay strictly within Marxist terminology, socialism. Socialism, rather than succeeding capitalism after crises and wars, as it was supposed to do, instead paved the way for the development of capitalism in the Third World. In some parts of the Third World, communist ideology and communist parties enabled capitalism to develop. In that way, communism in the Third World played the same functional role that the bourgeoisie played in the West. Therefore, socialism, rather than being a transition stage between capitalism and the utopia of communism, was in fact a transition system between feudalism and capitalism in some Third World countries.

This outcome is, in some ways, a testimony to the rightness of an apparently paradoxical position adopted by Russian "legal Marxists," who argued that the role of communist organizations in less-developed countries should be to help the development of capitalism.

How did this cunning of history come about? Why is it only now that we can clearly see the true role of communism?

The answer lies in the assumption that the Western path of development (WPD) is universal, which turns out to be wrong. This assumption made us unable to appreciate the remarkable difference in conditions between the parts of the world where bourgeois revolutions were autochthonous and those where foreign capital came principally to conquer and only in a secondary and accessory way to implement or transplant the institutions of capitalism as they had been created in the West. Indeed, if Western imperialism and colonialism had been stronger, and if their objective had been primarily to create capitalist institutions rather than to exploit (which was often made easier, as Rosa Luxemburg maintained, through exchange with precapitalist social formations), it is possible that the WPD would have been followed by the Third World and that colonialism would have transformed it into the West's own image. The *mission civilisatrice* would have been successful. And indeed, capitalist economies did become established in small, self-contained areas (such as Hong Kong and Singapore), and in the parts of the world where the local population was sparse or had been exterminated and where Europeans, dealing with other Europeans, were able to transplant their institutions (such as Argentina, Uruguay, Australia, and New Zealand).[1] But where Europeans could not transplant such institutions, or where exploitation was more profitable and keeping the old feudal institutions a better option, capitalist institutions grew only at the edges (in some cases literally, such as along the coast of Africa), and the rest of the population continued living under the previous order. Vietnam, India, and Indonesia, conquered by three different European empires, all exemplify this side-by-side existence of a thin layer of capitalism superimposed on an unchanged social system under which 90 percent or more of the population continued to live.

Marxist historiography, and no less a person than Marx himself in his writings on India, overestimated the willingness and ability of British colonialists to transform India into a capitalist society. As Marx wrote in June 1853:

> England, it is true, in causing a social revolution in Hindoustan, was actuated only by the vilest interests, and was stupid in the manner of enforcing then. But this is not the question. The question is, can mankind fulfill its destiny without a fundamental revolution in the social state of Asia? If not, whatever may have been the crimes of England she was the unconscious tool of history in bringing about that revolution.[2]

In another article written a few months later, he declared: "England has to fulfill a double mission in India: one destructive, another regenerating—the annihilation of the old Asiatic society, and the laying of the material foundations of western society in Asia."[3] But British capitalists failed to do so. India was just too big. Similarly, Bill Warren, in his book *Imperialism* (1980), took a very strong position in favor of WPD, consistent with the original Marxist view, arguing that the crucial mistake, namely the abandonment of the WPD, goes back to the Bolsheviks, who conflated the proletarian struggle with the anti-imperialist struggle. According to Warren, only the first one was legitimate from the Marxist point of view, and it should have been engaged equally in the West and the Third World. This mistake, in his view, led workers' movements in Third World countries to align themselves with the parts of the local bourgeoisie that were anticolonialist and thus to blunt the edge of social conflict.

And indeed the combining of the two struggles was the crucial decision—the decision that started with the Baku Meetings at the First Congress of the Peoples of the East, and continued with the Second Congress of the Communist International (Comintern), both in 1920; they broke off from the Comintern's hitherto Eurocentric view, the WPD. But it was not a mistake, as Warren believed. That decision meant that left-wing and communist movements in the Third World could legitimately combine social revolution and national liberation in a unique way that was, as I have argued, the key factor that allowed them to gain power. Where the cunning of history was, it was in not "revealing" to them that they were, as if "led by an invisible hand," bringing

Comintern's "eastern turn" and the worldwide diffusion of capitalism

in the conditions for the rise of their national capitalisms rather than, as they thought they were doing, ushering in a classless and internationalist communist society. In this context one can see that Lenin's and the Comintern's turn toward the "toilers of the East," along with the division of the world into the two camps of imperialist and colonized countries that it implied, was absolutely decisive for what happened next: not for bringing about communism, but for bringing about capitalism.[4] This interpretation allows us to claim—paradoxically, at first sight—that Lenin was probably the most important "capitalist roader" in history, since his idea to connect the proletarian struggle in the West to the movement for national liberation in Africa and Asia both departed from orthodox Western Marxism and unleashed the forces that some fifty or sixty years later would bring indigenous capitalism to countries as diverse as Vietnam, China, Angola, and Algeria. Without that decision there would have been no diffusion of capitalism across the world, or it would have taken place much more slowly.

Does this outcome entirely invalidate the Marxist view of history? I do not think so. The succession of the stages of economic development that played such a big role in Marxism was defined briefly by Marx in the preface to the *Critique of Political Economy,* and it remained unsettled until the end of Marx's and Engels's lives. But that particular succession of stages, which, as I have argued in this book, was wrong, was not the most important part of Marx's theory of historical materialism. As Eric Hobsbawm remarked, "The general theory of historical materialism requires only that there should be a succession of modes of production, though not necessarily . . . in any particular predetermined order. . . . If [Marx] had been mistaken in his observations [about the order in which socioeconomic formations would proceed], or if these had been based on partial and therefore misleading information, the general theory of historical materialism would remain unaffected."[5]

How does this interpretation then inform our view of the future? The first thing to realize is that there is no system that is an obvious successor to capitalism. My explanation of the true role of communism makes it clear that its role has been accomplished. Communism has fulfilled its function, and it is unlikely to have a role in the future of human history. It is not a system of the future, but a system of the past.

But the great advantage of Marxist analysis is that it urges us to consider each socioeconomic system as necessarily limited in time. Nothing remains unchanged as the underlying conditions of production evolve. In Marx's words, "A certain mode of production, or industrial stage, is always combined with a certain mode of cooperation, or social stage, and this mode of cooperation is itself a productive force."[6] We know that capitalism will evolve, too. Whether it will change in a dramatic way, such that either privately owned capital will cease to be dominant, or that wage labor will lose its importance, we do not know. It could be that thanks to the new types of technological progress, small-scale production organized by self-employed individuals, or small groups of people working with their own capital and borrowing at preferential rates from state-owned banks, will become the standard ways to organize production. Or there could be other combinations that would marginalize capitalism as Marx and Max Weber defined it. Nothing at present allows us to make such prognostications because capitalism today seems to be more powerful and omnipresent than ever in history, in both of the hyper-commercialized and globalized variants I have described—liberal meritocratic and political. As I argued in Chapter 5, capitalism has entered into the private sphere, including our homes, and affects our use of free time and personal property (which has now become capital), our relations with relatives, our marriage patterns, and so on. So we know that capitalism is stronger than ever, but we do not know if this represents its overall peak, or if it is only a local peak, with further expansion of capitalist relations in the future.

HYPERCOMMERCIALIZATION AND ADAM SMITH'S "INVISIBLE HAND"

I discussed in Chapter 5 the interaction between hypercommercialized globalization and our values and behaviors. Here I look at how the same type of issue was addressed, at the time of early capitalism, by Adam Smith, and the place of the "invisible hand" in Smith's argument.

The invisible hand type of argument relies on accepting what were thought, in the pre-Enlightenment, to be the destructive and insatiable passions of power, pleasure, and profit (to use David Wootton's [2018] classification) as long as, when controlled, they are able to result in a social good. Diverging from Aristotelian ethics and Christian morality, where the emphasis was on individual virtues like courage, self-control, and truthfulness, David Hume, Adam Smith, and others saw that if one gave a role to what were conventionally considered to be human vices, such as self-interest and ambition, one could harness them to the project of social betterment. If a person cannot become rich except by making someone else better off, or cannot attain greater power except by having that power be freely and temporarily delegated to him, then the conventional vices can be used as the engines to increase social happiness, wealth, and security. The "magic" that transforms individual vices into social virtues is Smith's invisible hand.

Social *summum bonum* can be achieved only by relying on individual interests, which in themselves are not always praiseworthy. Nor do the rewards always accrue to the virtuous. This contrast between the individual and the social level is laid out starkly by Mandeville, and to an even greater degree by Machiavelli, but is presented in a more nuanced way by Smith, perhaps because of his theism. This seems to be especially the case in *The Theory of Moral Sentiments,* where Smith comes close to Leibniz and the position that was ridiculed by Voltaire when he mocked the idea of "the best of all possible worlds" in *Candide:*

> The happiness of mankind, as well as of all other rational creatures, seems to have been the original purpose intended by the Author of nature, when he brought them into existence. No other end seems worthy of that supreme wisdom and divine benignity which we necessarily ascribe to him; and this opinion, which we are led to by the abstract consideration of his infinite perfections, is still more confirmed by the examination of the works of nature, which seem all intended to promote happiness, and to guard against misery. (*Theory of Moral Sentiments,* book 3, chap. 5, §7)

There is no contradiction between what one gets and what one deserves, continues Smith:

> If we consider the general rules by which external prosperity and adversity are commonly distributed in this life, we shall find, that notwithstanding the disorder in which all things appear to be in this world, yet even here every virtue naturally meets with its proper reward. (book 3, chap. 5, §8)

And if there is such a contradiction between the merit and the reward, this is an accident similar to an earthquake or a flood (although we do not know why the Author of nature allows for such accidents):

> By some very extraordinary and unlucky circumstance, a good man may come to be suspected of a crime of which he was altogether incapable, and upon that account be most unjustly exposed for the remaining part of his life to the horror and aversion of mankind. By an accident of this kind he may be said to lose his all, notwithstanding his integrity and justice; in the same manner as a cautious man, notwithstanding his utmost circumspection, may be ruined by an earthquake or an inundation. (book 3, chap. 5, §8)

The arguments I put forward in Chapter 5 regarding how hypercommercialized globalization affects our values and behavior, and reciprocally, how our values shape the currently existing commercialized societies, are in basic agreement with Smith's view of how individual self-interest becomes transmuted into a social good. But they are not in full and unconditional agreement.

My views depart from Smith's ultimately optimistic conclusion in two ways. First, I argue that an ever greater commodification of our lives leads to broader use of, and often unconstrained reliance on, the passions of power, pleasure, and profit. For these passions then to produce favorable social effects one must impose ever greater governmental "fencing-in," trying to stay, through legal constraints and tough legislation, one step ahead of possible abuses. This is not easy to achieve under the best imaginable circumstances, and it is even more difficult to achieve when those who hold power do not have an incentive to allow such governmental constraints to be introduced. Second, some of the extreme forms that such passions may take cannot be tamed by any method. This applies to activities that are from the very beginning illegal or unethical, and whose importance is probably greater in more commercially minded societies. These are then two instances where the Smithian transmutation of vices into virtues becomes difficult to effect in hypercommercialized societies.

One might then wonder to what extent the key postulates of Smithian transmutation are valid today. If at one point neither internal nor external checks are powerful enough to control and direct individual passions into socially productive channels, their free exercise may indeed lead to destructive outcomes.

SOME METHODOLOGICAL ISSUES
AND DEFINITIONS

In this appendix I provide more detail on several topics discussed in the book: how global inequality is measured (Section 1.2 and Figure 1.1), how the share of capital in total net income is estimated (Section 2.2a), and why income convergence between rich and poor countries is expected (Section 3.2b and Figure 3.2).

Measurement of Global Inequality

Global inequality refers to income inequality among all world citizens, measured at a given point in time. It is methodologically not different from income inequality within, say, the United States. The only difference is that the area over which we calculate global inequality is larger. But the methodology and the tools of measurement (e.g., the use of the Gini coefficient, the most popular measure of inequality) are the same.[1]

The data on global inequality normally come from nationally representative household surveys that are then combined into an overall world income distribution. (Obviously, if we had a global household survey, creating a global income distribution would be easier.) National surveys provide incomes of households expressed in national currencies. These amounts are converted into so-called international dollars (also called PPP, or purchasing power parity, dollars) that in principle have the same purchasing power in any country. This is done in order to adjust incomes earned in poorer countries, whose price level is generally lower than that of richer countries (e.g., the same quantity of food is cheaper in India than in Norway). This procedure makes national income data mutually comparable.

The just-described methodology can be used only for the period after the mid- to late 1980s because household surveys for some important parts of the world did not exist before then. Household surveys were not introduced in many African countries until the 1980s, China's surveys are only available starting in 1984, and the surveys conducted in the Soviet Union were not published until the late 1980s. So for the earlier periods, going all the way back to 1820, much rougher estimates have to be used. In their pioneering work, François Bourguignon and Christian Morrisson (2002) divided the world into thirty-three regional blocs and within each of these blocs applied the same estimated income distribution to all countries, at approximately twenty-year intervals. Thus all the countries that were included in a given regional bloc (in a given year) were supposed to have the same income distribution. This led to a significant simplification, but it was the best that could be done given the general lack of data on historical income distributions. Some newer work, using somewhat different historical distributions, has confirmed the main results obtained by Bourguignon and Morrisson (van Zanden et al. 2014; Milanovic 2011).

For mean country incomes (which are necessary in order to anchor a given distribution), Bourguignon and Morrisson used Angus Maddison's (2007) 1990 GDP per capita estimates for most of the countries in the world from 1820 to the end of the twentieth century.

In my Figure 1.1, for the period up to 1988, I take the original Bourguignon-Morrisson distributions and definitions of the regional blocs but replace the 1990 Maddison GDPs per capita with new GDP per capita estimates produced by the Maddison Database Project using 2011 PPP estimates, which are the most recent available.[2] What this recalculation does is to impose the original distributions upon the much improved estimates of historical GDPs per capita. For the period after 1988, I use national household surveys (as explained before) and convert national currency units into 2011 international (PPP) dollars.

It is important to note that inequality is calculated in terms of disposable (after-tax) income and is calculated across all individuals, where each individual is assigned the average per capita income for his or her household (e.g., if the total household after-tax income is 400, and there are four household members, each is assigned an income of 100). This approach is maintained for all calculations, from 1820 to 2013.

Measurement of Capital Share in Total Net Income

National income is divided between owners of property or capital (capitalists) and suppliers of labor (workers). The distribution of national income between capital and labor is called functional distribution of income to distinguish it from inter-personal distribution, discussed, for example, in the previous section in regard to global income distribution. Capital income is composed of all income received from the property a person owns: dividends, interest, and rents. National income can be expressed in gross terms (including depreciation of capital) or net terms (excluding depreciation). Consequently the share of capital in national income could be either net or gross. Empirical studies generally use gross capital share, which has recently been shown to display a steeper increase than the net share in the United States (Rognlie 2015). However, over the past two decades, the use of either measure tends'to show an increasing capital share (as discussed in Section 2.2a). This holds for both advanced and emerging market economies, although the effect is stronger among the former (Dao et al. 2017).

There are three difficult measurement or accounting issues that need to be solved in order to calculate capital share. The first is the division of self-employment (small business) income between capital and labor. The self-employed realize a net income, but since they are the providers of capital themselves and are workers too, it is not clear how their income should be apportioned between the two factors of production. The division is often done as half-half or as two-thirds for labor, one-third for capital. It is clear that such apportioning is arbitrary, or conventional, but it is also likely that, when the share of self-employed income does not vary much, the apportioning rule will have a minimal impact on the changes in the calculated labor and capital shares. The problems are more important when self-employment income itself changes. Then the apportioning rule may influence the evolution of the calculated capital share.

The second is a more recent problem and has to do with very high salaries and stock-like incomes received by top managers. Since CEOs or other managers, however well paid, are still workers, it seems clear that their income should be included in the labor share. There is, however, no unanimity on this point, as some economists argue that because CEO incomes mimic the stock market performance (say, if salaries or bonuses are linked to share prices), they should be treated as capital income. This is an unresolved issue. The opposite argument, in favor of treating such salaries as labor income, is a strong one, because salaries are disbursed only in the case of a person's physically being present and working. The fact that such incomes are high is immaterial: they may be high because of monopoly power or other infringements on competition, but this is a separate issue unrelated to the rules of apportioning.

The third issue is the treatment of imputed income from housing. This is especially important because housing represents a large share of total wealth (in the United States, between a quarter and 30 percent [Wolff 2017]), and for many middle-class families, housing is the only significant asset they own (Kuhn, Schularick, and Steins 2017, 37). Imputed income from housing, that is, rent that owners "pay" to themselves for an apartment or house, is a clear income from property and is included in capital income. However, not all countries report imputed housing values. In addition, the imputed value of housing is difficult to ascertain: households may tend to underestimate it, and hedonic regressions based on the observation of some key housing parameters may not always be reliable. But if the capital share is calculated only from the production side (that is, based on the distribution of nonfinancial and financial corporations' net income between capital and labor), imputed income from housing may be left out.

Income Convergence

One of the standard theoretical and empirical results in growth economics is that the rate of growth of an economy is negatively correlated with its income level.[3] This means that we expect, at a given period of time, say over one to five years, that rich economies will tend to grow more slowly than poor ones. The result is also known in empirical economics as unconditional convergence. When countries' growth rates are regressed on a number of variables that affect growth, such as capital-labor ratios, educational level of the population, institutions (democracy, rule of law, proportional or majoritarian political system), and participation of women in the labor force, the coefficient on the level of income is almost always negative—implying that richer countries will, ceteris paribus, tend to grow more slowly. The conclusion is that if two countries had all other characteristics alike but differed only by their income level, the poorer one would grow faster. This is called conditional convergence.

An intuitive understanding of that result is that as countries move closer to the technological frontier given by the best technology that exists at any given point in time, their growth increasingly depends on new inventions in technology and innovations in the organization of production. Innovations and inventions are normally difficult to make, and it is often thought that such productivity-enhancing innovators cannot produce more than 1 to 1.5 percent of annual growth. But poorer countries have much more room to grow because they can use, copy, or imitate the technologies that already exist.

This relationship between the rate of growth and income level has a direct application to how we view the fast growth rates of countries like China and Vietnam, as compared with the slow growth rates of the United States and Japan (as illustrated in Figure 3.2). It can indeed be argued that as China and Vietnam get richer and become more mature economies, their growth performance will slow down. The historical examples of Japan and South Korea lend some additional support to that hypothesis. This makes direct growth comparisons between poorer Asian economies and richer Western economies biased in favor of the former.

On the other hand, one could argue that what matters politically is comparative growth rates in real time and not what might hypothetically happen in the future. Also, even if the currently fast-growing Asian economies decelerate to the rate of growth exhibited by the West in some twenty to forty years, it will not affect the attractiveness of these economies to other countries that may wish to eliminate the income gap that separates them from the rich world as quickly as China, Vietnam, Singapore, and others have done. In conclusion, Asian economies, even if their growth decelerates in the future, might present the best model for other countries trying to catch up.

NOTES

1. The Contours of the Post–Cold War World

1. Between 1970 and 2016, total world GDP has expanded by almost five times in real terms (from $22 to $105 trillion in 2011 PPP [purchasing power parity]), while world population has doubled (from 3.5 to 7 billion).

2. Results were reported by YouGov in 2016. See Jeff Desjardins, "What People Think of Globalization, by Country," Visual Capitalist, November 9, 2017, http://www .visualcapitalist.com/globalization-by-country/.

2. Liberal Meritocratic Capitalism

1. André Orléan (2011, 23) uses a similar definition, distinguishing capitalist economy from market economy (*économie marchande*) by the presence of wage labor in the former. Peer Vries (2013) does the same but adds the "projection of power abroad" as a central feature of capitalism (a topic which we shall consider in Chapter 3).

2. I introduced a similar classification of capitalisms in Milanovic (2017).

3. Which requires that saving out of labor income is negligible.

4. Note that we assume that the proportions of income from capital and labor are constant across income distribution, not absolute amounts of income. Thus one person will get 7 units of income from labor and 3 units of income from capital; another

person, respectively, 14 and 6. Their total incomes are different, but the shares of the two factors are the same.

5. And since richer individuals save more, and capital-abundant individuals tend to be rich, there is an additional dynamic impetus to higher inequality.

6. Theoretically, however, this need not be so. A capitalist system, and even a rising share of net income from capital, is compatible with equal proportions of capital and labor income received by all income classes. This would break the link between individual "capital-abundance" and rank in income distribution.

7. Laborers also did not save, which was certainly the case historically when wages were close, or just slightly above, subsistence level.

8. There is some dispute about the extent to which they can be called workers, because part of their income mimics returns from assets (as for example, for individuals whose salary is linked to the performance of their company's equity), but it is still legitimate to call such income a salary or wage, because it is received only when one performs a labor function. Note that this is different from being paid in equity; income from these shares, or capital gains realized from these shares, is capital income.

9. See Piketty (2014), chap. 8, esp. figs. 8.3 and 8.4; Piketty and Saez (2003); Atkinson, Piketty, and Saez (2011); and Bakija, Cole, and Heim (2010), among others.

10. Dahrendorf ([1963] 1978, 113) speculated that social intergenerational mobility was relatively high in the United States, Britain, and Germany and that "the rate of mobility seems to correspond roughly to the degree of industrialization in a country."

11. I do not think that this view should be especially controversial. "Pure preference" will be different in an aristocratic society, where societal orders are hierarchically arranged, than in a more democratic society.

12. For some technical issues in the measurement of capital share, see Appendix C.

13. It is not always clear what should be included in the capital share. The issue is explained in Appendix C.

14. On monopoly power and rising capital share, see Kurz (2018). He finds that the "surplus income" (the share of monopoly profit in output value) increased in the United States from virtually 0 in 1986 to 22 percent in 2015 (table 7). On monopsony power, see Azar, Marinescu, and Steinbaum (2017).

15. See Branko Milanovic, "Bob Solow on Rents and Decoupling of Productivity and Wages," Globalinequality blog, May 2, 2015, http://glineq.blogspot.com/2015/05/bob-solow-on-rents-and-decoupling-of.html.

16. The market power, or rent-seeking, explanation for the rising share of capital versus labor has been adduced by a number of economists, including by Angus Deaton in an interview with editors of the ProMarket blog on February 8, 2018: https://promarket.org/angus-deaton-discussed-driver-inequality-america-easier-rent-seekers-affect-policy-much-europe/.

17. The corporate profit rate in 2015 was at the highest level in the past half century (Wolff 2017, 27).

18. According to Goldman Sachs Research, "We estimate that the rise in product market and labor market concentration has depressed annual wage growth by 0.25 per-

centage points per year since the early 2000s" (quoted in Alexandra Scaggs, "On Juggernaut Companies and Wage Growth," *Financial Times,* February 4, 2018, version).

19. Anticipated or chronic hyperinflation, such as in Brazil in the 1970s, does not affect capital owners very much, as they are able to hedge and even to do better than poorer households, which, for daily needs, have to operate with cash, whose value is evaporating.

20. Note that people who are in the top wealth decile are not necessarily the same as the people who are in the top income decile.

21. The implicit assumption, which is empirically corroborated, is that rankings by wealth and income are strongly positively correlated—that is, that people with high incomes are also people with high wealth.

22. Ginis are calculated from individual data in household surveys, dividing total labor income by the number of individuals in the household and then calculating Gini across individuals and thus defined values. The approach is the same for income from capital. Note that this calculation shows how important capital and labor incomes are for households and directly relates to national accounts data. It is different from a calculation of wage inequality based only on earners. For example, in the latter calculation, two high-earning individuals who are married to each other are treated as independent people, whereas in a household-based calculation their incomes are summed up.

23. Income from capital includes dividends, interest, rents, and so on, but not realized capital gains (or capital losses).

24. The results shown here are actually underestimates of capital concentration, since the household surveys from which these results come tend not to include the most affluent capital-rich individuals, or, in order to avoid some possible loss of confidentiality, the surveys do "top-coding" (not reporting incomes above a certain ceiling) or "swapping" (swapping very high capital and labor incomes among the richest individuals so that individuals cannot be identified). Fiscal data tend to show somewhat higher concentration of income from capital, but they have their own shortcomings: the units can be at times families and at times individuals simply because of changes in tax rules, or there may be sudden movements between capital income reported in tax returns and corporate profits (using one or the other depending on what is taxed less, as happened in the United States with the Tax Reform Act of 1986).

25. The existence in rich countries of an important part of the population without assets is not unique to the United States. Grabka and Westermeier (2014) estimate that 28 percent of German adults have zero or negative net wealth, while the bottom half of the Swedish population has negative wealth (Lundberg and Walderström 2016, table 1).

26. Carried interest is taxed as a capital gain, at a rate of about 20 percent. Interest from savings accounts is taxed as ordinary income, where the top rate is around 40 percent.

27. Bas van Bavel (pers. comm.) gave me the example of BNP Paribas Fortis wealth management fund, which distinguishes between its retail, priority, private banking, and

wealth management clients. For the last group, whose investments must be at least 4 million euros, the number of investment options is much greater, and management fees (as a percent of invested assets) are lower.

28. This analysis looks only at male-female marriages, since the number of same-sex marriages during this period was negligible.

29. The result cannot be explained by the greater work participation of women because the sample is in both cases composed only of people who have non-zero earnings. Thus the possibility that in 1970 more men were marrying women who were not working does not affect the relative shares of the top decile of male earners marrying the top or bottom decile of female earners.

30. Decancq, Peichl, and Van Kerm (2013) found that the US Gini increased from 0.349 to 0.415 between 1967 and 2007, but if the marriage pattern in 2007 had been the same as in 1967, the counterfactual Gini would have been only 0.394. Increased homogamy thus added more than 2 Gini points to inequality (0.415 − 0.394). The extent to which homogamy increases inequality, while positive, is not exactly clear. In an early estimation, Greenwood et al. (2014a) found that assortative mating explains the lion's share of increased inequality in the United States between 1960 and 2005. They retracted that finding later and in a corrigendum (Greenwood et al. 2014b) estimated the effect on inequality to have been between 0.1 and 1 Gini point out of the 9 Gini points by which observed inequality increased.

31. Fiorio and Verzillo (2018) found that assortative mating in Italy is very strong among men and women belonging independently to the top 1 percent. Women in the top 1 percent of income distribution of women are twenty-five times more likely than median income women to marry men who are in the top 1 percent of men's income distribution. They argue, however, that the effects on overall inequality are small and that homogamy is limited to the very top of the Italian income distribution.

32. In a revealing discussion tucked away in a footnote to *Law, Legislation and Liberty*, vol. 2, pp. 188–189, Hayek mentions the perception of greater equality of opportunity in the United States using his own (or rather his son's) example. While Hayek was in London, having fled the Nazis, he decided to send his son outside of England to live with a family. He chose the United States rather than Sweden or Argentina because he believed that the United States provided greater equality of opportunity for a foreigner: success was less influenced by parental background. Hayek then intriguingly notes that high social status was an advantage for himself in the United Kingdom but would not be equally so in the United States, where he was then relatively unknown. But when starting from a clean slate, his son's chances were much better in America than in Argentina. Hayek also notes that this was based on a tacit assumption that his son would not be placed with a black family, for then all advantages of American greater mobility would turn into the opposite.

33. The same idea was recently propounded by Nassim Taleb in *Skin in the Game* (2018). He calls it "ergodicity," meaning that during one's lifetime or, in the intergenerational case, over several generations, people should—if there is full mobility—spend equal times at different parts of the income distribution. That is, all would have a

20 percent chance (over that longer time horizon) to be in the bottom quintile and a 20 percent chance to be in the top quintile.

34. Relative mobility is a measure of changes in position in income distribution over generations: say, if the father's position was at the fiftieth percentile and the son's at the sixtieth percentile, then there has been upward mobility. Note that since relative mobility deals with positions, each upward move must correspond to an equal downward move. The "ideal" situation would be full orthogonality (no relationship) between parents' and children's income positions.

35. In their analysis, Chetty et al. (2017b) exaggerate the decline in US absolute mobility. Their baseline scenario shows 92 percent of children in the initial period (the cohort born in 1940) to have greater incomes than their parents, and only 50 percent of children having so at the end of the period (the cohort born in 1984). However that calculation is based on comparing household total income, which is inappropriate when household size has been declining. After they adjust for that by looking at per capita income, the decline becomes much smaller; it goes from 92 percent to 62 percent. Further, they use gross income rather than disposable income. With the increase of redistributive social transfers and taxes over the period, absolute income mobility likely decreased even less. Davis and Mazumder (2017, 12) find much lower, and not statistically significant, decline in US absolute intergenerational mobility.

36. Some parts of the text in this section rely on the posts I published on my blog "Global Inequality" in 2017 (http://glineq.blogspot.com/).

37. For the United States in 1990, Tinbergen forecast the income ratio of university-trained to average-income recipients to be between 0.83 (i.e., university would carry a negative premium of 17 percent) and 1.07. For the Netherlands, the premium would still be substantial (around 2 to 1), but would have been halved compared to its 1970 level (Tinbergen 1975, table 6.7).

38. That countries must deal differently with citizens who own moveable property or can themselves move easily abroad than with those who cannot was noted by Montesquieu (as Hirschman reminds us in *The Passions and the Interests* [1977, 94]). Adam Smith was of the same opinion because "the proprietor of stock is properly a citizen of the world and is not necessarily attached to any particular country. He would be apt to abandon the country in which he was exposed to a vexatious inquisition, in order to be assessed to a burdensome tax, and would remove his stock to some other country where he could either carry on his business or enjoy his fortune more at his ease" (*Wealth of Nations,* book 5, chap. 2).

39. In such a utopian world, compulsory social insurance might still exist. Taxes and transfers would not be zero, but they could be relatively small, and their objective would be income-smoothing rather than redistribution or poverty alleviation.

40. We can expect, both because of the increasing number of years of compulsory education and the natural ceiling on the maximum number of years of education, that individual differences in the stock of schooling (years of education) will become smaller and smaller. This is already the case in rich countries. For example, around year 2000, the Gini coefficient for years of education was 0.6 in India, 0.43 in Brazil (which is

undergoing the transition from low to medium level of schooling), and only 0.16–0.18 in the highly educated United States and Sweden (Thomas, Wang, and Fan 2001).

41. For example, an investor whose total financial investments during a year remained below a certain threshold could be protected against any net losses. (If there were net losses, they could be used implicitly as a tax credit.) It could be argued that this guarantee might lead small investors to take unreasonable risks because the upside would be their own, while the downside would be guaranteed by the government. This could be adjusted by making the guarantee valid only if the losses did not exceed, say, 30 percent, and it would also apply only to sufficiently small investors. This would limit government overall liability and discourage excessively risky behavior.

42. Isabel Sawhill (2017) suggests that the treatment of very high CEO compensations as wages (and thus having them reduce taxable corporate profits) be limited only to the companies that engage in profit- or equity-sharing. This is an intriguing idea because it would link the interests of top management to that of workers. The UK Labour Party proposes a scheme whereby companies employing more than 250 workers would be obliged to hand over between 1 and 10 percent of shares to their workers.

43. The idea of reducing poverty and inequality through one-off grants, in order to safeguard democracy, goes back to Aristotle: "For the duty of the truly democratic politician is just to see that people are not destitute; for destitution is a cause of deterioration of democracy. Every effort therefore must be made to perpetuate prosperity. And, since this is to the advantage of the rich as well as of the poor, all that can be got from the revenues should be collected into a single fund and distributed to those in need, if possible enough for the purchase of a piece of land, but if not, enough to start a business or work on the land" (*Politics,* book 6, chap. 5. [1976, 246]). A very similar proposal was made by Thomas Paine in *Agrarian Justice,* published in 1797.

44. Moral suasion may be another way to (possibly) achieve this. The richest universities could be asked to sign a Giving Pledge whereby a certain percentage of their annual income realized through tax-free return on endowments would be earmarked for a special fund to be used for public education. Note that the tax-free status of private college endowments means that forgone taxes on such endowments, at the state level, are often greater than the tax-funded contributions for public colleges. Thus, indirectly, states may contribute more to private than to public education.

45. Among other sources, see Milanovic (2016, 194–199).

46. One example is that of British pensions. By the late 1970s, public pensions accounted for 90 percent of all received pensions, and private occupational pensions for only 10 percent. By 2013, occupational pensions were more important than public pensions (calculated from British microdata available in Luxembourg Income Study database, https://www.lisdatacenter.org/).

47. An interesting case is a relative lack of success of the German "green card" system in attracting, on a permanent basis, highly skilled migrants. Such migrants might prefer, if they looked at their incomes only, a much more unequal American system than a more benign and equal West European one.

48. Aristotle, *Politics,* book 3, chap. 8 (1976, 117).

49. For example, if 90 percent of the rich favor a certain change, it has an almost 50 percent chance of being considered; if 90 percent of people around median income care about an issue, it has a 30 percent chance of being addressed (Gilens 2015).

50. Contributions from members of this group of the rich are therefore four thousand times greater than those of average citizens. See Thomas B. Edsall, "Why Is It So Hard for Democracy to Deal with Inequality?" *New York Times,* February 15, 2019, based on data from Bonica et al. (2013).

51. It would be an interesting topic to study jointly the distributions of capital income or wealth and political contributions across the same individuals. The data for both exist, but they come from separate surveys, and the link between top contributors and top wealth-holders has not, to my knowledge, been studied except for the wealthiest four hundred Americans on the *Forbes* list. For them, Bonica and Rosenthal (2016) found that between 1984 and 2012, the share of contributors among the wealthiest four hundred Americans was always more than 70 percent and went up to 81 percent in 2012, and the wealth elasticity of political contributions was slightly above 1 (meaning that each percentage point increase in wealth was accompanied by about a 1 percent increase in contributions).

52. Trevor Timm, "Money Influences Everybody. That Includes Hillary Clinton," *Guardian,* April 14, 2016.

53. This does not mean, as is sometimes crudely interpreted, that politicians are blank slates on which the rich can draw any policy they like. The point is that there is a selection process whereby the rich "select" the candidates who are sympathetic to their interests and whom they can also influence further in that "desirable" direction.

54. Real (i.e., inflation-adjusted) cost of tuition and fees at private universities has increased by 2.3 times between 1988 and 2018. See Emmie Martin, "Here's How Much More Expensive It Is for You to Go to College That It Was for Your Parents," CNBC, November 29, 2017, https://www.cnbc.com/2017/11/29/how-much-college-tuition-has -increased-from-1988-to-2018.html. Over the same period, US real median per capita income has increased by around 20 percent (calculated from Luxembourg Income Study database, https://www.lisdatacenter.org/).

55. "Some Colleges Have More Students from the Top 1 Percent Than the Bottom 60," The Upshot, *New York Times,* January 18, 2017. For the paper from which this article is drawn, see Chetty et al. (2017a).

56. If poor and middle-class families have more children per family, the advantage of the rich is even greater than 60 to 1.

57. For discussion of the educational system in the social reproduction of the class system see Bowles and Gintis (1976).

58. This text was written before the scandal about extensive bribes paid by parents to get their children admitted to top schools was revealed in February 2019. See Jennifer Medina, Katie Benner, and Kate Taylor, "Actresses, Business Leaders and Wealthy Parents Charged in U.S. College Entry Fraud," *New York Times,* March 12, 2019.

59. Things are not very different in France: in 2017, only 2.7 percent of students in the French top schools (the *grandes écoles)* had parents from the lower end of the

socioeconomic ladder; see Philippe Aghion and Benedicte Berner, "Macron's Education Revolution," Project Syndicate, May 7, 2018, https://www.project-syndicate.org /commentary/macron-education-reforms-by-philippe-aghion-and-benedicte-berner -2018-03.

60. It has been very difficult until recently to obtain any information from top US universities about the income or wealth of students' parents. This shut-down of information contrasts strongly with the fact that all top US schools maintain heavily staffed departments whose sole role is precisely to learn as much as possible about the financial status of parents and also of their former alumni in order to correctly calibrate the amount of money they ask as contributions.

61. The only other country for which such estimates are available is the United Kingdom. Atkinson (2018) finds the ratio of inherited wealth to GDP to have decreased from 20 percent at the beginning of the twentieth century to some 5 percent in the 1980s (the trough) and to have gone up to about 8 percent since then. This still puts it somewhat below the French level. Atkinson also confirms Piketty's finding of a rising μ, that is, relative wealth of decedents.

62. The percentage of billionaires who inherited their wealth in advanced economies (within which the United States plays a preponderant role) also went down over the same period, from 42 percent to 37 percent (Freund 2016, 22).

63. "The governing class tries . . . to defend its power and avert the danger of an uprising . . . in various ways. . . . the [governing classes] uses derivation [ideology] to keep [the oppressed] quiet telling them that 'all power comes from God,' that it is a 'crime' to resort to violence, that there is no reason for using force to obtain what, if it is 'just,' may be obtained by 'reason.' The main purpose of such derivations is to keep [the oppressed] from giving battle on their own terrain, the terrain of force, and to lead them to other ground—the field of cunning—where there defeat is certain" (Pareto 1935, chap. 12, 1534).

3. Political Capitalism

1. I am dealing here with communism-in-power, an actual socioeconomic system, not with communism as an ideology.

2. Berdyaev 2006 (based on lectures delivered in Moscow in 1924).

3. This locus classicus for the critique of what he terms "the doctrine of historical laws of succession" is Karl Popper's *The Poverty of Historicism*: "Historicism is . . . an approach to the social sciences which assumes that historical prediction is their principal aim, and which assumes that this aim is attainable by discovering the 'rhythms' or the 'patterns,' the 'laws' or the 'trends' that underlie the evolution of history" ([1957] 1964, 3).

4. Note that this usage of "socialism" is very different from a more colloquial use of "socialist" for capitalist economies that have a large welfare state. I think it is a misleading characterization and I will not use it.

5. Trade and, by implication, capitalism, have been associated with peace since the time of Montesquieu.

6. Marx's letter to Vera Zasulich is available at https://www.marxists.org/archive /marx/works/1881/zasulich/zasulich.htm. See also Marx's 1877 letter to the editors of *Otechestvennye Zapiski:* "I arrived at this result: If Russia continues to proceed along the path followed up to 1861 [abolition of serfdom], she will lose the finest opportunity that history has ever offered to a people, only to succumb to all the vicissitudes of the capitalist regime," https://www.marxists.org/history/etol/newspape/ni/vol01/no04/marx .htm. See also Avineri (1968).

7. Furthermore, the concept of the Asiatic mode of production is inapplicable to a number of Asian societies, including China, that displayed small-scale peasant commodity production combined with a state that exercised much lower fiscal pressure (as a share of GDP) than Western states at the same time (see Ma 2011, 9–21). In other words, there was no alienation of producers from their means of production, nor was the state a de facto landlord, nor was there unbearable fiscal pressure or widespread forced labor—all characteristics that we would associate with the Asiatic mode of production. As Peer Vries (2013, 354) notes, Qing China came much closer to Adam Smith's idea of a market economy with free competition than did Europe at the same time.

8. In 1885, Jules Ferry, a left-wing French politician who was among the most ardent supporters of French colonialism, defined three objectives of French colonial policy; the third was that "the higher races had a duty to civilize the lower" (Wesseling 1996, 17).

9. The rest of the Third World, which was colonized but did not go through communist revolutions, could be considered to be following the standard liberal path to a developed capitalist economy. The examples of India, Nigeria, and Indonesia are consistent with that view.

10. In "The British Rule in India" (1853), Marx wrote: "We must not forget that these idyllic village communities [being destroyed by British imperialism], inoffensive though they may appear, had always been the solid foundation of oriental despotism, that they restrained the human mind within the smallest possible compass, making it the unresisting tool of superstitions . . . depriving it of all grandeur and historic energies" (Marx 2007, 218).

11. There is an interesting parallelism here between this view of externally induced transition to socialism and Lenin's view that proletarian consciousness can be brought to workers only externally, that is through the action of professional revolutionaries. In both cases, there are no autonomous endogenous forces that would lead the subjects (Third World countries or workers) to revolution.

12. Warren (1980, 105). Mao Zedong explicitly endorsed this view in *On New Democracy,* published in 1940: "No matter what classes, parties or individuals in an oppressed nation join the revolution, and no matter whether they themselves are conscious of this point or understand it, so long as they oppose imperialism, their revolution becomes part of the proletarian-socialist world revolution" (quoted in Chi Hsin [1978], 223).

13. Note that the underdevelopment of the Third World with which we are concerned here is relative to the West. This is what matters, and not that the Third World was as poor as the West was at some earlier point in time. Relative poverty implies technological backwardness and military weakness, and therefore vulnerability to foreign conquest.

14. "The Foolish Old Man Who Removed the Mountains," in *Selected Works of Mao Tse-tung*, vol. 3 (Beijing: Foreign Languages Press, 1969), 272, (as quoted in Kissinger [2011], 111).

15. Quoted in Tooze (2014, 104).

16. The inequality extraction ratio (actual inequality as a proportion of the maximum inequality that would exist under conditions of everyone but a very small elite living at a subsistence level) was, according to calculation by Sarah Merette (2013), between 75 and 80 percent, respectively, in Tonkin (North) and Cochinchina (South) in 1929. (A 100 percent extraction ratio would indicate that the entire local population lived at the subsistence level and the colonizers appropriated all of the surplus.) Note that the percentage of colonists was extremely small in both parts of Vietnam: 0.2 percent in Tonkin and 0.4 percent in Cochinchina. The French, moreover, left large Vietnamese landholdings untouched. So feudal relations of production were intact, and foreign exploitation was at the peak, with most of the local population living at the subsistence level.

17. Chris Bramall (2000) described as the main achievement of the Maoist era "suppression of growth-retarding interest groups" (as quoted in Gabriel [2006], 171).

18. Wang (1991, 269). See my review at http://glineq.blogspot.com/2018/02/i-wont -go-to-moscow-until-revolution.html.

19. The use of the term was attributed to Chen Dixiu, the first general secretary of the Chinese Communist Party (1921–1922). See Wang (1991, 174).

20. There are similarities with the role of the state in Germany and Japan—but these countries were not under foreign rule, so the nationalist element was expressed differently, through imperialism rather than national liberation.

21. This is based on the fact that industry accounts for about a third of China's GDP, and thus the SOEs' share translates into slightly less than 7 percent of the overall GDP. The rest of the state sector's share comes from transportation and services, such as banking and communication. In October 2018, the Chinese vice premier, Liu He, stated that the private sector accounted for 60 percent of China's GDP ("Xi Reaffirms Support for Private Firms," *China Daily*, October 22, 2018, 1). This is consistent with the figure of around 20 percent share of the SOEs, because the "missing" 20 percent is contributed by collectives and cooperative enterprises (including township and village enterprises), foreign-funded firms, and those founded by funds from Hong Kong and Macao.

22. In the 1980s, the state sector accounted for 85 percent of fixed investment, with the rest being done by the collective firms often controlled by local governments (World Bank 2017, 8).

23. A nice, although by its declared objective Western-centric, review of ideological discussions that led to the adoption of reform programs in China can be found in

Gewirtz (2017). See my review at http://glineq.blogspot.com/2017/09/how-china -became-market-economy-review.html.

24. It will be noticed that the contradiction is due to the clash of the first two systemic characteristics.

25. The People's Congress is the richest parliament in the world, with an estimated total wealth of its members of 4.12 trillion yuan, or $660 billion at the early 2018 exchange rate. See "Wealth of China's Richest Lawmakers Rises by a Third: Hurun," Reuters, March 1, 2018, https://www.reuters.com/article/us-china-parliament-wealth /wealth-of-chinas-richest-lawmakers-rises-by-a-third-hurun-idUSKCN1GD6MJ.

26. Even China formally has a multiparty system, with non-Communist parties playing a strongly circumscribed and essentially ceremonial role.

27. Malaya's struggle for independence from the United Kingdom was indeed violent, with an element of civil war between communist-led guerilla and the others. So in that sense Singapore's experience, while part of Malaya, was no different. But its own secession from Malaya was accomplished peacefully.

28. The countries that were part of the Soviet Union do not fit in this scheme not only because their colonial status was (to say the least) unclear, but because after 1991 they have moved toward liberal capitalism, even if in some of them (including Belarus, Russia, Uzbekistan, Kazakhstan, and Azerbaijan) a quasi- or fully single-party system has been maintained.

29. Even if we exclude China their share of world output increased strongly, from 1.7 percent in 1990 to 2.7 percent in 2016.

30. It is estimated that 16 percent of China's population are people without *hukou* who nevertheless live in urban areas (a datum presented at the China Development Forum conference in Beijing in September 2018).

31. Very good reviews of the data sources used to study incomes and income inequality in China can be found in Gustafsson, Li, and Sato (2014) and Xie and Zhou (2014). An excellent overview of the official National Bureau of Statistics surveys, from their inception in the 1950s to 2013, is provided in Zhang and Wang (2011).

32. There is additional evidence for the decline in the wage premium. Zhuang and Li (2016, 7) show that from 2010, wage increases in low-skill sectors have always exceeded wage increases in high-skill sectors.

33. This result is confirmed by what is probably the largest household survey ever undertaken in China, the mini-census of 2005, which interviewed almost one million households: it reported a Gini of 48.3 (see Xie and Zhou 2014, table 1).

34. However, the Congressional Budget Office (2014, table 2), gives the capital income and capital gains plus business income share in top 1 percent total income as 58 percent (in fiscal year 2011).

35. A study by Gong, Leigh, and Meng (2012), based on partial microdata from urban household surveys, found the intergenerational correlation of fathers' and sons' incomes to be 0.64, which is at the high end of what similar studies find for the United States. Van der Weide and Narayan (2019) confirm the decline in China's intergenerational education mobility and find it to be about the same as in the United States.

However, given that the results of similar studies for other countries have not produced stable coefficients, these results should be taken with a dose of caution. Concerning wealth inequality, Ding and He (2018) showed, based on the most reliable source of household wealth coming from the China Household Income Project, that in 2002 (the latest year they have) the Gini for financial net worth in China was 0.81; this can be compared with a US Gini for net financial wealth of about 0.9 in the same period (see Wolff 2017, table 2.0).

36. For the "new" middle class, the public sector is still dominant: in 2006, more than 60 percent of managers and professionals were employed by the public sector (Li n.d., table 3). The "old" middle class is old in the sense that its functional equivalents (small owners) existed in prerevolutionary China and even in the 1960s.

37. As of 2017, 66 out of 100 largest Chinese fugitives from justice were in the United States and Canada. Chinese abduction of one of them recently produced tension in US-Chinese relations until the FBI finally agreed to cooperate with the Chinese authorities in arresting and surrendering the worst offenders. See Mimi Lau, "China's Graft-Busters Release List of 100 Wanted Fugitives in Operation Sky Net," *South China Morning Post,* April 23, 2015, http://www.scmp.com/news/china/policies-politics/article/1773872/chinas-graft-busters-release-list-100-wanted-fugitives.

38. Quoted in Arrighi (2007, 15).

39. This approach was recommended by Zhao Ziyang, former general secretary of the Chinese Communist Party, who wrote in his "secret" memoirs (published after his death): "without an independent judiciary the court could not judge a case with a disinterested attitude" and "without political reform to put checks on the Communist party's rule, the corruption problem could not be resolved" (2009, 265, 267).

40. "Is China Succeeding in the War against Corruption," interview with Bernard Yeung, ProMarket blog, April 1, 2017, https://promarket.org/china-succeeding-war-corruption-qa-bernard-yeung/.

41. Xi's own family, according to an exposé published in *Bloomberg News* in 2012, seems to enjoy a lifestyle that is at odds both with what they profess and with the official incomes they have, but it is not likely that investigation of corruption would go that high, at least as long as Xi is in power. See "Xi Jinping Millionaire Relations Reveal Fortunes of Elite," *Bloomberg,* June 29, 2012, https://www.bloomberg.com/news/articles/2012-06-29/xi-jinping-millionaire-relations-reveal-fortunes-of-elite.

42. As an officially published book on corruption puts it, "severe punishment might not necessarily build a clean government, but without severe punishment there will be [no end to] corruption" (Xie 2016, 23).

43. The data are public and are reported by the Chinese authorities.

44. Or, as Pei (2016) argues, they may sell the positions to people who would be loyal to them, thus creating a network that could be useful in generating future corrupt income.

45. Smith praises the Navigation Act in the section that deals with special cases when protection can be acceptable (book 4, chap. 2), going so far as to say that "the Act of Navigation is, perhaps, the wisest of all the commercial regulations of England."

46. In Smith's opinion, such a system existed, in his time, only in Holland.

47. The term was introduced by Kees van der Pijl (2012).

48. Li (n.d., table 2) puts the size of the Chinese middle class at less than 20 percent of the urban population.

49. These are terms the Chinese apparently used to refer to foreigners, depending on whether they were more or less advanced (which in practice meant whether they accepted Chinese suzerainty or not); see Jacques (2012).

50. On the European "coercion-intensive" path, see also Pomeranz (2000, 195, 202–203).

51. "China is a civilization pretending to be a state" (Lucien Pye quoted in Jacques 2012, 245).

52. See, for example, the long review article by Xu (2011) on Chinese institutions.

53. The beginning of the responsibility system, which would eventually cover all of China, goes back to twenty farm households in Fengyang Xiaogang village in Anhui Province who, like medieval conspirators, swore to stick by each other and secretly signed a document in which they agreed to divide the land into individual plots and deliver the required grain quotas to the government while keeping the rest for themselves. The possibility that such "capitalist-roaders" would be severely punished was not negligible. So the farmers vowed that "[they] will not regret [their decision] even if [they] have to face the death penalty. The rest of the members promise to take our kids until 18 years old" (Wu 2015, 32). The original contract is presently kept in the National Museum of China.

54. Or as a Chinese friend put it, "Western governments are like scientists, while the Chinese government is like a very experienced and sophisticated artisan; this renders mass production, that is, transfer of its knowledge, more difficult" (Li Yang, pers. comm.).

55. China is currently the nation with the largest number of outward foreign tourists and the largest tourism spending (exceeding by more than twice the second-ranked United States; data of the World Tourist Organization for 2016).

56. Travel time is sixteen days from Chongqing to Duisburg, Germany, over land, compared with thirty-six to forty days by sea from Shanghai to Rotterdam (Pomfret 2018).

57. Unless things get so much out of order as they did in Zimbabwe.

58. Stated in the Lowell Lectures delivered in March 1941, reprinted in Swedberg (1991, 387).

59. See Jacques (2012, 480). See also my review of Jacques's book at http://glineq .blogspot.com/2018/01/the-aloofness-of-pax-sinica.html.

60. See an excellent discussion of how international institutions, from the postal union to the World Trade Organization, have been created by the West, in Mark Mazower's *Governing the World* (2012).

4. The Interaction of Capitalism and Globalization

1. A slightly different but equally appropriate definition of rent is that of Marx: "it . . . is [an income] by no means determined by the actions of its recipient, but . . . rather by the independent developments . . . in which the recipient takes no part" (*Capital,* vol. 3, part 6, chap. 37; see http://www.marxists.org/archive/marx/works/1894 -c3/ch37.htm).

2. Plus, in some cases, profit from whatever is produced elsewhere using capital owned by people with the same citizenship.

3. See Milanovic (2015), where the value of each country's citizenship is compared not only for all country dyads but for all combinations of countries and income deciles (e.g., the value of Swedish citizenship to a Brazilian is different depending on whether he is at the bottom or the top of the Brazilian income distribution).

4. Although at times a "better" citizenship may be more urgently needed by the old when, for example, citizenship gives the right to free health care or nursing home accommodation.

5. Slaves were also subcitizens. In Imperial Rome slavery was a juridical, not an economic category (see Veyne 2001), but slaves' rights were curtailed, compared with the rights of free citizens, even in cases where they were rich. Even freedmen's rights were not in all respects the same as those of freely born citizens.

6. The United Kingdom is an exception to this general lack of concern—for obvious reasons, since it controlled an enormous amount of territory populated by people with much lower incomes. In 1948, it confirmed free movement of people within the Commonwealth (which in principle existed even before World War I), but then twenty years later rescinded it with the Commonwealth Immigration Act. Avner Offer (1989) noted the often complex and ambivalent attitude of Great Britain toward the movement of the "colored" population into "self-governing" territories like Australia and Canada, which were nominally equal to India but frequently rejected free movement of labor. The self-governing territories were the most concerned about accepting nonwhite labor, perhaps because large Indian inflows would have tilted the balance of political power against the white population.

7. Zygmant Bauman (in "Le coût mondial de la globalisation," cited in Wihtol de Wenden [2010, 70]) correctly made the point that the right to mobility is a new superior good. People from rich countries can move freely, whereas people from poor countries are stuck wherever they are.

8. At first, however, it might increase migration by removing lack of money as a constraint to moving abroad.

9. Lifting currently existing barriers to the free circulation of international labor would, according to one calculation, more than double world income (Kennan 2014). According to Borjas (2015, table 1), the gain under the central (neither optimistic nor pessimistic) scenario is almost 60 percent of world GDP. In all such calculations, the gains come from the increased marginal product of migrant labor that can avail of much better infrastructure and higher capital stock once it is in a richer country.

10. Studies of World Bank and IMF loans invariably find a close to zero net effect on growth of the recipient countries (Rajan and Subramanian 2005). This despite the fact that the rates of return on individual projects financed by foreign aid or concessional loans are often positive (Dalgaard and Hansen 2001).

11. See, for example, a discussion of the decrease of the risk premium, the so-called empire effect, in Ferguson and Schularick (2006).

12. Some of these tools may be anachronistic (e.g., national balance of payments and especially bilateral national balances) because today's globalization differs substantially from the first one. Many of our ways of thinking economics are still derived from globalization as it was in the past.

13. This is why the term "global fragmentation" of production is also used (Los, Timmer, and de Vries 2015).

14. Institutions mattered, however, for capital exporters.

15. The physical presence of labor may still be necessary for some occupations, but the key point is that there would be fewer of such occupations.

16. We assume, as before, that significantly reducing income gaps between nations is not a realistic short- or medium-term option.

17. Aristotle, *Nicomachean Ethics,* book 8, argues that within each community there is a *philia* (affection; goodwill), but that the *philia* diminishes, as in concentric circles, as we move farther from a very narrow community.

18. There are, unfortunately, no empirical studies looking at the link between globalization and corruption. The closest, to my knowledge, is a paper by Benno Torgler and Marco Piatti (2013), who found, in a cross-country study, that both an index of a country's globalization and an index of a country's corruption are positively correlated with the number of billionaires.

19. These surveys are different from surveys of "experienced corruption," which are, in my opinion, better, but are even less available.

20. The results from a natural experiment revealed why most of the accounts in tax havens are held (Johannesen 2014). In 2005, when the European Union convinced the Swiss government to impose withholding tax on interest earned by EU residents holding Swiss bank accounts, the number of such accounts declined by about 40 percent within only four months.

21. Some other estimates of money held in tax havens have been slightly higher; Becerra et al. (2009), for example, estimated $6.7 trillion versus Zucman's $5.9 trillion. For the estimates up to 2015, see Alstadsaeter, Johannesen, and Zucman (2017).

22. International Monetary Fund, *Balance of Payment Statistics Yearbook 2017,* table A-1; IMF Committee on Balance of Payments Statistics, *Annual Report 2010,* table 2.

23. Freund identified billionaires as being politically connected "if there are news stories connecting his or her wealth to past position in government, close relatives in government, or questionable licenses" (2016, 24). The group also includes billionaires whose firms are privatized state enterprises (because of the obvious need for the government to acquiesce to such transfers) and billionaires whose wealth comes from

oil, natural gas, coal, and other natural resources. Again, in this case, the control over the physical area where the resources are frequently depends on government permission.

24. Calculated from the data kindly supplied by Caroline Freund and Sarah Oliver.

25. This is Machiavelli's view. While liberty leads to wealth ("for experience shows that cities never increased in dominion or in riches except while they have been in liberty," he stated in a letter to Francesco Vettori [quoted in Wootton 2018, 40]), wealth is the source of corruption. This is why republican liberty (which we would call democracy) can be found only in poor agricultural societies like the Republican Rome and medieval German cities, but not in a commercial society like Machiavelli's Florence.

26. Jack Abramoff became a rather infamous case of a lobbyist who, because of multiple shady deals and service to dubious clients, was eventually found guilty and jailed for six years. But, I am told by the people who have worked in the same "industry," that what Abramoff did was not exceptional; it might have just been more blatant.

27. This kind of corruption, limited to a few top leaders, is not something that can be considered as generalized corruption. Moreover, these advantages were not transferrable to the next generation.

28. In a book on corruption in Nigeria, Ngozi Okonjo-Iweala (2018) gives the example of electronic transactions between different ministries as one of the measures introduced to combat corruption.

29. British capital controls in the 1960s and 1970s are held responsible for the creation of financial offshore areas like the Channel Islands, where currency controls could be evaded.

30. José Piñera, "President Clinton and the Chilean Model," Cato Policy Report, January / February 2016, https://www.cato.org/policy-report/januaryfebruary-2016/president-clinton-chilean-model.

31. See "Mauritius Largest Source of FDI in India, Says RBI," Economic Times, January 19, 2018, https://economictimes.indiatimes.com/articleshow/62571323.cms.

32. In a review of Oliver Bullogh's book Moneyland: Why Thieves and Crooks Now Rule the World and How to Take It Back (2018), Vadim Nikitin (London Review of Books, February 21, 2019) cites a part of the book where a London PR man defines his objectives regarding the corrupt foreign clients he serves as to make them "unkillable" by having them become "philanthropists," and "unwriteabout-able" by threating expensive defamation suits. The method works well.

33. Black, Kraakman, and Tarassova (2000, 26) write that "After Bank Menatep collapsed in mid-1998, Khodorkovski transferred its good assets to a new bank, Menatep-St. Petersburg, leaving depositors and creditors to pick at the old bank's carcass. To ensure that the transactions couldn't be traced, Khodorkovski arranged for a truck containing most of Bank Menatep's records for the last several years to be driven off a bridge into the Dybna river. Where presumably they will remain." They also describe the purchase of Yukos shares and the allegation that some $4.4 billion of government funds handled by Khodorkovsky's bank "never arrived at their intended destination" (p. 14).

34. As of 2018, Leonid Blavatnik was the third richest person in the United Kingdom; he was knighted for his services to philanthropy.

35. The relative income hypothesis of consumption proposed by James Duesenberry in 1949 was based on similar reasoning: that our consumption responds to what we perceive as normal or desirable consumption within our community.

36. A Serbian friend who worked in a food-catering business for US forces in Iraq told me, with probably slight exaggeration, that the story among the contractors was that for the same job an American would be paid $100, an East European $10, and an African $1.

37. Once, just before a World Cup soccer final, I bought a very expensive scalped ticket from one of the soccer officials from an African nation who had probably gotten the ticket for free. He did not feel any embarrassment in selling it, nor did I feel any in buying it. I thought that he must have (legitimately) compared his normal low salary with that of an identical soccer official in say, Switzerland, and decided that he had the right to make some money on the side. It is hard to argue he did not.

5. The Future of Global Capitalism

1. In *The Spirit of Laws,* Montesquieu wrote, "Le commerce guérit des préjugés destructeurs: et c'est presque une règle générale que, partout où il y a des moeurs douces, il y a du commerce; et que, partout où il y a du commerce, il y a des moeurs douces" (*Spirit of the Laws,* book 20, chap. 1). ["Commerce is a cure for the most destructive prejudices; for it is almost a general rule, that whereever we find agreeable manners, there commerce flourishes; and that wherever there is commerce, there we meet with agreeable manners." From Online Library of Liberty, https://oll.libertyfund .org/titles/montesquieu-complete-works-vol-2-the-spirit-of-laws#a_1820107.] Michael Doyle, one of the main authors of the liberal peace hypothesis, discusses the commercial pacifism of Adam Smith and Schumpeter in *Ways of War and Peace* (1997).

2. At any given point in time, cross-country studies show a strong positive correlation between GDP per capita and mean reported happiness (Helliwell, Huang, and Wang 2017, 10) and also at an individual level within countries, between own income and reported own happiness (Clark et al. 2017, table 5.2). Of all the correlates of life satisfaction, calculated across numerous countries, income is the strongest (Graham, Laffan, and Pinto 2018, fig. 1).

3. "But how destructive soever this system may appear, it could never have imposed upon so great a number of persons, nor have occasioned so general an alarm among those who are the friends of better principles, had it not in some respects bordered upon the truth" (*The Theory of Moral Sentiments,* part 7, section 2, chap. 4).

4. David Wootton writes: "The two works [*The Theory of Moral Sentiments* and *The Wealth of Nations*] do not fit quite so neatly together, for one is about how we ought to behave toward our family, friends, and neighbors (who evoke our benevolent feelings), and the other about how we should interact with strangers we meet in the marketplace

(to whom we owe no particular duty of care—caveat emptor is an attitude we can legitimately adopt to strangers, but not to family, friends, and neighbors). . . . [There is] a tension between the *amoral* world of market forces, and the moral world of human interactions. *The Wealth of Nations* establishes the extent to which our choices are constrained by market forces, and these constraints limit our opportunities for admirable moral behavior" (Wootton 2018, 174–175; my emphasis).

5. "Business with its continuous work has become a necessary part of their [capitalists'] lives. That is in fact the only possible motivation, but it at the same time expresses what is, seen from the view-point of personal happiness, so irrational about this sort of thing, where a man exists for the sake of his business, instead of the reverse" (Weber 1992, 70).

6. It may be useful to clarify that Weber did not see Protestantism as coming *ex post* to tame the greed of capitalists, but that its religious values stimulated this kind of behavior. So the direction of causation, according to Weber, is from religion to capitalist values; the values do not arise for instrumental reasons.

7. "Herein lay, in fact, the main justification of the Capitalist System. If the rich had spent their new wealth on their own enjoyments, the world would long ago have found such a régime intolerable. But like bees they saved and accumulated, not less to the advantage of the whole community because they themselves held narrower ends in prospect" (*The Economic Consequences of the Peace,* chap. 2, section 3).

8. "When the limitation of consumption is combined with this release of acquisitive activity, the inevitable practical result is obvious: accumulation of capital through ascetic compulsion to save" (Weber 1992, 172).

9. A more contemporary example of a tacit contract, currently in the danger of unraveling, is found in the Nordic countries, where wage compression was combined with a high share of capital in net income—but with an understanding that profits would be reinvested to maintain high aggregate demand and full employment (Moene 2016).

10. Harriet Sherwood, "'Christianity as Default Is Gone': The Rise of a Non-Christian Europe," *Guardian,* March 21, 2018.

11. An exception may be the recent attempts by the Catholic Church under Pope Francis to reinforce ethical considerations in business life. See, for example, Hannah Brockhaus, "Pope Francis: The Church Cannot Be Silent about Economic Suffering," April 12, 2018, *Crux,* https://cruxnow.com/vatican/2018/04/12/pope-francis-the-church-cannot-be-silent-about-economic-suffering/.

12. Quoted in Tara Isabella Burton, "Prominent Evangelical Leader on Khashoggi Crisis," *Vox,* October 17, 2018, https://www.vox.com/2018/10/17/17990268/pat-robertson-khashoggi-saudi-arabia-trump-crisis.

13. Rawls thought that nonostentatious behavior by the better-off was important for inevitable inequalities in income and wealth to be accepted by those who are poorer without provoking unjustified envy or resentment: "In everyday life the natural duties are honored so that the more advantaged do not make an ostentatious display of their higher estate calculated to demean the condition of those who have less" (1971, 470).

14. Data from household surveys conducted in the early 2000s. The same finding is reflected in the percentage of children over twenty-five who live with their parents: it is less than 10 percent in Denmark, less than 20 percent in other (very rich) Nordic countries, and about 30 percent in the United States, United Kingdom, and Germany, and it increases as one moves south and east. In Italy, Spain, Taiwan, and Greece, it is between 70 and 80 percent (calculated from Luxembourg Income Study data, around year 2013, https://www.lisdatacenter.org/).

15. The internalization of these activities often puts most of the burden on women.

16. Another way of seeing how sharing and excluding are interconnected is to recall Montesquieu's quip that a fully virtuous man can have no friends because friendship, like sharing, implies a special preference given to someone, a preference that cannot be spread across the entire community.

17. It is estimated that in the mid-nineteenth century only 5 to 15 percent of those working in the Yangtze Delta, the most developed part of China, were wage laborers, while almost three-quarters of those working in the English countryside at the same period were wage laborers (Vries 2013, 340).

18. In *Postcapitalism*, Paul Mason explains the rise of new commodities (like the commercialization of leisure) by a tendency of profits to go to zero and the inability to fully protect the property rights of some new commodities (like software). As profits dissipate, capitalism disappears. The only solution that remains for capitalists, according to Mason, is the commercialization of daily life. This gives them a new "field of action." Ultimately, every human interaction will have to be commodified; mothers, for example, will charge each other a penny to push each other's kids on a playground swing. But this can't continue, Mason argues. There is a natural limit to what humans will accept in terms of commodification of daily activities: "You would have to treat people kissing each other for free the way they treated poachers in the nineteenth century" (Mason 2016, 175). As will become apparent later in this chapter, I am less convinced than Mason that this type of commercialization faces natural limits. Activities that public custom thought beyond the pale to be commercialized have gradually become so, and this is now seen as normal. There is no reason this should not continue happening into the future.

19. Jan de Vries (2008) introduced the term "industrious" to indicate that the movement from household production to wage labor increased dramatically the annual number of hours worked. Thus, the Industrial Revolution was characterized not only by greater output per hour of work, but also by a much greater labor input. See also Pomeranz (2000, 94) and Allen (2009, 2017).

20. Weber (1992, 161).

21. I thank Carla Yumatle for this comment.

22. Daniel Markovits, "A New Aristocracy," Yale Law School Commencement Address, May 2015, https://law.yale.edu/system/files/area/department/studentaffairs/document/markovitscommencementrev.pdf (italics in the original).

23. One possible counterargument is to see forces of decommodification reflected in the demand for open-source software and free (single-payer) health care in the United

States, trends that may become more important in the future. It is a possibility: nobody knows what will happen in the future. However, I think that the arguments presented here, based on the internal logic of the system (not least on the set of values it promotes), point in the opposite direction.

24. I saw the effect of wealth on commodification first hand when I worked on African household surveys, where a number of activities that are routinely monetized in rich economies are performed "for free" at home and had to have their values imputed; otherwise we would grossly underestimate the consumption level of households in many African countries.

25. In Nassim Taleb's words: "If you are a Stone Age historical thinker called on to predict the future in a comprehensive report for your chief tribal planner, you must project the invention of the wheel or you will miss pretty much all of the action. Now, if you can prophesy the invention of the wheel, you already know what a wheel looks like, and thus you already know how to build a wheel" (Taleb 2007, 172).

26. World Bank (2019, p. 22, fig. 1.1). Jobs are classified as "at risk" if the probability of being automated is estimated at more than 0.7.

27. Jean-Baptiste Say, *Cours complet d'économie politique,* 2:170, quoted in Braudel (1979, 539).

28. See Keynes's description of Jevons in his *Essays in Biography* (1972, 266) "[Jevons's] conclusions were influenced . . . by a psychological trait, unusually strong in him, which many other people share, a certain hoarding instinct, a readiness to be alarmed and excited by the idea of exhaustion of resources. Mr. H. S. Jevons [his son] has communicated to me an amusing illustration of this. Jevons had similar ideas as to the approaching scarcity of paper . . . he acted on his fear and laid in such large store not only of writing-paper, but also of thin brown packing paper, that even today, more than fifty years after his death, his children have not used up the stock he left behind."

29. See van Parijs and Vanderborght (2017) and Standing (2017).

30. World Bank (2019, 110). For the monthly UBI amounts in Mongolia and Iran, see World Bank, World Development Report 2019, "The Changing Nature of Work," working draft, April 20, 2018, p. 89, https://mronline.org/wp-content/uploads/2018/04/2019-WDR-Draft-Report.pdf.

Saudi Arabia, like several other Gulf sheikdoms, is distributing a part of the oil rent to its citizens under various cash transfer schemes. I am not sure whether such windfall bounties, which are dependent on the price of oil and the benevolence of the rulers, could be fully assimilated to the more regular unconditional transfers that UBI implies.

31. In a recent paper, Hauner, Milanovic, and Naidu (2017) found strong evidence that all of the individual components mentioned by the authors of the Hobson neo-Marxist theory of imperialism (John Hobson, Rosa Luxemburg, and Vladimir I. Lenin) were indeed present in the runup to World War I: wealth and income inequality in key belligerent countries were at their historical peak; "core" imperialist countries rapidly acquired foreign assets, which were almost entirely owned by the wealthiest 1 to 5 percent of the population; these assets yielded superior returns compared with domestic assets; and the countries that had the greatest amounts of them had the largest

military (in proportion to their population). Thus all the ingredients for a war were present.

32. The number of war-related deaths is calculated from the Correlates of War (COW) project (http://www.correlatesofwar.org/). Between 1901 and 2000, about 166.5 million people have died in inter-state wars, almost 64 million in civil wars, and less than 1 million in imperial and colonial wars. The COW project calls the latter "extra-systemic wars" because they involved a recognized systemic actor (say, the United Kingdom or Russia) fighting a nonsystemic actor (say, Sikh or Polish rebels). "Systemic" simply means that both actors are internationally recognized states. The approximate number of births in the twentieth century is calculated from an estimate made by the US Population Reference Bureau; see table 1 in "How Many People Have Ever Lived on Earth," https://www.prb.org/howmanypeoplehaveeverlivedonearth/.

33. If that happened, Marx's observation that appears as the epigraph to Chapter 4 would be confirmed.

34. Rawls writes: "Imagine . . . that people seem willing to forego certain political rights when the economic returns are significant. It is this kind of exchange which the two principles [extensive individual liberty compatible with the same liberty for all, and economic inequality acceptable only if to the advantage of the poorest] rule out; being arranged in serial order they do not permit exchanges between basic liberties and economic and social gains" (1971, 55).

35. Based on Leijonhufvud (1985) and Bowles and Gintis (1986).

36. This drop in inequality is evident not only when we use synthetic inequality indicators like the Gini coefficient, which look at income levels across the entire global income distribution (as shown in Figure 1.1), but even when we focus on the share of the global top 1 percent. Despite the fact that the income share of the global top 1 percent has tended to grow while global income inequality went down, most recently even the global top 1 percent share has been reduced (see *World Inequality Report 2018*, 56, figure 2.1.9).

37. The role of Africa in global inequality has so far been limited because its population has been much less than Asia's. Around 2005, Africa's contribution to global inequality was about 10 percent. That number is bound to rise with the increase in population, so the evolution of global inequality will increasingly depend on what is happening in Africa.

38. Adam Smith, *The Wealth of Nations*, book 4, chap. 7.

Appendix A

1. "The colony of a civilised nation which takes possession either of a waste country, or of one so thinly inhabited that the natives easily give place to the new settlers, advances more rapidly to wealth and greatness than any other human society" (Adam Smith, *The Wealth of Nations*, book 4, chap. 7).

2. "The British Rule in India," *New York Tribune,* June 25, 1853, in Marx (2007, 218–219).

3. "The Future Results of British Rule in India," *New York Tribune,* August 8, 1853, in Marx (2007, 220).

4. "Capitalism has grown into a world system of colonial oppression and of the financial strangulation of the overwhelming majority of the people of the world by a handful of 'advanced' countries" (Lenin, *Collected Works,* 19:87, quoted in Sweezy [1953, 24]).

5. Eric Hobsbawm, "Introduction," in Marx (1965, 19–20).

6. Karl Marx, "The German Ideology," in Tucker (1978, 157).

Appendix C

1. For more methodological detail, see Milanovic (2005).

2. See Maddison Project Database 2018, https://www.rug.nl/ggdc /historicaldevelopment/maddison/releases/maddison-project-database-2018.

3. Empirically, the result was presented in Baumol (1986), one of the first papers to look at the growth performance of OECD countries. Innumerable papers published since have confirmed the convergence (see, e.g., Barro 1991, 2000).

REFERENCES

Acemoglu, Daron, and James A. Robinson. 2006. *Economic Origins of Dictatorship and Democracy.* Cambridge: Cambridge University Press.

Acemoglu, Daron, and James A. Robinson. 2012. *Why Nations Fail: The Origins of Power, Prosperity, and Poverty.* New York: Crown.

Achen, Christopher, and Larry Bartels. 2017. *Democracy for Realists: Why Elections Do Not Produce Responsive Government.* Princeton, NJ: Princeton University Press.

Akcigit, Ufuk, Salomé Baslandze, and Stefanie Stantcheva. 2015. "Taxation and the International Mobility of Inventors." NBER Working Paper No. 21024, National Bureau of Economic Research, Cambridge, MA, March. Published 2016 in *American Economic Review* 106(10): 2930–2981.

Allen, Robert C. 2009. *The British Industrial Revolution in Global Perspective.* Cambridge: Cambridge University Press.

Allen, Robert C. 2011. "Technology and the Great Divergence." Discussion Paper Series No. 548, Department of Economics, University of Oxford. https://www.economics.ox.ac.uk/materials/papers/5001/paper548.pdf. Published 2012 as "Technology and the Great Divergence: Global Economic Development since 1820." *Explorations in Economic History* 49(1): 1–16.

Allen, Robert C. 2017. *The Industrial Revolution: A Very Short Introduction.* Oxford: Oxford University Press.

Alstadsaeter, Annette, Niels Johannesen, and Gabriel Zucman. 2017. "Who Owns the Wealth in Tax Havens? Macro Evidence and Implications for Global Inequality." NBER Working Paper No. 23805, National Bureau of Economic Research, Cambridge, MA, September.

Alvaredo, Facundo, Anthony B. Atkinson, and Salvatore Morelli. 2018. "Top Wealth Shares in the UK over More Than a Century." *Journal of Public Economics* 162: 26–47.

Aristotle. 1976. *The Politics,* trans. and with an introduction by T. A. Sinclair. Harmondsworth, UK: Penguin Classics.

Arrighi, Giovanni. 2007. *Adam Smith in Beijing: Lineages of the Twenty-First Century.* London: Verso.

Atkinson, Anthony. 2015. *Inequality: What Can Be Done?* Cambridge, MA: Harvard University Press.

Atkinson, Anthony B. 2018. "Wealth and Inheritance in Britain from 1896 to the Present." *Journal of Economic Inequality* 16(2): 137–169.

Atkinson, Anthony B., Thomas Piketty, and Emmanuel Saez. 2011. "Top Incomes in the Long Run of History." *Journal of Economic Literature* 49(1): 3–71.

Avineri, Shlomo, ed. 1968. *Karl Marx on Colonialism and Modernization.* New York: Doubleday.

Azar, José, Ioana Marinescu, and Marshall Steinbaum. 2017. "Labor Market Concentration." NBER Working Paper No. 24147, National Bureau of Economic Research, Cambridge, MA, December.

Bai, Chong-En, Chang-Tai Hsieh, and Zheng (Michael) Song. 2014. "Crony Capitalism with Chinese Characteristics." Unpublished manuscript, May. http://china.ucsd.edu /_files/pe-2014/10062014_Paper_Bai_Chong.pdf.

Bakija, Jon, Adam Cole, and Bradley T. Heim. 2010. "Jobs and Income Growth of Top Earners and the Causes of Changing Income Inequality: Evidence from U.S. Tax Return Data." Unpublished manuscript. https://web.williams.edu/Economics/wp/ BakijaColeHeimJobsIncomeGrowthTopEarners.pdf.

Baldwin, Richard. 2016. *The Great Convergence: Information Technology and the New Globalization.* Cambridge, MA: Belknap Press of Harvard University Press.

Barkai, Simcha. 2016. "Declining Labor and Capital Shares." Unpublished manuscript. http://home.uchicago.edu/~barkai/doc/BarkaiDecliningLaborCapital.pdf.

Barro, Robert J. 1991. "Economic Growth in a Cross Section of Countries." *Quarterly Journal of Economics* 106(2): 407–443.

Barro, Robert. 2000. "Inequality and Growth in a Panel of Countries." *Journal of Economic Growth* 5(1): 5–32.

Baumol, William J. 1986. "Productivity Growth, Convergence, and Welfare: What the Long-Run Data Show." *American Economic Review* 76(5): 1072–1085.

Becerra, Jorge, Peter Damisch, Bruce Holley, et al. 2009. "Delivering on the Client Promise." Global Wealth 2009, Boston Consulting Group, September. Executive summary at https://www.bcg.com/documents/file29101.pdf.

Bekkouche, Yasmine, and Julia Cagé. 2018. "The Price of a Vote: Evidence from France, 1993–2014." CEPR Discussion Paper No. 12614, Centre for Economic Policy Research, London, January. https://cepr.org/active/publications/discussion_papers /dp.php?dpno=12614#.

Berdyaev, Nikolai. 2006. *The Meaning of History.* New Brunswick, NJ: Transaction.

Black, Bernard, Reinier Kraakman, and Anna Tarassova. 2000. "Russian Privatization and Corporate Governance: What Went Wrong?" Stanford Law School John M. Olin Program in Law and Economics Working Paper No. 178. Published 2000 in *Stanford Law Review* 52(6): 1731–1808.

Bonica, Adam, Nolan McCarty, Keith T. Poole, and Howard Rosenthal. 2013. "Why Hasn't Democracy Slowed Rising Inequality?" *Journal of Economic Perspectives* 27(3): 103–123.

Bonica, Adam, and Howard Rosenthal. 2016. "Increasing Inequality in Wealth and the Political Expenditures of Billionaires." Unpublished manuscript.

Borjas, George. 1987. "Self-selection and the Earnings of Immigrants." *American Economic Review* 77(4): 531–553.

Borjas, George J. 2015. "Immigration and Globalization: A Review Essay." *Journal of Economic Literature* 53(4): 961–974.

Bourguignon, François, and Christian Morrisson. 2002. "Inequality among World Citizens: 1820–1992." *American Economic Review* 92(4): 727–744.

Bournakis, Ionnis, Michela Vecchi, and Francesco Venturini. 2018. "Off-shoring, Specialization and R&D." *Review of Income and Wealth* 64(1): 26–51.

Bowles, Samuel, and Herbert Gintis. 1976. *Schooling in Capitalist America: Education Reform and the Contradictions of Economic Life.* New York: Basic Books.

Bowles, Samuel, and Herbert Gintis. 1986. *Democracy and Capitalism: Property, Community and the Contradiction of Modern Social Thought.* New York: Basic Books.

Bowley, Arthur. 1920. *The Change in the Distribution of National Income, 1880–1913.* Oxford: Clarendon Press.

Bramall, Chris. 2000. *Sources of Chinese Economic Growth: 1978–1996.* Oxford: Oxford University Press.

Braudel, Fernand. 1979. *Civilization and Capitalism 15th–18th Century,* vol. 3: *The Perspective of the World,* trans. Sian Reynolds. New York: Harper and Row.

Bregman, Rutger. 2017. *Utopia for Realists: How We Can Build the Ideal World.* New York: Little, Brown.

Broadberry, Stephen, and Alexander Klein. 2008. "Aggregate and Per Capita GDP in Europe, 1870–2000: Continental, Regional and National Data with Changing Boundaries." Unpublished manuscript. Published 2012 in *Scandinavian Economic History Review* 60(1): 79–107.

Broadberry, Stephen, and Alexander Klein. 2011. "When and Why Did Eastern European Economies Begin to Fail? Lessons from a Czechoslovak / UK Productivity Comparison, 1921–1991." *Explorations in Economic History* 48(1): 37–52.

Brunori, Paolo, Francisco H. G. Ferreira, and Vito Peragine. 2013. "Inequality of Opportunity, Income Inequality and Economic Mobility: Some International Comparisons." IZA Working Paper No. 7155, IZA Institute of Labor Economics, Bonn, January. http://ftp.iza.org/dp7155.pdf.

Calvino, Italo. 1994. "Apologo sull'onestà nel paese dei corrotti." In *Romanzi e racconti,* ed. Mario Berenghi and Bruno Falcetto, vol. 3, 290–293. Milan: Mondadori.

Capussela, Andrea Lorenzo. 2018. *The Political Economy of Italy's Decline.* Oxford: Oxford University Press.

Carlin, Wendy, Mark Schaffer, and Paul Seabright. 2012. "Soviet Power Plus Electrification: What Is the Long-Term Legacy of Communism?" Working Paper 43-212, Department of Studies on Economic Development, Universita degli studi de Macerata, June. Published 2013 in *Explorations in Economic History* 50(1): 116–147.

Chen, Shaohua, and Martin Ravallion. 2007. "Absolute Poverty Measures for the Developing World, 1981–2004." *Proceedings of the National Academy of Sciences of United States of America* 104(43): 16757–16762.

Chetty, Raj, John N. Friedman, Emmanuel Saez, Nicholas Turner, and Danny Yagan. 2017a. "Mobility Report Cards: The Role of Colleges in Intergenerational Mobility." NBER Working Paper No. 23618, National Bureau of Economic Research, Cambridge, MA, rev. July.

Chetty, Raj, David Grusky, Maximilian Hell, Nathaniel Hendren, Robert Manduca, and Jimmy Narang. 2017b. "The Fading American Dream: Trends in Absolute Income Mobility since 1940." *Science* 356(6336): 398–406.

Chi, Wei. 2012. "Capital Income and Income Inequality: Evidence from Urban China." *Journal of Comparative Economics* 40(2): 228–239.

Chiappori, Pierre-André, Bernard Salanié, and Yoram Weiss. 2017. "Partner Choice, Investment in Children and the Marital College Premium." *American Economic Review* 107(8): 2109–2167.

Chi Hsin. 1978. *Teng Hsiao-ping: A Political Biography.* Hong Kong: Cosmos Books.

China Statistical Yearbook. 2017. National Bureau of Statistics, Beijing.

Clark, Andrew, Sarah Flèche, Richard Layard, Nattavudh Powdthavee, and George Ward. 2017. "The Key Determinants of Happiness and Misery." In *World Happiness Report 2017,* ed. John Helliwell, Richard Layard, and Jeffrey Sachs, 122–143. New York: Sustainable Development Solutions Network.

Congressional Budget Office. 2014. "The Distribution of Household Income and Federal Taxes, 2011." CBO Report, Washington, DC, November 12. https://www .cbo.gov/publication/49440.

Corak, Miles. 2013. "Inequality from Generation to Generation: The United States in Comparison." In *The Economics of Inequality, Poverty, and Discrimination in the 21st Century,* ed. Robert Rycroft. Santa Barbara, CA: Praeger.

Crabtree, James. 2018. *A Billionaire Raj: A Journey through India's New Gilded Age.* New York: Tim Duggan Books of Crown Publishing.

Credit Suisse Research Institute. 2013. "Global Wealth Report 2013." October. https://www.files.ethz.ch/isn/172470/global_wealth_report_2013.pdf.

Creemers, Rogier. 2018. "Party Ideology and Chinese Law." Unpublished manuscript, July 30. https://papers.ssrn.com/sol3/papers.cfm?abstract_id=3210541.

Dahrendorf, Ralf. (1963) 1978. "Changes in the Class Structure of Industrial Societies." In *Social Inequality,* ed. André Béteille. Reprint. Harmondsworth, UK: Penguin.

Dalgaard, C. J., and H. Hansen. 2001. "On Aid, Growth and Good Policies." *Journal of Development Studies* 37(6): 17–41.

Dao, Mai Chi, Mitali Das, and Zoka Koczan, and Weiching Lian. 2017. "Why Is Labor Receiving a Smaller Share of Global Income?" IMF Working Paper wp/17/169, International Monetary Fund, Washington DC, July. https://www.imf.org/en

/Publications/WP/Issues/2017/07/24/Why-Is-Labor-Receiving-a-Smaller-Share-of
-Global-Income-Theory-and-Empirical-Evidence-45102.

Dasgupta, Rana. 2015. *Capital: The Eruption of Delhi*. New York: Penguin.

Davis, Gerald F. 2016. *The Vanishing American Corporation: Navigating the Hazards of a
New Economy*. N.P.: Berrett-Koehler.

Davis, Jonathan, and Bhashkar Mazumder. 2017. "The Decline in Intergenerational
Mobility after 1980." Federal Reserve Bank of Chicago Working Paper No. 17-21,
revised January 29, 2019. https://www.chicagofed.org/publications/working-papers
/2017/wp2017-05.

Decancq, Koen, Andreas Peichl, and Philippe Van Kerm. 2013. "Unequal by Marriage?
Assortativeness and Household Earnings Inequality: A Copula-Based Decomposi-
tion." Unpublished manuscript. http://economics.mit.edu/files/8479.

de Vries, Jan. 2008. *The Industrious Revolution: Consumer Behavior and the Household
Economy, 1650 to the Present*. Cambridge: Cambridge University Press.

Ding, Haiyan, and Hui He. 2018. "A Tale of Transition: An Empirical Analysis of
Income Inequality in Urban China, 1986–2009." *Review of Economic Dynamics*
29: 108–137.

Ding, Haiyan, Zhe Fu, and Hui He. 2018. "Transition and Inequality." Unpublished
manuscript, IMF Seminar, August 22 version.

Doyle, Michael W. 1997. *Ways of War and Peace: Realism, Liberalism, and Socialism*.
New York: Norton.

Easterly, Bill, and Stanley Fischer. 1995. "The Soviet Economic Decline." *World Bank
Economic Review* 9(3): 341–371.

Economy, Elizabeth C. 2018. "China's New Revolution: The Reign of Xi Jinping."
Foreign Affairs 97(3): 60–74.

Ellul, Jacques. 1963. *The Technological Society*. New York: Vintage Books.

Elsby, Michael W. L., Bart Hobijn, and Ayşegül Şahin. 2013. "The Decline of U.S.
Labor Share." Brookings Papers on Economic Activity, Brookings Institution,
Washington, DC, October 18 version. https://www.brookings.edu/bpea-articles/the
-decline-of-the-u-s-labor-share/.

Feldstein, Martin, and Shlomo Yitzhaki. 1982. "Are High-income Individuals Better
Stock Market Investors?" NBER Working Paper No. 948, National Bureau of
Economic Research, Cambridge, MA, July.

Ferguson, Niall, and Moritz Schularick. 2006. "The Empire Effect: The Determinants
of Country Risk in the First Age of Globalization, 1880–1913." *Journal of Economic
History* 66(2): 283–312.

Fiorio, Carlo V., and Stefano Verzillo. 2018. "Looking in Your Partner's Pocket before
Saying 'Yes!' Income Assortative Mating and Inequality." Working Paper 2/2018,
Dipartmento di Economia, Università degli Studi di Milano, February. http://wp
.demm.unimi.it/files/wp/2018/DEMM-2018_02wp.pdf.

Fisher, Irving. 1919. "Economists in Public Service: Annual Address of the President."
American Economic Review 9(1) supp.: 5–21.

Frank, André Gunder. 1966. "Development of Underdevelopment." *Monthly Review*
18(4): 17–31.

Fraser, Nancy. 2012. "Can Society Be Commodities All the Way Down? Polanyian Reflections on Capitalist Crisis." FMSH-WP-2012–18, Fondation Maison des sciences de l'homme, Paris, August. https://halshs.archives-ouvertes.fr/halshs-00725060/document. Published 2014 in *Economy and Society* 43(4): 541–558.

Freeman, Richard B. 2006. "People Flows in Globalization." *Journal of Economic Perspectives* 20(2): 145–170.

Freeman, Richard B. 2014. "Who Owns the Robots Rules the World." *IZA World of Labor*: 5, May. https://www.sole-jole.org/Freeman.pdf.

Freund, Caroline. 2016. *Rich People Poor Countries: The Rise of Emerging Market Tycoons and Their Mega Firms.* Washington, DC: Peterson Institute for International Economics.

Freund, Caroline, and Sarah Oliver. 2016. "The Origins of the Superrich: The Billionaire Characteristics Database." PIIE Working Paper 16-1, Peterson Institute for International Economics, February. https://piie.com/system/files/documents/wp16-1.pdf.

Fukuyama, Francis. 1992. *The End of History and the Last Man.* New York: Free Press.

Fukuyama, Francis. 2011. *The Origins of Political Order.* New York: Farrar, Straus and Giroux.

Gabriel, Satyananda J. 2006. *Chinese Capitalism and the Modernist Vision.* London: Routledge.

Gernet, Jacques. 1962. *Daily Life in China on the Eve of Mongol Invasion, 1250–1276.* New York: Macmillan; repr. Stanford University Press.

Gewirtz, Julian. 2017. *Unlikely Partners: Chinese Reformers, Western Economists, and the Making of Global China.* Cambridge, MA: Harvard University Press.

Gilens, Martin. 2012. *Affluence and Influence: Economic Inequality and Political Power in America.* Princeton, NJ: Princeton University Press.

Gilens, Martin. 2015. "Descriptive Representation, Money, and Political Inequality in the United States." *Swiss Political Science Review* 21(2): 222–228.

Gilens, Martin, and Benjamin I. Page. 2014. "Testing Theories of American Politics: Elites, Interest Groups, and Average Citizens." *Perspectives on Politics* 12(3): 564–581.

Goldin, Claudia, and Lawrence F. Katz. 2010. *The Race between Education and Technology.* Cambridge, MA: Belknap Press of Harvard University Press.

Gong, Honge, Andrew Leigh, and Xin Meng. 2012. "Intergenerational Income Mobility in Urban China." *Review of Income and Wealth* 58(3): 481–503.

Grabka, Markus, and Christian Westermeier. 2014. "Anhaltend hohe Vermögensungleichheit in Deutschland." *DIW Wochenbericht* 9: 151–164. https://www.diw.de/documents/publikationen/73/diw_01.c.438708.de/14–9.pdf.

Graham, Carol, Kate Laffan, and Sergio Pinto. 2018. "Well-being in Metrics and Policy." *Science* 362(6412): 287–288.

Greenwood, Jeremy, Nezih Guner, Georgi Kocharkov, and Cezar Santos. 2014a. "Marry Your Like: Assortative Mating and Income Inequality." *American Economic Review* 104(5): 348–353.

Greenwood, Jeremy, Nezih Guner, Georgi Kocharkov, and Cezar Santos. 2014b. "Corrigendum to 'Marry Your Like: Assortative Mating and Income Inequality.'" http://pareto.uab.es/nguner/ggks_corrigendum.pdf.

Greenwood, Jeremy, Nezih Guner, and Guillaume Vandenbroucke. 2017. "Family Economics Writ Large." NBER Working Paper No. 23103, National Bureau of Economic Research, Cambridge, MA, January.

Gustaffson, Björn, Shi Li, and Hieroshi Sato. 2014. "Data for Studying Earnings, the Distribution of Household Income and Poverty in China." IZA Working Paper 8244, IZA Institute of Labor Economics, Bonn, June. Published 2014 in *China Economic Review* 30: 419–431.

Hallward-Driemeier, Mary, and Gaurav Nayyar. 2018. *Trouble in the Making? The Future of Manufacturing-Led Development.* Washington, DC: World Bank Group. https://www.worldbank.org/en/topic/competitiveness/publication/trouble-in-the -making-the-future-of-manufacturing-led-development.

Harrington, Brooke. 2016. *Capital without Borders: Wealth Managers and the One Percent.* Cambridge, MA: Harvard University Press.

Hauner, Thomas, Branko Milanovic, and Suresh Naidu. 2017. "Inequality, Foreign Investment and Imperialism." Munich Personal RePEc Archive (MPRA), Working Paper 83068, 30 November. https://mpra.ub.uni muenchen.de/83068/1/MPRA _paper_83068.pdf.

Helliwell, John F., Haifang Huang, and Shun Wang. 2017. "Social Foundations of World Happiness." In *World Happiness Report 2017,* ed. John Helliwell, Richard Layard, and Jeffrey Sachs, 8–47. New York: Sustainable Development Solutions Network.

Hirschman, Albert O. 1977. *The Passions and the Interests: Political Argument for Capitalism before Its Triumph.* Princeton, NJ: Princeton University Press.

Hobson, John. 1902. *Imperialism: A Study.* London: J. Nisbet. Reprint Ann Arbor: University of Michigan Press, 1965.

Jacques, Martin. 2012. *When China Rules the World,* 2nd ed. London: Penguin.

Johannesen, Niels. 2014. "Tax Evasion and Swiss Bank Deposits." *Journal of Public Economics* 111: 46–62.

Karabarbounis, Loukas, and Brent Neiman. 2013. "The Global Decline of the Labor Share." NBER Working Paper No. 19136. National Bureau of Economic Research, Cambridge, MA, June (rev. October). Published 2014 in *Quarterly Journal of Economics* 129(1): 61–103.

Kennan, John. 2014. "Freedom of Movement for Workers." *IZA World of Labor* 2014: 86, September. https://wol.iza.org/uploads/articles/86/pdfs/freedom-of-movement -for-workers.pdf.

Keynes, John Maynard. 1919. *The Economic Consequences of the Peace.* London: Macmillan.

Keynes, John Maynard. 1930. "The Economic Possibilities for Our Grandchildren," parts 1 and 2. *The Nation and Athenaeum* 48, October 11 and 18.

Keynes, John Maynard. 1972. *Essays in Biography.* London: Macmillan.

Kissinger, Henry. 2011. *On China*. New York: Penguin.

Kristov, Lorenzo, Peter Lindert, and Robert McClelland. 1992. "Pressure Groups and Redistribution." *Journal of Public Economics* 48(2): 135–163.

Krouse, Richard W. 1982. "Polyarchy and Participation: The Changing Democratic Theory of Robert Dahl." *Polity* 14(3): 441–463.

Kuhn, Moritz, Moritz Schularick, and Ulrike Steins. 2017. "Income and Wealth Inequality in America, 1949–2016." Discussion Paper 20547, Centre for Economic Policy Research, London, September.

Kurz, Mordecai. 2018. "On the Formation of Capital and Wealth: IT, Monopoly Power and Rising Inequality." Unpublished manuscript, dated June 25, 2017, rev. May 11, 2018. https://papers.ssrn.com/sol3/papers.cfm?abstract_id=3014361.

Lakner, Christoph. 2014. "Wages, Capital and Top Incomes: The Factor Income Composition of Top Incomes in the USA, 1960–2005." Chap. 2 of "The Determinants of Incomes and Inequality: Evidence from Poor and Rich Countries." PhD diss., Oxford University.

Lakner, Christoph, and Branko Milanovic. 2016. "Global Income Distribution: From the Fall of the Berlin Wall to the Great Recession." *World Bank Economic Review* 30(2): 203–232.

Landes, David. 1998. *The Wealth and Poverty of Nations: Why Some Are So Rich and Some So Poor*. New York: Norton.

Leijonhufvud, Axel. 1985. "Capitalism and the Factory System." In *Economics as a Process: Essays in the New Institutional Economics,* ed. Richard N. Langlois. Cambridge: Cambridge University Press.

Levy, Harold O., and Peg Tyre. 2018. "How to Level the College Playing Field." *New York Times,* April 7.

Li, Cheng. 2016. *Chinese Politics in the Xi Jinping Era*. Washington, DC: Brookings Institution Press.

Li, Chunling. n.d. "Profile of Middle Class in Mainland China." Unpublished manuscript.

Lin, Justin Yufu, and Celestin Monga. 2017. *Beating the Odds: Jump-starting Developing Countries*. Princeton, NJ: Princeton University Press.

Los, Bart, Marcel P. Timmer, and Gaaitzen de Vries. 2015. "How Global Are Global Value Chains? A New Approach to Measure International Fragmentation." *Journal of Regional Science* 55(1): 66–92.

Lundberg, Jacob, and Daniel Walderström. 2016. "Wealth Inequality in Sweden: What Can We Learn from Capitalized Income Tax Data?" Unpublished manuscript, April 22. http://www.uueconomics.se/danielw/Research_files/Capitalized%20 Wealth%20Inequality%20in%20Sweden%20160422.pdf. Published 2018 in *Review of Income and Wealth* 64(3): 517–541.

Luo, Xubei, and Nong Zhu. 2008. "Rising Income Inequality in China: A Race to the Top." Policy Research Working Paper No. 4700, World Bank, Washington, DC, August.

Ma, Debin. 2011. "Rock, Scissors, Paper: The Problem of Incentives and Information in Traditional Chinese State and the Origin of Great Divergence." Economic History

Department Working Papers 152 / 11, London School of Economics. http://eprints
.lse.ac.uk/37569/.

Machiavelli, Niccolò. 1983. *The Discourses*. Edited with an introduction by Bernard
Crick, using the translation of Leslie J. Walker, S.J., with revisions by Brian
Richardson. London: Penguin.

Maddison, Angus. 2007. *Contours of the World Economy, 1–2030 AD: Essays in
Macro-economic History*. Oxford: Oxford University Press.

Maddison Project. 2018. See Jutta Bolt, Robert Inklaar, Herman de Jong, and Jan
Luiten van Zanden, "Rebasing 'Maddison': New Income Comparisons and the
Shape of Long-Run Economic Development," Maddison Project Working Paper 10,
https://www.rug.nl/ggdc/historicaldevelopment/maddison/research.

Daniel Markovits, "A New Aristocracy," Yale Law School Commencement Address,
May 2015. Available at https://law.yale.edu/system/files/area/department/studentaf-
fairs/document/markovitscommencementrev.pdf (accessed August 31, 2018).

Marx, Karl. 1965. *Pre-Capitalist Economic Formations,* trans. Jack Cohen. New York:
International Publishers.

Marx, Karl. 1973. *Grundrisse: Foundations of the Critique of Political Economy,* trans.
Martin Nicolaus. London: Penguin.

Marx, Karl. 2007. *Dispatches for the New York* Tribune: *Selected Journalism of Karl
Marx,* ed. James Ledbetter. London: Penguin.

Mason, Paul. 2016. *Postcapitalism: A Guide to Our Future*. New York: Farrar, Straus and
Giroux.

Mazower, Mark. 2012. *Governing the World: The History of an Idea*. New York: Penguin.

Meade, James. 1964. *Efficiency, Equality, and the Ownership of Property*. London: Allen
and Unwin.

Merette, Sarah. 2013. "Preliminary Analysis of Inequality in Colonial Tonkin and
Cochinchina." Unpublished manuscript, June.

Milanovic, Branko. 1989. *Liberalization and Entrepreneurship: Dynamics of Reform in
Socialism and Capitalism*. Armonk, NY: M. E. Sharpe.

Milanovic, Branko. 2005. *Worlds Apart: Measuring International and Global Inequality*.
Princeton, NJ: Princeton University Press.

Milanovic, Branko. 2011. "A Short History of Global Inequality: The Past Two
Centuries." *Explorations in Economic History* 48(4): 494–506.

Milanovic, Branko. 2012. "Global Inequality Recalculated and Updated: The Effect of
New PPP Estimates on Global Inequality and 2005 Estimates." *Journal of Economic
Inequality* 10(1): 1–18.

Milanovic, Branko. 2015. "Global Inequality of Opportunity: How Much of Our
Income Is Determined by Where We Live?" *Review of Economics and Statistics*
97(2): 452–460.

Milanovic, Branko. 2016. *Global Inequality: A New Approach for the Age of Globalization*. Cambridge, MA: Belknap Press of Harvard University Press.

Milanovic, Branko. 2017. "Increasing Capital Income Share and Its Effect on Personal
Income Inequality." In *After Piketty: The Agenda for Economics and Inequality,* ed.

Heather Boushey, J. Bradford DeLong, and Marshall Steinbaum. Cambridge, MA: Harvard University Press.

Mill, John Stuart. 1975. *Three Essays.* Oxford: Oxford University Press.

Moene, Kalle. 2016. "The Social Upper Class under Social Democracy." *Nordic Economic Policy Review* 2: 245–261.

Novokmet, Filip, Thomas Piketty, and Gabriel Zucman. 2017. "From Soviets to Oligarchs: Inequality and Property in Russia 1905–2016." WID.world Working Paper Series 2017/9, July. Published 2018 in *Journal of Economic Inequality* 16(2): 189–223.

OECD. 2011. *Divided We Stand: Why Inequality Keeps Rising.* Paris: OECD Publishing.

Offer, Avner. 1989. *The First World War: An Agrarian Interpretation.* Oxford: Oxford University Press.

Offer, Avner, and Daniel Söderberg. 2016. *The Nobel Factor: The Prize in Economics, Social Democracy, and the Market Turn.* Princeton, NJ: Princeton University Press.

Okonjo-Iweala, Ngozi. 2018. *Fighting Corruption Is Dangerous: The Story behind the Headlines.* Cambridge, MA: MIT Press.

Orléan, André. 2011. *L'empire de la valeur: refonder l'économie.* Paris: Seuil.

Overbeek, Hans. 2016. "Globalizing China: A Critical Political Economy Perspective on China's Rise." In *Handbook of Critical International Political Economy: Theories, Issues and Regions,* ed. Alan Cafruny, Leila Simona Talani, and Gonzalo Pozo-Martin, 309–329. London: Palgrave Macmillan.

Pareto, Vilfredo. 1935. *The Mind and Society,* vol. 4 [*Trattato di Sociologia Generale*]. New York: Harcourt Brace.

Pei, Minxin. 2006. *China's Trapped Transition.* Cambridge, MA: Harvard University Press.

Pei, Minxin. 2016. *China's Crony Capitalism.* Cambridge, MA: Harvard University Press.

Piketty, Thomas. 2014. *Capital in the Twenty-First Century,* trans. Arthur Goldhammer. Cambridge, MA: Harvard University Press.

Piketty, Thomas, Li Yang, and Gabriel Zucman. 2017. "Capital Accumulation, Private Property and Rising Inequality in China, 1978–2015." WID.world Working Paper Series 2017/6, April. https://wid.world/document/t-piketty-l-yang-and-g-zucman -capital-accumulation-private-property-and-inequality-in-china-1978-2015-2016/.

Piketty, Thomas, and Emmanuel Saez. 2003. "Income Inequality in the United States, 1913–1998." *Quarterly Journal of Economics* 118(1): 1–39.

Piñera, José. 2016. "President Clinton and the Chilean Model." Cato Policy Report, Cato Institute, Washington, DC, January/February. https://www.cato.org/policy -report/januaryfebruary-2016/president-clinton-chilean-model.

Pomeranz, Kenneth. 2000. *The Great Divergence: China, Europe and the Making of the Modern World Economy.* Princeton NJ: Princeton University Press.

Pomfret, Richard. 2018. "The Eurasian Landbridge: Linking Regional Value Chains." *VoxEU,* CEPR Policy Portal, Centre for Economic Policy Research, London, May 1. https://voxeu.org/article/eurasian-landbridge-linking-regional-value-chains.

Popper, Karl. (1957) 1964. *The Poverty of Historicism.* New York: Harper and Row.

Rajan, Raghuram G., and Arvind Subramanian. 2005. "Aid and Growth: What Does the Cross Country Evidence Really Show?" NBER Working Paper 11513, National Bureau of Economic Research, Cambridge, MA, February, rev. 2007.

Rawls, John. 1971. *A Theory of Justice.* Cambridge, MA: Belknap Press of Harvard University Press.

Rawls, John. 1999. *The Law of Peoples.* Cambridge, MA: Harvard University Press.

Raworth, Kate. 2018. *Doughnut Economics: Seven Ways to Think Like a 21st Century Economist.* White River Junction, VT: Chelsea Green.

Ray, Debraj. 2014. "Nit-Piketty: A Comment on Thomas Piketty's *Capital in the Twenty-First Century.*" Unpublished manuscript, May 25, https://www.econ.nyu.edu /user/debraj/Papers/Piketty.pdf.

Rognlie, Matthew. 2015. "Deciphering the Fall and Rise in the Net Capital Share: Accumulation or Scarcity?" Brookings Papers on Economic Activity, Spring. https://www.brookings.edu/wp-content/uploads/2016/07/2015a_rognlie.pdf.

Rotman, David. 2015. "Who Will Own the Robots?" MIT Technology Review, June 16. https://www.technologyreview.com/s/538401/who-will-own-the-robots/.

Samuelson, Paul. 1976. *Economics.* New York: McGraw Hill.

Sapio, Flora. 2010. *Sovereign Power and the Law in China.* Leiden: Brill.

Sapir, André. 1980. "Economic Growth and Factor Substitution: What Happened to the Yugoslav Miracle?" *Economic Journal* 90(358): 294–313.

Sawhill, Isabel. 2017. "Post-Redistribution Liberalism." *Democracy: A Journal of Ideas* 46, Fall.

Schäfer, Armin. 2017. "How Responsive Is the German Parliament?" Blog post, July 26. http://www.armin-schaefer.de/en/how-responsive-is-the-german-parliament/.

Shiroyama, Tomoko. 2008. *China during the Great Depression: Market, State, and the World Economy, 1929–1937.* Cambridge, MA: Harvard University Asia Center.

Solimano, Andres. 2018. "Global Mobility of the Wealthy and Their Assets in an Era of Growing Inequality." Paper presented at the Investment Migration Council (IMC) Forum, Geneva, June 4–6.

Stamp, Josiah. 1926. "Inheritance as an Economic Factor." *Economic Journal* 36(143): 339–374.

Standing, Guy. 2017. *Basic Income: And How We Can Make It Happen.* New York: Penguin.

Stewart, Matthew. 2018. "The 9.9% Is the New American Aristocracy," *Atlantic,* June. (Published with the title "The Birth of a New American Aristocracy.")

Swedberg, Richard, ed. 1991. *The Economics and Sociology of Capitalism.* Princeton, NJ: Princeton University Press.

Sweezy, Paul. 1953. *The Present as History.* New York: Monthly Review Press.

Taleb, Nassim Nicholas. 2007. *The Black Swan: The Impact of the Highly Improbable.* New York: Random House.

Taleb, Nassim Nicholas. 2018. *Skin in the Game: Hidden Asymmetries in Daily Life.* New York: Random House.

Thomas, Vinod, Yan Wang, and Xibo Fan. 2001. "Measuring Education Inequality—Gini Coefficients of Education." Policy Research Working Paper No. WPS 2525, World Bank, Washington, DC, January. http://documents.worldbank.org/curated /en/361761468761690314/pdf/multi-page.pdf.

Tinbergen, Jan. 1975. *Income Distribution: Analysis and Policies.* Amsterdam: North-Holland.

Tooze, Adam. 2014. *Deluge: The Great War, America and the Remaking of the Global Order, 1916–1931.* New York: Penguin.

Torgler, Benno, and Marco Piatti. 2013. "Extraordinary Wealth, Globalization, and Corruption." *Review of Income and Wealth* 59(2): 341–359.

Tucker, Robert C., ed. 1978. *The Marx-Engels Reader,* 2nd ed. New York: Norton.

van der Pijl, Kees. 2012. "Is the East Still Red? The Contender State and Class Struggles in China." *Globalizations* 9(4): 503–516.

van der Weide, Roy, and Ambar Narayan. 2019. "China versus the United States: Different Economic Models but Similarly Low Levels of Socio-economic Mobility." Unpublished manuscript.

van Parijs, Philippe, and Yannick Vanderborght. 2017. *Basic Income: A Radical Proposal for a Free Society and a Sane Economy.* Cambridge, MA: Harvard University Press.

van Zanden, Jan-Luiten, Joerg Baten, Peter Foldvari, and Bas van Leeuwen. 2014. "The Changing Shape of Global Inequality, 1820–2000: Exploring a New Dataset." *Review of Income and Wealth* 60(2): 279–297.

Veyne, Paul. 2001. *La société romaine.* Paris: Seuil.

Vonyó, Tamas. 2017. "War and Socialism: Why Eastern Europe Fell Behind between 1950 and 1989." *Economic History Review* 70(1): 248–274.

Vries, Peer. 2013. *Escaping Poverty: The Origins of Modern Economic Growth.* Göttingen: V & R Unipress.

Wang Fan-hsi. 1991. *Memoirs of a Chinese Revolutionary,* trans. Gregor Benton. New York: Columbia University Press.

Wang Hui. 2003. "Contemporary Chinese Thought and the Question of Modernity (1997)." In Wang, *China's New Order,* ed. Theodore Huters. Cambridge, MA: Harvard University Press.

Warren, Bill. 1980. *Imperialism: Pioneer of Capitalism,* ed. John Sender. London: New Left Books.

Weber, Max. 1978. *Economy and Society,* ed. Guenther Roth and Claus Wittich. Berkeley: University of California Press.

Weber, Max. 1992. *The Protestant Ethic and the Spirit of Capitalism,* trans. Talcott Parsons. Reprint. London: Routledge.

Weitzman, Martin, and Colin Xu. 1993. "Chinese Township Village Enterprises as Vaguely Defined Cooperatives." CEP Discussion Paper no. 155, Centre for Economic Performance, London School of Economics and Political Science, June. http://cep.lse.ac.uk/pubs/download/DP0155.pdf.

Wesseling, H. L. 1996. *Divide and Rule: The Partition of Africa, 1880–1914,* trans. Arnold J. Pomerans. Westport, CT: Praeger.

Wihtol de Wenden, Catherine. 2010. *La question migratoire au XXI siècle: migrants, réfugiés et relations internationales.* Paris: Presses de Sciences Po.

Wolff, Edward N. 2017. *A Century of Wealth in America.* Cambridge, MA: Harvard University Press.

Wootton, David. 2018. *Power, Pleasure, and Profit: Insatiable Appetites from Machiavelli to Madison.* Cambridge, MA: Belknap Press of Harvard University Press.

World Bank. 2011. *Inside Inequality in the Arab Republic of Egypt: Facts and Perceptions across People, Time, and Space.* Report No. 86473. Washington, D.C. http://documents.worldbank.org/curated/en/707671468247494406/pdf/864730PUB0ISB N00Box385175B00PUBLIC0.pdf.

World Bank. 2017. "China: Systematic Country Diagnostic: Towards a More Inclusive and Sustainable Development." Report No. 113092, Washington DC. http://documents.worldbank.org/curated/en/147231519162198351/pdf/China-SCD -publishing-version-final-for-submission-02142018.pdf.

World Bank. 2019. *The Changing Nature of Work.* World Development Report 2019. http://pubdocs.worldbank.org/en/816281518818814423/2019-WDR-Concept-Note.pdf.

World Inequality Report 2018, coordinated by Facunto Alvaredo, Lucas Chancel, Thomas Piketty, Emmanuel Saez, and Gabriel Zucman. Paris, December 2017.

Wu, Guoyou. 2015. *The Period of Deng Xiaoping's Reformation.* Beijing: Xinhua Publishing House / Foreign Language Press.

Wu, Ximing, and Jeffrey Perloff. 2005. "China's Income Distribution, 1985–2001." *Review of Economics and Statistics* 87(4): 763–775.

Xia, Ming. 2000. *The Dual Developmental State: Development Strategy and Institutional Arrangements for China's Transition.* Aldershot, UK: Ashgate.

Xie, Chuntao. 2016. *Fighting Corruption: How the CPC Works.* Beijing: New World Press.

Xie, Yu, and Xiang Zhou. 2014. "Income Inequality in Today's China." *Proceedings of the National Academy of Sciences* 111(19): 6928–6933.

Xu Chenggang. 2011. "The Fundamental Institutions of China's Reforms and Development." *Journal of Economic Literature* 49(4): 1076–1151.

Yang, Li, Filip Novokmet, and Branko Milanovic. 2019. "From Workers to Capitalists in Less than Two Generations: A Study of Chinese Urban Elite Transformation between 1988 and 2013." Unpublished manuscript.

Yonzan, Nishant. 2018. "Assortative Mating and Labor Income Inequality: United States 1970–2017." Unpublished manuscript.

Yonzan, Nishant, Branko Milanovic, Salvatore Morelli, and Janet Gornick. 2018. "Comparing Top Incomes between Survey and Tax Data: US Case Study." LIS "Inequality Matters" Newsletter, Issue 6, pp. 10–11, LIS Cross-National Data Center in Luxembourg, June. https://www.lisdatacenter.org/newsletter/nl-2018-6-h-4/.

Zhang, Yi, and Ran Wang. 2011. "The Main Approach of the Proposed Integrated Household Survey of China." Paper presented at the 4th meeting of the Wye City Group on Statistics of Rural Development and Agriculture Household Income, Rio de Janeiro, November 9–11.

Zhao Ziyang. 2009. *Prisoner of the State.* New York: Simon and Schuster.

Zhuang Juzhong and Li Shi. 2016. "Understanding Recent Trends in Income Inequality in the People's Republic of China." ADB Economics Working Paper Series, No. 489, Asian Development Bank, July. https://www.adb.org/publications /understanding-recent-trends-income-inequality-prc.

Zucman, Gabriel. 2013. "The Missing Wealth of Nations: Are Europe and the U.S. Net Debtors or Net Creditors?" *Quarterly Journal of Economics* 128(3): 1321–1364.

Zucman, Gabriel. 2015. *The Hidden Wealth of Nations: The Scourge of Tax Havens,* trans. Teresa Lavender Fagan. Chicago: University of Chicago Press.

ACKNOWLEDGMENTS

Details of book writing are, like those of many other activities, hard to recall after it is all over. One only dimly remembers when he or she had the first idea for the book, how the ideas changed, were abandoned or revised, how the process of writing proceeded, what was written when. Every time at the completion of a manuscript, I have had that same feeling: that the book got written almost miraculously.

In this case, however, I remember that I glimpsed the idea for the structure of the book in a conversation I had with Ian Malcolm, the editor of this book for Harvard University Press, in the summer of 2017 in London. I had previously wanted to write a short book on the place of communism in global history, but only during our lunch in London did I see how I could combine this idea with the other topics on which I also wanted to write. The reinterpretation of the historical role of communism is now in the first part of Chapter 3.

Chapter 3, which deals with political capitalism and China, was read and commented on in writing by (in alphabetical order) Misha Arandarenko, Christer Gunnarsson, Ravi Kanbur, Debin Ma, Kalle Moene, Mario Nuti, Henk Overbeek, Marcin Piatkowski, Anthea Roberts, John Roemer, Bas van Bavel, Peer Vries, Li Yang, and Carla Yumatle (who also commented on Chapter 5).

Chapter 2, which deals with liberal meritocratic capitalism and the United States, was read and commented on in writing by (again in alphabetical order) Misha Arandarenko, Andrea Capussela, Angus Deaton, Salvatore Morelli, Niels Planel, John Roemer, Paul Segal (who also commented on Chapter 1), and Marshall Steinbaum.

I benefited enormously from their comments. In each case I went, I hope carefully, through each individual comment.

I am also grateful for the provision of various data and unpublished calculations to Minxin Pei, Marcin Piatkowski, Nishant Yonzan, and Chunlin Zhang. I discussed the structure of the book with Glen Weyl, too.

The entire manuscript was read by two excellent anonymous reviewers, whose comments I took practically in entirety. It was of course read by Ian Malcom, who provided a number of most valuable critiques and improvements. As in my previous book, outstanding editing and questioning of my statements was done by Louise Robbins. Anne McGuire checked all the references. I am very grateful and indebted to all of them.

The manuscript was also read (on their request) by two outstanding scholars of inequality, Jamie Galbraith and Thomas Piketty. I am very gratified by their interest.

The book was written while I was teaching at the Graduate Center, City University of New York, and closely working, within the Stone Center on Socio-Economic Inequality, with Janet Gornick. As before, Janet's support and help were absolutely crucial. Whenever I traveled I would leave the most recent version of the manuscript with Janet: I knew it would be published if anything happened to me. I am very appreciative of Janet and the Graduate Center for letting me take a sabbatical during a part of the time during which I wrote the book.

As many times before, I am grateful to my wife and to my (by now) two adult sons. They will see the outcome of things about which I write at the end of Chapter 5.

INDEX

Acemoglu, Daron, 73
Achen, Christopher, 56
Adam Smith in Beijing (Arrighi), 92–93, 113
Adverse selection, of migrants, 55
Africa: Chinese role in economic development in, 125–126, 214; global inequality and, 9, 213–214, 257n37
Agriculture, capitalism and Chinese, 87–88
Akcigit, Ufuk, 54
Alaska, annual grants in, 202
Albania, China and, 122
Algeria, political capitalism in, 96, 97
Alienation, commodification and, 193
Allen, Robert, 149
Amazon (company), 183
American Community Survey, 37
American Dream, 40–41
American Economic Association, 48
Amorality: hypercommercialized capitalism and, 176–187; hyperglobalization and, 163–164
Angola, political capitalism in, 96, 97
Anthropomorphism, robots and, 197–201
Anticorruption campaign, in China, 108–109
Antiglobalization stance of left-wing parties, 157

Anti-immigration policies, 156
Apple (company), 183
Aristotle, 4, 67, 119, 159
Arrighi, Giovanni, 92–93, 113, 115
Art galleries, moral money laundering and, 169–170
Asia: globalization and economic success of, 2, 5–11, 153–154; political capitalism and, 5–6; support for globalization in, 9; Western conquest of, 76. *See also individual countries*
Asian Infrastructure Investment Bank, 127
"Asiatic mode of production," 74, 75, 245n7
Assets: deconcentrating ownership of, 46; liberal meritocratic capitalism and higher rate of return on rich people's, 31–34
Assortative mating, liberal meritocratic capitalism and, 18–19, 36–40
"Athens" laws, 68
Atkinson, Anthony, 48
Atomization: global capitalism and, 187–190; relation to commodification, 190, 192
Autarky, 95; defying commercialized world by embracing, 187; limits on corruption and, 164
Authoritarian capitalism. *See* Political capitalism

275